A Writing Life

Helen Garner and Her Work

Bernadette Brennan

TEXT PUBLISHING MELBOURNE AUSTRALIA

textpublishing.com.au

The Text Publishing Company
Swann House
22 William Street
Melbourne Victoria 3000
Australia

First published in 2017 by The Text Publishing Company
Reprinted 2017 (twice)

Book design by Imogen Stubbs
Cover photograph © Julian Kingma
Typeset by J&M Typesetting

Printed and bound in Australia by Griffin Press, an accredited ISO/NZS 1401:2004 Environmental Management System printer

National Library of Australia Cataloguing-in-Publication entry
Creator: Brennan, Bernadette, author.
Title: A writing life : Helen Garner and her work/by Bernadette Brennan.
ISBN: 9781925498035 (paperback)
ISBN: 9781925410396 (ebook)
Subjects: Garner, Helen, 1942–
Garner, Helen, 1942—Correspondence.
Women authors, Australian—20th century.
Australian literature—Women authors—History and criticism.
Australian literature—20th century—History and criticism.

This book is printed on paper certified against the Forest Stewardship Council® Standards. Griffin Press holds FSC chain-of-custody certification SGS-COC-005088. FSC promotes environmentally responsible, socially beneficial and economically viable management of the world's forests.

Dr Bernadette Brennan is an academic and researcher in contemporary Australian writing, literature and ethics. She is the author of a number of publications, including a monograph on Brian Castro, and editor of two collections: *Just Words? Australian Authors Writing for Justice* (UQP 2008), and *Ethical Investigations: Essays on Australian Literature and Poetics* by Noel Rowe (Vagabond 2008). She lives in Sydney.

Contents

*Tell me what the artist is, and I will tell you of what
he has been conscious. Thereby I shall express to you at
once his boundless freedom and his 'moral' reference.*

HENRY JAMES, PREFACE TO
The Portrait of a Lady (1881)

Introduction:
Sketching an Outline

Helen Garner began to fidget. She glanced at the moderator, Michael Cathcart, then at the American writer David Shields. The 2012 NonfictioNOW Conference had brought Garner, Shields, Margo Jefferson and José Dalisay together on a panel. The catalyst for Garner's agitation was Shields' assertion that 'because we experience almost no reality in our actual lives, we crave the real'. In reply Garner said that, living next door to her three young grandchildren, she did experience real things. She thought there was nothing more real than the company of children and seeing how they understood the world. 'It seems to me,' she said, 'there is a world and there is a reality.'

Throughout her work, Garner has explored the reality of the world around her: the fraught complexity of relationships, the social experiments of communal living, the balance between personal freedom and moral responsibility, the rule of law and, always, questions about sex and power. Significantly, she has also ventured into aspects of the real that by their nature defy easy elucidation: spirituality and death.

Thirty years ago Garner told Jennifer Ellison that she would never be so famous as to be recognised when she walked into a room. Now, aged seventy-four, and author of thirteen books, two screenplays, and a multitude of articles, essays and reviews, Garner is one of the best-known and, some would say, best-loved writers in Australia. That admiration is inspired by a sense that she is honest, authentic and familiar to readers. She appears to write so much of herself into her nonfiction, and many of her own experiences inform her fiction. Garner admits to striking up conversations with strangers on public transport, hungry for their tales of experience. Who can forget the poignant moment in her essay on the outpouring of grief over Jill Meagher's violent rape and murder, where she both weeps and laughs with an emotional father over the photo of his newborn daughter: 'Thank you for telling me! Thank you for listening!'

And yet, Garner's work continues to polarise opinion. Some readers maintain the rage against what they perceive to be her ill-informed betrayal of feminism in *The First Stone*. Others rail against the ways in which she cannot but insert herself into textual dramas of pain and loss. Where some readers find and applaud her candour, others see a kind of ruthless egotism. Some critics remain exasperated by her refusal to stay within delineated genres. *Monkey Grip* and *The Spare Room*, they insist, are not novels. *The First Stone*, they argue, is fiction.

Garner has always been a boundary-crosser. Refusing the constraints of literary genre, she has sought to write across and craft her own versions of them. She admits to a 'me' character in all her work. That character is a carefully constructed self. In her fiction, she unsettles her readers' assumptions about protagonists by creating 'Helen' characters, most blatantly in 'Little Helen's Sunday Afternoon', 'Habe Dank' and *The Spare Room*. In so doing, she demonstrates the complexity of a constructed fictional self. The 'I' in her journalism and nonfiction is, as Janet Malcolm has argued about her own work, 'almost pure invention', a functionary connected tenuously to the actual writer. When she came to write *Joe Cinque's Consolation*, for example, Garner toyed with creating a third-person HG with access to the thoughts and memories of a first-person HG. In her journal she asked: 'Cd I create a 3rd person I? A m/aged writer HG? With sore feet & hair anxieties, the loneliness, & life experience & ability to get an imaginative grip on the Cinques' loss.'

In May 1985 Garner wrote a column for the *Australian Women's Weekly* in which she recounted the belittling response given by Doris Lessing to a reader who asked if Lessing's work was autobiographical. The question, wrote Garner, 'is the worst, most unanswerable, most infuriating question a writer has to confront'. Of course writers use their lives in their work, she said, but 'the word "autobiographical" is like a red rag to a bull because it seems to ignore the amount of hard slog we do, the endless work of observation and witnessing and things in our work that are pure invention'. There was no point in a writer trying to answer the autobiographical question: 'The only thing that can give an answer is the book itself.' Philip Roth illuminates her perspective: 'the intriguing biographical issue—and critical issue, for that matter—isn't that a writer will write about some of what has happened to him, but *how* he writes about it, which, when understood properly, takes us a long way to understanding *why* he writes about it.'

So how best to approach the *how* and the *why* of Garner's books, screenplays and essays? Given her experimentation with form, genre, voice and style, this study also crosses established critical boundaries. It can be neither a conventional biography nor a strict monograph. Garner's life and writing inform and shape each other to such a degree that it is not possible to understand one without the other. With a respectful nod to Janet Malcolm, this book is a literary portrait of Garner and her work. In her essay 'Forty-One False Starts', Malcolm constructs a portrait of the American artist David Salle. Through fragmentary entries, she traverses aspects of Salle's life, his art, published reviews and her interviews with him, adding a touch here, modifying something there. She has a profound respect for the absences, for what cannot be known, or need not be known. The essay is a portrait of a complex artist that acknowledges the impossibility of capturing the full essence of another human life.

After reading *True Stories* in 1996, the Sydney-based artist Jenny Sages contacted Garner to paint her with her four sisters for the Archibald Prize. Garner refused. She was convinced her sisters would never agree to such a request. Not to be deterred, Sages approached Garner again in 2002. This time Garner was receptive to the idea of an individual portrait. Sages spent a day photographing Garner, with her daughter and granddaughter, in her Fitzroy home. In these beautiful, intimate photographs Garner appears calm, open and vulnerable. Sages says of that day: 'It was a wonderful encounter. She is as spare and as honest as her work.' Garner remembers feeling very relaxed in Sages' presence. She was impressed that Sages never tried to make her smile. When she later sat for Sages in her Double Bay studio, the foundations of a respectful friendship were laid. Sages made thirty-seven charcoal drawings in preparation for her portrait. Garner enjoyed watching each emerge.

Sages' 'True Stories—Helen Garner' was completed in 2003. It now hangs in the National Portrait Gallery in Canberra. The portrait captures, through its combination of gesture and expression, many of Garner's seemingly contradictory traits: she is somewhat relaxed yet displays her characteristic anxious pose—her right hand raised to her temple. Her gaze is direct and almost too vividly open, suggesting that she is both surprised and a touch unimpressed, even resistant, to the whole project of portrayal. The lips are thin, not exactly pursed but firmly closed. It is a portrait of an alert, inquisitive, unglamorous woman who is at once strong and vulnerable.

I approached Garner in 2014 saying I wished to write a book

about her body of work and requested access to her embargoed archives at the National Library of Australia. Garner was worried about what was in the archive. She thought it best that we discuss my intentions. Why didn't I come to lunch at her home? So began two years of conversation. She established at the outset that she did not want a biography. I did not wish to write one, but I knew that the intersection and overlap of her life and art made discussion of the biographical essential to understanding her work. Garner gave me access to the NLA files, but went further in answering every query that I have put to her. She has admitted to anxious rumblings about this book.

Finding the right balance between discussion of a writer's personal life and published work can be fraught, particularly when the writer is as self-representational as Garner. More conventional biographies will no doubt be written in the future. The many volumes of Garner's diaries will provide rich material for researchers wishing to know more about her reading practices, private musings and intimate relationships, but Helen Garner the writer is best found in her books, essays and screenplays. As the author James Button says of his friend: 'Writing is how she tests her intuition, kindness and courage, how she feels alive. I always want to know what she's been reading and writing; it's the best guide I have to how and who she is.'

It is too simple to say that Garner's body of work is one book, but everything she has written is interrelated. Over a period of forty years she has revisited themes, relationships, situations, characters and questions. Because houses, and their domestic spaces of intimacy and negotiation sit at the core of all Garner's fiction, I originally thought to structure this study around Garner's primary spaces: bedrooms, kitchens, courtrooms and public institutions. There is much to be gained, for example, in reading the fluid bedrooms of the shared houses in Fitzroy and Carlton alongside the locked and dusty bedrooms of the house in *Cosmo Cosmolino* and the womb-like space in *The Spare Room*. Similarly, the negotiations in the kitchens of *Honour & Other People's Children* resonate with some of Garner's concerns in *This House of Grief*. Such readings, however, do not lend themselves to a full and coherent appreciation of Garner's development as a writer. As the critic Kerryn Goldsworthy noted in her 1996 monograph, *Helen Garner*, there is a 'close and immediate engagement in [Garner's] work with the circumstances of her own life, with the time and place in which the writing was produced, and with the representation of that time and place as manifested in the details of material culture and social practice'.

In the end I decided to structure this portrait so that each chapter, dedicated primarily to literary analysis, can be read as a room describing Garner's house of writing. Some rooms have alcoves, others debouch into wider spaces; all are connected by passageways. Goldsworthy's monograph is the only dedicated study of Garner's work to date. In the two decades since its publication Garner has published major works of nonfiction and her novel *The Spare Room*. Through close readings of these works and analysis of her restricted archives, I hope this book will contribute to a more robust picture of Garner and her writing life.

PART I:

Letters to Axel

I

Writing Home

There are no beloved historic objects in our family.
There is no family home.

HELEN GARNER, 'A SCRAPBOOK, AN ALBUM' (1993)

In 'Writing Home', the opening essay in *The Feel of Steel*, Garner ponders her father's insistence that he never had any attachment to material possessions, or the many houses in which he lived. Has this dismissal informed her own lack of a sense of home? At the time in which the essay is set, Garner is living with her third husband, Murray Bail, in Sydney. To understand what the concept of home might mean, she will have to confront her earliest memories. She is wary. Walking the streets of the 'beautiful' but 'foreign' city, she is assaulted by unbidden memories of her family's Ocean Grove house, before being 'yanked' back to the house of her birth in Geelong. Her language is filled with menace and fear. Fragmentary memories 'sneak up' and 'stab' her. Was she once the favoured child, held fast and loved? Do her parents remember that time? She daren't ask, for the answers may prove painful.

The issue of a favourite child is also addressed in an earlier essay. In 'A Scrapbook, An Album', first published in 1993, Garner interviews her four younger sisters, mapping their ferocious love for, and complex relationships with, each other. When the discussion veers towards their parents Garner attempts to refocus it back on their relationships as sisters. 'We are women,' she writes, 'who have always been fighting our father'. Garner's extended battle with her father has been one of the defining features of her adult life, and a central drama of her writing. She credits this struggle with both shaping and distorting her character. Garner's father rejected her for many years. They reconciled three years before he died, yet Garner continues to assert that her behaviour warranted such rejection.

Garner was born in Geelong in 1942. Wartime Geelong was a provincial, conservative town. Garner's parents, Bruce and Gwen Ford (née Gadsden), were middle-class, respectable folk. Bruce was complex and contradictory. He was 'a vivid, obstreperous character'; an 'impatient, rivalrous, scornful' man who dominated his timid, depressive wife and bullied his children. Neither parent had much formal education or interest in the arts, though Gwen's mother was an accomplished pianist and instilled in her a love of classical music. Bruce 'never read a book'. He left school at fifteen and began his working life as a wool classer, eventually becoming a wool merchant. Gwen, a primary-school physical education teacher, worked for only six months before marrying and becoming a mother to five daughters and a son. Helen was her first child.

From 1948 until 1952 the family lived on The Terrace at Ocean Grove, a coastal town south-west of Melbourne. In 'Sad Grove by the Ocean', Garner narrates select memories of the place, but resists probing her past too deeply: 'If I poked even one rational hole in the thick skin of that closed-off world, who knows what would come squirting out.' In her forties she returned to Ocean Grove, perceiving only ugliness and a sense of personal desolation. The door of her old family home was open but she made no attempt to enter: 'Why would I go in? It's just an ugly old house. If I went in my father would shout, "Shut the flaming door!" and my mother would say, "*Go outside.*"'

Parental responses of anger and dismissal were, according to Garner, the chorus of her childhood. She believes that her father loved her dearly, but that he could not negotiate their relationship when she became a teenager. Even before tensions about sexuality arose, the young Helen's literary interests and constant reading were a point of contention. 'Go outside.' 'Get your nose out of that book.' Indeed, as a university student in 1965 working in Geelong during term holidays, Helen wrote excitedly to her friend Axel Clark about coming to stay with his family in Canberra. She could 'get away from bookshop drudgery and parental disapproval, and be able to go to the library or read every day without being accused of bludging'.

Garner's memories of childhood are contradictory. She insists that being the eldest child marked and formed her. Through psychoanalysis, she later came to realise that she felt that her position in the family was usurped with each new sibling. She knows that there must have been a baby in the house for most years of her childhood, but she cannot remember ever changing a nappy or looking after a baby. Rather, she remembers retreating from the noise of the house to lose herself in books. On the other hand, she also remembers a happy childhood always playing with a gang of siblings. Ocean Grove was a place of barbecues, Frank Sinatra records, Film Fun comics and being sunburnt at the beach. It was at Ocean Grove that Helen rigged up a bucket to tip water on her father as he came through the gate from work. From her hiding spot she saw him laugh with shock and delight.

Why, then, did it hurt so much to return and gaze at Ocean Grove? Was it simply the landscape? Was it because on leaving that house the family returned to Retreat Road in Geelong and the laughter lessened? Was that the last house where Helen could sneak alone into her cubby and read and write by candlelight? Or was this, when she was between the ages of six and ten, the last time Helen felt that she truly belonged at home?

In 1960 an unworldly Helen Ford was the head prefect and dux of The Hermitage, a prestigious Anglican school for girls in Geelong. In the humorous and poignant essay 'At Nine Darling Street', she recounts her frumpish prudery and social inadequacy at a school dance in the big city of Melbourne. Yet the next year, aged nineteen, she arrived at the University of Melbourne and was catapulted into the intellectual, sexual and social revolutions it had to offer. 'Fordie', as her close friends called her, enrolled in English and French. By her own admission, she was an unimpressive student, rarely attending tutorials and never keeping up with the prescribed reading. She lived on campus at Janet Clarke Hall, the first residential college in Australia for women students. It required every applicant to sit an external exam in homecraft. Helen revelled in the heady freedom. Her circle of friends and lovers included architecture students who introduced her to American writers, so while she may not have been reading George Eliot and Milton in preparation for class, she was reading F. Scott Fitzgerald and Hemingway.

Helen forged an abiding friendship with Axel Clark, son of the historian Manning Clark, who was also enrolled in a Bachelor of Arts and was living at the neighbouring Trinity College. When she returned to her parents' house during term breaks she wrote to Axel every few days. In January 1963, she complained: 'Gosh I'm sick of being so far away from all my people. I think I have stopped considering my family as "my people".' She supposed Axel to be more at ease in Canberra because his parents were 'in close touch with university life' and noted: 'There is such a tremendous gap between my parents' interests and my own that there is no hope of bridging it. It hurts to notice that my father bores me and I bore him.'

Helen's early letters to Axel are about relationships, drunken parties, common friends, student poverty, dreams and difficult family dynamics. Elements of these letters, by virtue of their author's age and experience, are banal and repetitious. Yet these letters also demonstrate Helen's inquiring imagination and her hunger for ideas about life and writing. Interwoven with gossip about friends, lovers and marriage proposals, are enthusiastic discussions of literature, particularly poetry. She cites Eliot, Yeats, Brennan, Slessor, Blake, Keats, Browning, Shakespearean sonnets; she appreciates the brilliance of Wordsworth's 'Ode on Immortality'; she admits to weeping through *King Lear* and at the conclusion of *Antony and Cleopatra*; she is 'tremendously impressed' by Graham Greene's *Brighton Rock* and loves Hardy's *Return of the Native* and *Jude the Obscure*. While reading *Jude*, she signs off as Susanna Florence Mary Bridehead. Once she remarks: 'no, I'm not like Sue Bridehead, but I understand her!—and I am like her in that passage about wanting to captivate and then when it is done, being too frightened to know what to do next.'

The similarities do not end there. The headstrong, well-read Sue Bridehead wants to find a new way of living as a sexual, independent woman in the late nineteenth century, a way that does not involve marriage. Marriage kills true love and intimacy, both of which involve so much more than simply sexual relations. Sue has 'tight-strained nerves', she speaks her mind, and 'everything she did seemed to have its source in feeling. An exciting thought would make her walk ahead so fast that he could hardly keep up with her; and her sensitiveness on some points was such that it might have been misread as vanity.' Like Helen, Sue wants to be loved more than she can love herself. Her father casts her out of the family home because he believes her to be morally lax. When tragedy strikes, late in the novel, Sue returns to her Anglican faith. She punishes herself harshly as a means of expiating her sense of shame: 'I cannot humiliate myself too much. I should like to prick myself all over with pins and bleed out the badness that's in me!' Shame and disgust are familiar words in Garner's lexicon. They are experienced by all the female protagonists in her fiction and by the narrators of her nonfiction.

Helen squandered opportunities for rigorous undergraduate study because she was young, egocentric and irresponsible. She failed third year, and achieved only a third-class honours degree. Her sense of academic inadequacy fuelled her early insecurities about becoming a writer. It has often placed her on a defensive footing when challenged about the subject matter of her work, whether that be domestic relationships or a father's murder of his children. Crucially, it feeds into her sense of inferiority when faced with academic or legal authority.

Garner submitted two theses for her honours degree. For French she wrote on the work of the mediaeval poet François Villon, for English, Christopher Brennan. With self-deprecating humour she has recounted how in the 1990s she ran into an academic who had taught English at Melbourne University thirty years earlier. The academic had said she'd recently gone back to re-read Garner's final thesis on Brennan and observed that it showed no evidence whatsoever of any early talent. It was interesting, therefore, to discover—particularly given Inga

Clendinnen's attack on Garner's methodology in *Joe Cinque's Consolation*—the following account of an undergraduate history essay, written to Axel in August 1963: 'I got a beaut comment on my Modern A essay on Voltaire and the Calas case. I went to see Mrs Clendinnen…She had written on it: "A clear and intelligent argument, well-supported. You have an eye for the telling quotation."'

When I told Garner about this letter she was taken aback. She did not remember being taught by Clendinnen, and was gratified that she had written a good essay: 'My memories of university work are of nothing but failure and incapacity & shame and crippling silence in tutes. The idea that I ever even wrote "an argument", let alone that anyone commented on it, favourably or otherwise, provokes utter astonishment and disbelief.' Perhaps she was energised by the topic: the philosophic and moral questions raised by Voltaire's account of a controversial trial that resulted in a young man's father being put to death after a questionable verdict of murder.

Letters from 'Fordie' are scattered throughout Axel Clark's papers in the National Library of Australia archives. Altogether 188 of them survive, sent largely between 1962 and 1967, and 1985 and 1986. Garner was surprised when I told her about these letters. She wondered why Axel had kept them. After I suggested that perhaps he knew that one day she would be a successful writer she replied:

> I am suddenly remembering that I once showed Axel
> a short story I'd written. The first one I ever wrote.
> I didn't even know what a 'short story' was. I don't know

if I'd ever read one. Though I must have read *Dubliners*, I suppose. And I certainly wouldn't have dreamt that anything I wrote might be 'published', whatever that was. This must have been in maybe 1964 or '5…Axel read it right there at the table, returned the pages to order, looked at me with a calm face, and stuck up his thumb. I don't remember him saying anything. Just that thumbs-up gesture. That would have been the first comment anyone ever gave me on my 'writing' as distinct from a letter or an essay.

Axel graduated with first-class honours in English in 1965 and enrolled in a Master of Arts at the University of Sydney. Helen's letters to him continued unabated, though it seems Axel was a less frequent correspondent.

By 1966, Helen was teaching English and French at Werribee High School. She was back living with her parents in Geelong. Bruce Ford's once bright and charming personality had given way to an 'unpredictable possessiveness…brutal rudeness, scorn and erratic acts of cruelty'. In 1966 his overbearing control became untenable for Helen. He read her letters from Axel, and from two other young men. He insulted the correspondents, confiscated the letters and a packet of the Pill, and attempted to show some letters to one lad's parents. The intrusion and betrayal were too intimate. Helen left home the next day. She described her father's 'vengeful rage' to Axel, concluding: 'I think he is going to forbid the little kids to see me.'

So began a prolonged period of estrangement.

*

In *The Poetics of Space*, French philosopher Gaston Bachelard explores how we inhabit imaginatively the intimate spaces of our childhood home. The house, according to Bachelard, 'is our first universe', a dynamic space where thoughts, memories and dreams coalesce. Bachelard insists that a great many of our memories find refuge in our houses' cellars, garrets, 'nooks and corridors', and that 'all our lives we come back to them in daydreams'. He suggests that psychoanalysts should pay more attention to the 'localization of our memories', a methodology he defines as topoanalysis. 'Topoanalysis', as an auxillary of psychoanalysis, 'would be the systematic psychological study of the sites of our intimate lives', he explains.

Perhaps Garner's resistance to re-entering the childhood house where she was told to *go outside* reflects the continuing wound of her exile from the family. Two decades later she wrote that she 'can't understand why it hurts so much to look at Ocean Grove', and that the events of childhood 'have a hard shell of inevitability over them [that] resist historical explanation', so there is no point in asking why they happened. With Bachelard in mind, we might ask what happens to a child in a family that owns no 'beloved historical objects', who has no family home? Does that child grow up to insist, as Garner does, that she is 'hopeless at history, the past is a kind of blank—even my own and I forget everything'? Does she conduct, again and again, a topoanalysis of intimate spaces? Does she enter her sisters' bedrooms and kitchens armed with a tape recorder?

In 'A Scrapbook, An Album', the middle sister tells the story of two Papuan missionaries who visited the family home and who were impressed by her material sacrifice in coming to work with them. She replies: 'Yes, but in that house I have not learnt what I need to know.' In the bedrooms, kitchens, bathrooms and corridors of the large, communal houses in Melbourne's Carlton or Fitzroy, or the spare room of a later house, Garner seeks what she needs to know. In these works, she fashions new configurations of family. In different ways, they all narrate tales of fraught belonging and painful rejection.

When I suggested to Garner that Bachelard's approach might illuminate how houses operate in her work as 'image, symbol, site and space', she told me about visiting her sister Marie, ten days before her death in 2003, and finding her drawing the houses of their childhood. Garner retrieved her diary from that time and began to read it aloud. She stopped. 'I think I had better photocopy these pages for you,' she said. They read:

> Marie had been trying to draw up floor plans of houses our family had lived in…She'd put in little drawings of important scenes taking place in one house or another: Mum huddling by the fire at Retreat Rd after she'd had all her teeth pulled out; Dad standing in the doorway of our bedroom at The Terrace in 1953, holding a newspaper & announcing in sombre tones, 'THE KING—IS DEAD.' Her memory of Strachan Ave was vestigial—an L-shaped block with a mother & a father on the doorstep & two children, she & I, lying in parallel single beds & wearing brown knitted pixie bonnets b/c we had mumps. I sat down with the clipboard on my knee & slaved away trying to reproduce my own memories of the houses. They seemed architecturally more accurate but totally lacked her sense of atavistic drama.

Our conversation swerved to David Malouf's *12 Edmondstone Street*, Garner's favourite among Malouf's books because it seems 'so true'. In *12 Edmondstone Street* the child narrator rediscovers and maps the spaces of his childhood house, which is also the house of his body, the house of wonder, desire and sexual discovery. The hero of the piece is the burglar, reimagined by the boy as someone, like a writer, who can see unexpected 'threads between things' and is unafraid to penetrate the most intimate spaces.

In August 1966 Helen moved into a single room, with a kitchenette in one corner and a fireplace in the other, at 870 Swanston Street, Carlton. The following year she travelled to England, where she became reacquainted with Bill Garner, whom she had met at university. Together they travelled through parts of Europe and Ireland. In Dublin, Helen bought an 1818 edition of Montaigne's essays for one shilling and sat down to read it where 'Wilde and Swift and Berkeley had trodden'. On returning to England, she secured a teaching position at St Angela's Ursuline School in East London.

Helen and Bill returned to Melbourne in 1968. In the summer, they married. Bruce Ford attempted to stop the wedding by informing the Anglican Minister that Helen was not a virgin. He then forbade any family members to attend. Helen's mother and her sister Linda defied him. Bill began his Master of Arts in political philosophy at Monash University and was a part-time tutor in philosophy at Melbourne University.

He and Helen moved into Kerr Street, Fitzroy, offsetting their rent by sharing with two others. Friends remember a house full of people and parties. In September 1969 Helen gave birth to their daughter, Alice. She continued to be largely estranged from her parents. Her mother, under Bruce's veto, did not come to the hospital.

Nineteen sixty-eight is the year most associated with youth rebellion and student protest, particularly in Paris and Chicago. Anti-Vietnam protests were escalating in Australia and illicit drugs were becoming more freely available but the country remained firmly under conservative rule and conservative values. Perhaps in choosing to marry at that time Garner displayed that she was more of the head prefect than the immoral radical her father believed her to be. Perhaps it was just the times. The publisher Hilary McPhee was married in her third year of university aged twenty-one, the writer Drusilla Modjeska married at twenty and the playwright David Williamson at twenty-three. But within three years Garner's marriage was over. Bill moved into the Tower, an overcrowded space of frenetic sexual and creative activity behind the Pram Factory in Carlton. Helen and Alice moved to Falconer Street, Fitzroy North, 'the *Monkey Grip* house'.

Undoubtedly, one great attraction of marriage for Garner was the opportunity to form a new family. In 2002 Charlotte Wood interviewed a number of women writers about their attitudes to marriage and changing their surnames. Garner explained that through marriage she sought to overcome some of the painful clashes with her father, and achieve a sense of belonging to another family. She told Wood that she happily surrendered the name Ford: 'I was rather keen to get away from that name because it was very much connected to my way of being when I was a student, mostly sexually, which I look back on with some dismay.' She has never contemplated reverting to her maiden name: 'I feel that Ford was my child name, and then my really stupid, self-destructive youth name. Garner is my grown-up name.'

Bill and Helen married at about the same time as the La Mama Group, soon to be known as the Australian Performing Group (APG), was becoming established at the Pram Factory. It was a heady time. A rollcall of those involved includes many leading playwrights, directors, actors and administrators of Australian theatre and television. Bill became immersed in the performance scene. As Garner later commented: 'I was one of the La Mama widows. I was married to Bill Garner and we had a baby and everything was going swimmingly, then La Mama started up…He went up to La Mama and basically never came back.'

For all its supposed egalitarian ethos, the group at the Pram Factory was a tense, factional clique. Garner remembers feeling 'left out and lonely': 'It was a closed group. You couldn't even be involved in their social life.' She was part of the APG women's collective, which spent months in consciousness-raising workshops before writing and producing *Betty Can Jump*, an experimental feminist theatre piece. *Betty Can Jump* drama-tised how it felt to be a woman from convict times through to the seventies. It played to packed houses for seven weeks in November and December 1971. The production caused ructions within the male-dominated APG and added to escalating tensions within the group. In the 1994 documentary on the Pram Factory, Garner noted that *Betty Can Jump* coincided with the break-up of her marriage and she was 'pretty angry'. By way of shorthand, she suggested that any complaint about one's personal fate was viewed by the leftist men at the APG as a kind of 'bourgeois individualism'.

This production, and the audience responses to it, helped to shape Garner's early writing. In the 1972 winter issue of *dissent: a radical quarterly*, she published an extended piece on the process and performance of *Betty Can Jump*. She wrote of the difficulty in 'wrestling with our feelings and experiences' and trying to 'mould them into theatrical form'. This need to find the right shape or form persists throughout Garner's oeuvre. Prior to opening night, the women performed for the men of the APG. It was, according to Garner, a hollow, humiliating experience. Their personal statements appeared 'facile and self-indulgent'. Things that the women felt profoundly in rehearsals were somehow lost in translation to the stage. The men, untouched by the performance, made no response whatsoever. Total silence. Garner was ashamed to realise that, despite months of workshops, the actors' first concern had been to impress men and gain their approval.

Through the ensuing weeks of performance, she learned about the capacity of diary entries to capture mood and experience. She discovered that brevity and structure were powerful tools of communication. Garner also appreciated the need for women to record their experiences or risk remaining forever silenced. Some nights the female performers were subjected to grotesque sexual heckling from men in the audience, but women watching the show felt a shock of recognition. These responses confirmed for Garner that women's interior experiences were valid and needed to be articulated.

The APG strove to produce Australian theatre true to the Australian vernacular, accents and experience. Garner does something similar in her writing. In *Monkey Grip* her characters go to the outside 'dunny', they 'spew' and say 'fair dinkum', and they walk and cycle through the recognisable streets and parks of Fitzroy and Carlton. Many of Garner's friends who feature in the novel enjoyed seeing their lives and suburbs portrayed. A generation later, Christos Tsiolkas remembers the 'buzz' he felt as a young man recognising the geography and landscape of Garner's work, and of seeing his world reflected in a book.

By 1972, Garner was teaching at Fitzroy High School. As she details in 'Why Does the Women Get All the Pain?', one springtime afternoon her first-form class on Ancient Greece descended fairly quickly, thanks to the graphically defaced images of Greek athletes in the students' textbook, into a sex education lesson. Garner invited her students to write down any questions they had. She offered to end the discussion if anyone was uncomfortable, and proceeded to answer with brutal honesty everything these thirteen-year-olds asked.

For a single beat I see the situation from a distance: *a kid has just asked his teacher if she sucks cocks.* I should be thunderstruck, outraged—but twenty-nine kids are gazing at me, waiting, their faces open and alight. Why lie? They trust me. They want to know the truth.

Garner first published this article anonymously in *Digger* in November 1972. *Digger* was a countercultural paper founded by the publisher Phillip Frazer and produced by a collective that included Garner, Bruce Hanford, Ponch Hawkes, Colin Talbot, Garrie Hutchinson, Virginia Fraser and Isabelle Rosemberg. Beatrice Faust, Michael Gawenda, Bobby Sykes, Bob Gould and Frank Moorhouse were some of the contributors. The sixteen-page broadsheet appeared fortnightly and cost 30 cents. Its readership included politically aware young adults, many of whom had grown up reading Frazer's earlier publications such as *Go-Set* and *Revolution*.

The next issue of *Digger* carried a letter titled 'Sexual Virtuosity', in which the writer praised Ms X's courage and honesty in the classroom, acknowledged that she had treated the students with respect, but argued that in refusing to engage with issues of homosexuality the teacher had probably furthered the sense of alienation for some of the students. Garner, as Ms X, responded. She wrote that she had talked about homosexuality; she had articulated her 'own uncertain experience of homosexual love', while feeling out of her depth. Her own experience of a lesbian relationship, she wrote, was 'emotionally ecstatic but physically puzzling'. The same issue of *Digger* celebrated Gay Pride Week. Here Garner published a half-page article,

'Bisexuality: Joining the Middle', with a prominent by-line. It was not her finest piece of journalism. She was 'ga-ga with love' for a woman, she embraced the idea of sex with a woman, 'but then we never did get it on', she wrote.

The day after publication an outraged school caretaker challenged Garner in the staffroom. She readily admitted to writing the initial article as Ms X. For two weeks she continued to teach and take her students to the Fitzroy Baths, unaware that the wheels of her demise were in motion. On 7 December, she met with the school principal, was shown his draft report to the Department of Education and, in typical Garner manner, corrected his spelling. She was expecting a slap on the wrist and possible school transfer. Eight days later, she was sacked for using 'popular four-letter words' to discuss 'the male and female sexual organs, and the sexual act'. Garner insisted that she did not realise speaking in this manner was a political act. She was simply being honest.

Maybe. Or maybe not. Even if Garner did not recall the obscenity charges laid against the editors of *Oz* magazine in Sydney in 1963 and 1964, she would have known about the raid on *Oz*'s London offices following the 1970 publication of the 'School Kids Issue', replete with a cover featuring a stylised lesbian orgy and 'four-letter words'. In 1971, the *Oz* editors, Richard Neville, Jim Anderson and Felix Dennis, were charged in London with obscenity and conspiring to 'debauch and corrupt the morals of young children'. Garner may also have been aware of the onstage arrest, in Queensland in 1969, of Norman Staines for saying 'Fuckin'' at the conclusion of Alex

Buzo's *Norm and Ahmed*. In that same year, closer to home, the actors in La Mama's production of John Romeril's *Whatever Happened to Realism* were also charged with obscenity. When police removed them from the theatre to the Carlton police station, a crowd gathered outside the station chanting: 'Shit, fuck, bum, cunt.' Language was political.

The *Digger* collective were waging a war on censorship. The third issue led with Beatrice Faust's three-page verbal and pictorial study of pornography. The Victorian police raided *Digger*'s office and served an obscenity writ. Garner's article about the sex education lesson ran in the sixth issue. It too attracted a writ. A magistrate fined *Digger* $750 for the pornographic pictures and $500 for Garner's story. On appeal Judge Martin, of Melbourne's County Court, found that the pictures were 'undesirable' rather than obscene and quashed the fine. He was, however, appalled by Garner's blatant language and increased that fine to $750.

'Why Does the Women Get All the Pain?' is the only one of Garner's *Digger* essays to be included in *True Stories*. It is an extremely important piece, not only because it got her sacked and kickstarted her writing career, but also because it goes some way to explaining her complex responses to institutional power and the academy in *The First Stone*. Garner knew the worth of her story at the time. She asked Axel if he had read the piece, saying she thought it was 'a bottler'.

In addition to book and movie reviews, Garner wrote nearly twenty feature articles for *Digger*. While the paper was defiantly political, Garner's interest remained largely with the politics of women's experiences. She highlighted the plight of unmarried pregnant girls in various refuges. She explained methods of contraception. She lamented the lack of female playwrights and roles for women at the Pram Factory. She attended Women's Electoral Lobby meetings and railed against the male politicians who dominated debate and set the agenda. She explained how collective households work, how the presence of children affects the dynamics of the collective, and how those households fall apart. All of these pieces provided rich groundwork for her future novels. But her heart wasn't in it. In 'The Art of the Dumb Question', she admits that she was ill at ease writing for *Digger*: 'Things I wrote then felt false to me. I was bluffing. I secretly knew myself to be hopelessly bourgeois.' She resigned in September 1974, exhausted and unwell. Diagnosed with hepatitis, she took to her bed and read *War and Peace* and Isaac Babel's stories. She 'howled' over Lionel Trilling's suggestion that Babel's work 'hinted that one might live in doubt, that one might live by means of a question'.

Garner survived 1975 living on the Supporting Mothers' Benefit topped up with small contributions from Bill Garner and her parents. With Alice at school, she spent her mornings in the domed Reading Room of the State Library of Victoria shaping her diary into what she thought might become a novel. In the afternoons she read. She also made her one and only acting debut, playing the part of Jo, an obsessive-compulsive speed queen in Bert Deling's film *Pure Shit*. Relations with her father remained strained. In April she wrote to Axel that her father's '<u>most peculiar</u> attitude towards sex' was unchanged. When Garner went to stay at her parents' beach house in Anglesea, he made a five-hour round trip from his farm in Shelford in order to find out who was with her. He 'tiptoed' in unannounced at ten in the morning, only to find her in the bath with Alice. She noted: 'I am quite sure that my disastrous relationship with my father has a lot to do with the fact that I always fall in love with men a fair bit younger than I am.' Her current lover, she wrote, was in jail in Bangkok.

Axel had sent her some of his poems. She sent him one of hers in return, remarking 'all events described are true, unfortunately':

> This is the day the junkies' child
> Drowned in the river, undefiled.
> This is the day the junkies said
> 'We've learned our lesson now he's dead.'
>
> Out in the kitchen, without a qualm,
> I watched him stick it in his arm.
> Blood ran back, blood ran down;
> I heard him swear, I saw him frown.
> I stood leaning against the shelf
> And watched my man make love to himself.
>
> This is the day the rain fell down.
> I rode my bike across the town.
> I rode my bike across the town;
> The rain fell down, the rain fell down.

She signed off: 'My name is Helen.' She wanted Axel to stop calling her 'Fordie'.

In the latter half of 1975 Garner turned this poem into the song 'White Eyes'. Andrew Bell wrote the score. Jane Clifton sang it. It was the first of her songs to be performed by the rock 'n' roll band Stiletto, made up of Bell, Clifton, Janie Conway, Marnie Sheehan and Eddie van Roosendael.

2

'The blind, needing self':
Monkey Grip

In the journal…I create myself. The journal
is a vehicle for my sense of selfhood.

SUSAN SONTAG, 'ON KEEPING A JOURNAL' (1957)

I have started work on a novel and expect it to take AT LEAST a year.
I go to the public library every morning while the kids are at school.
It's the most enjoyable work I've ever done in my life.

HELEN GARNER, LETTER TO AXEL CLARK (4 DECEMBER 1975)

In the same year that Garner decided to try to shape her diary into what would become *Monkey Grip*, Hilary McPhee and Diana Gribble established McPhee Gribble, their pioneering publishing house in Jolimont Lane, East Melbourne. It was a time of great optimism in the Australian arts community, and many expatriates had come home in the three years since Gough Whitlam's election victory in 1972. In 1973 the Australia Council, established under John Gorton, doubled its funding and established its various boards. Independent publishing houses were on the increase. The post-1968 generation had new, exciting stories to tell, and new ways to tell them. In *The Americans, Baby*, published in 1972, Frank Moorhouse employed the discontinuous narrative form to weave together confronting stories of social change, fraught gender politics and sexual transgression. Two years later Peter Carey, in *The Fat Man in History*, also sought to shock his readers, but in a different way. Carey's fabulist tales played with the established boundaries of fiction and reality, and drew attention to the fictive process. And *Mother I'm Rooted: An Anthology of Australian Women Poets*, edited by Kate Jennings, marked a truly revolutionary shift for, and celebration of, Australian women's voices when it was published in 1975 by Outback Press.

Jennings selected poems that articulated female experience 'uncontaminated by trends, fashions and the politics of the poetry world': poems about 'childbirth, babies, menstruation, housework, feminine conditioning and female perceptions'. The anthology provoked a heated debate about literary standards. Were these subjects worthy of poetic treatment? Garner's contribution to the anthology was an untitled poem celebrating the good-natured spirit of a treasured friend within the domestic setting of a shared household. She went on to chart in *Monkey Grip* the complex female experiences of motherhood, sexuality and desire, within the changing social contexts of the seventies, and to explode notions of literary decorum.

In her memoir, *Other People's Words*, Hilary McPhee remembers Garner arriving at the Jolimont Lane bunker in 1976 'to tell us rather diffidently that she thought she might have written a novel'. McPhee and Gribble each read the manuscript overnight and were impressed by the originality of the voice. McPhee judged the manuscript to be 'a bit bumpy and awkward in places but there was no straining after effect, no literary flourishes'. Like the audience members at *Betty Can Jump*, the vast majority of female readers of *Monkey Grip* would be gripped by the shock of recognition. As McPhee explains: 'It was as if Nora was speeding into a present that many of us were trying to make sense of, inventing the rules as we went along, copping the hurt and the uncertainty that things would be alright.'

Monkey Grip was published in hardcover on 16 September 1977, at a recommended retail price of $7.75. The first print run of 2500 copies sold out quickly, the next 4000 even faster. There was excitement about this book. But the reviewers were split, and many were savage in their attacks. At best the book was regarded as 'tremendous' and 'truthful', a 'good old-fashioned love story'; it described a new way of loving and living beyond marriage and the nuclear family. For others it was 'immoral and sordid', 'careless and unstructured', 'perverse', 'repetitious', certainly 'not a book for the prudish'. Jan McGuinness, in the *Herald*, could not resist noting that Garner was once the 'Head prefect at Tamie Fraser's old school' and was the teacher 'at the centre of a storm over a frank talk on sex'. Now here she was, 'Helen the Stirrer', 'a refugee from middle class conservatism', writing a 'controversial book about junkies and the counter culture'. Many critics were made uncomfortable by both the form and the explicit subject matter. What was to be made of a woman writing about the need for, and joy of, fucking—or what Peter Pierce termed 'the scatological verb'? How were

'Mr and Mrs Average from the suburbs' supposed to react to a narrative written from within the drug culture? John Larkin, writing in the *Age* in October 1977, argued that the book was getting the 'wrong kind of publicity' and pleaded the need for careful reading. In treating it like a drug directory, he noted, readers were being distracted from recognising how the book offered a sensitive distillation of 'the incredible eddying…of human relationships'.

The most vitriolic attacks made no distinction between Garner as author and Nora as protagonist. Peter Corris was repelled by what he saw as Garner's 'audacious' egocentrism: 'Helen Garner has published her private journal rather than written a novel. The "I" of the book, Nora, is indisputably the author herself and the other characters are identifiable members of the *Digger*…Pram Factory set in Melbourne.' He wondered if Garner was able to write about anything other than herself. Similar responses have marked Garner's critical reception for nearly forty years. To an extent, Corris was correct. The characters were recognisable. Garner admits freely that they were all versions of actual people, including herself. She maintains that she circulated the manuscript around the relevant households prior to publication and that no one complained.

Mark Rubbo, who ran the bookshop Readings, remarked that 'half of Carlton was buying the book to see if they were in it. Journalist John Halpern had just created a furore by naming the real-life identities of the characters in Frank Hardy's *Power Without Glory* and he was threatening to do the same with *Monkey Grip*.' The fact that the novel was heavily autobiographical is less startling than the attacks levelled at it for being so. A compulsive diarist, Garner has always written autobiographically as a means of making sense of her experiences and her world. Joan Didion's words could be Garner's: 'I write entirely to find out what I'm thinking, what I'm looking at, what I see and what it means. What I want and what I fear.' Nearly twenty-five years later Garner challenged critics like Corris in her essay defiantly titled 'I':

> Why the sneer in 'All she's done is publish her diaries'? It's as if this were cheating. As if it were lazy. As if there were no work involved in keeping a diary in the first place: no thinking, no discipline, no creative energy; no intelligent or artful ordering of material; no choosing of material, for God's sake; no shaping of narrative; no ear for the music of human speech; no portrayal of the physical world; no free movement back and forth in time; no leaping between inner and outer; no examination of motive; no imaginative use of language.

Reading *Monkey Grip* as poorly disguised reality not only dismisses the creative process of shaping the story, it also ignores how and why the diarised basis for this novel contributes to its meaning. A diary often consists of episodic entries that record immediate experience. Writing only for the self, the diarist is free to record emotions, moods and thoughts. In her 1947 chapbook *On Writing*, Anaïs Nin noted:

> in the Diary I only wrote of what interested me genuinely, what I felt most *strongly* at the moment, and I found this fervor, this enthusiasm produced a vividness which often

> withered in the formal work...The Diary...being written
> at white heat, developed a love of the living moment, of
> the immediate emotional reaction to experience, which
> revealed the power of recreation to lie in the sensibilities
> rather than in memory or critical intellectual perception.

It is precisely these kinds of crafted sensibilities that Garner develops and foregrounds in the finished novel which retains, for the most part, the vivid immediacy of private jottings.

In *Monkey Grip*, Nora tells her story. The narrative covers a year of her life from one baking, hot Melbourne summer to the next. Nora is a single mother who lives in various collective households in Melbourne's Fitzroy with her seven-year-old daughter, Gracie, and negotiates relationships with housemates, friends and lovers. Nora loves Javo, a part-time actor and a heroin addict. They exist in a world of free love, awash with sex, drugs, and rock'n'roll, but Nora is nowhere near as cool as she pretends to be, and Javo is unreliable. Their relationship unfolds—much like a diary—through fragmentary scenes, letters, intense moments and painful absences. And, like a diary, their relationship is about the now, rather than any projected future.

In a monkey grip, the harder one tries to pull away, the more firmly one is held. For much of the narrative Nora is held in such a clasp; she aspires to be free but is addicted to loving Javo. Her perspective lures the reader into a vortex, where it is possible to feel swamped by her (self)obsessions and insecurity. The narrative pace slows. Will Javo return? Will Javo survive? Nora frets. The reader can only wait. Short, staccato sentences proliferate. And then, with a quiet knock or sudden appearance, Javo is back. Nora has her fix; the tone lifts, the sentences lengthen and flow. The narrative is on a high. Until the next withdrawal. In its cyclic surge and retreat, the story can be read as repetitious and going nowhere. From a different perspective, it represents the ebb and flow of relationships and the endless cycle of dependency on drugs or love.

Garner's fluctuating narrative structure was bold and new in Australian fiction. Frank Moorhouse had championed the discontinuous narrative (aspects of which can be traced back to Henry Lawson) in which stories, characters and relationships were not developed sequentially, but presented as fragmentary, improvised and unreliable. Moorhouse's characters appear and reappear at various times across a body of stories. A number of critics made favourable comparisons between Moorhouse and Garner but, in suggesting that Garner provided simply a female equivalence to the 'impolite, brashly explorative side of Australian life', they missed the innovative nature of her novel.

Garner read Moorhouse while living in Paris in 1978 and wrote to Axel praising his skill, but identifying 'a coldness' in the stories that made her 'nervous'. Both Moorhouse and Garner were writing new forms of Australian realism, trying to capture the turbulent experiences of a generation of educated, urban youth. Both questioned conventional ways of telling a story, thereby inviting closer attention to how fiction is created. Both broke taboos on content and language. Yet their approaches to gender and location were very different. In *Real Relations*, Susan Lever pinpoints some crucial differences relating to gender:

> Garner's women characters share with the urban characters in Moorhouse's short stories a commitment to questioning prevalent sexual attitudes, but the sexual revolution makes more complex demands on them because sex cannot be disentangled from its implications for the female body, including maternity, abortion, and menstruation. Where Moorhouse's...accounts of sex retained some of the masculine hubris of conventional pornography, Garner managed to recreate the vulner-ability of a female sexual perspective...she demonstrated that there was another way to write about sex—carefully and explicitly, weighing the act's emotional significance from a woman's point of view.

Moorhouse's urban tribes are made up predominantly of male characters who drink in Sydney's Balmain and Newtown pubs and are influenced strongly by the libertarian philosophy of John Anderson, a legendary professor at Sydney University. By contrast, Garner's characters are at home in the nightclubs and pubs of Melbourne's Fitzroy and Carlton. Jane Clifton, upon whom the character of Angela is based, suggested to me that the potent combination of theatre in La Mama and the APG, vibrant pub band culture, sociopolitical awareness and shared households, made their milieu and their lifestyle unlike anywhere else.

Monkey Grip traces Nora's emotional responses to her world, marking the contrast between her private reflections and public persona. Nora knows she is 'a fast faker', she fears appearing 'uncool'. She suffers from 'terminal naivety' when it comes to loving a junkie. At times she is overwhelmed by the responsibility of being a mother to Gracie—she doesn't feel like a 'real grown-up'—yet she is both mother and lover to Javo. She enjoys being the steady centre around which he hovers and, at some level, she needs to feel that he is always on the point of breaking away. She eschews notions of fidelity and commitment, yet longs 'stupidly for something [and]…someone steady and complete'.

Nora does not like herself much. She recognises that she is vain, stubborn and in need of constant validation. Melbourne critic and bookseller Sean O'Beirne identified the core of *Monkey Grip* when he wrote recently: 'This honest book about Australia can…take you far inside, closer to the blind, needing self.' *Monkey Grip* is a story about a naïve, blind, needy Nora groping towards some self-awareness and maturity. At the outset she rolls in the water at the Fitzroy baths 'where the sign read AQUA PROFONDA'. Drawn powerfully to Javo, she thinks she is 'only testing the water with [her] toe', but she is already in over her head.

At one point Nora and another character talk about 'what it means to be alive in 1975, what change is and might be, how we see ourselves fitting in (or not) to this society'. While their discussion may have canvassed the end of the Vietnam War, the invasion of East Timor or the dismissal of the Whitlam government, we remember that '*Monkey Grip*'s particular moment in history places it not in grand politics, but the politics of sexual liberation'. Nineteen seventy-five was International Women's Year. As a sexually liberated woman and mother, Nora tries to establish workable patterns of living, parenting and loving among new configurations of family. Her predicament and confusion were shared increasingly by women of her generation across the Western world. Feminist presses, bookshops, journals and reading groups were being established. Writing that privileged intimate female experience proliferated. So too did feminist literary theory. In 1975 French philosopher Hélène Cixous published 'Le Rire de la Méduse', translated the following year as 'The Laugh of the Medusa', in which she called for women to write themselves—their bodies, sexuality, desires—into their texts. Cixous 'wished that women…might exclaim: I, too, overflow; my desires have invented new desires, my body knows unheard-of songs'.

Nora exclaims such things. Yet it was not Cixous who galvanised Garner to write; it was her belief that her story was big enough to become a novel. For Garner the real issue with theory—here and throughout her work—is the glaring gap she feels between feminist theoretical positions and her lived experience. In *Monkey Grip* she explores that gap largely through Nora and Angela, who espouse sexual freedom yet experience jealousy and long for 'romantic, exclusive' relationships.

In a climate of new sexual politics, characters swap and change partners, as Nora describes, 'like a very complicated dance to which the steps had not yet been choreographed, all of us trying to move gracefully in spite of our ignorance'. Clifton remembers there being rosters for everything, including sex and the break-up of couples. A written request for permission to sleep with someone was known as 'getting a Carlton letter'. Clifton,

Garner and Ponch Hawkes have all spoken of the damaging repercussions of those open, experimental years. Hawkes writes:

> I did despicable things to other women in the name of sexual freedom. You went with it, all this stuff you said you believed, all this rhetoric about being open and having free relationships. The consequences were it was very hurtful to people who then couldn't say they were very hurt, or act hurt and who had to see you the next day or the same day, in the hall—and wear it.

Even today, Garner is troubled by the hurt she caused through what she defines as her thoughtless and cruel egotism. *Monkey Grip* introduces a theme that runs throughout Garner's life and work: how should one balance the desire for personal freedom with ethical responsibility.

A confluence of factors contributed to *Monkey Grip*'s production and success, not least the establishment of McPhee Gribble. Garner had sent an early, and quite different, version of the manuscript to Colin Talbot at Outback Press for his opinion. Talbot remembers thinking there needed to be 'more story'—there was at that stage no story of Javo—in order to make the 'passion on the page' more believable. Garner believes that many male publishers would have either rejected her manuscript or required a radical change in structure. Judy Brett was the first to point out that *Monkey Grip* would not have been published a decade earlier and probably would not have been written even a short five years later. Reforms to Australia's censorship laws, championed first by Don Chipp in

1970 and then by Gough Whitlam in 1972, were essential for its publication. As for content, the sexual promiscuity of that time was taking place in a golden window of freedom post the Pill but pre HIV/AIDS.

At a 2012 Wheeler Centre discussion, Kerryn Goldsworthy postulated that part of *Monkey Grip*'s continuing appeal is driven by a nostalgia for seemingly more innocent days. It is a novel about being young, about dinking kids on bikes, baking by the pool or on hot salty beaches, hurtling down the freeway bound for Sydney, having different lovers and dancing till dawn high on drugs and sex and love. Some writers of the next generation claim *Monkey Grip* taught them to write. Tegan Bennett Daylight, initially disorientated by 'such unstructured fiction', read the book repeatedly because she 'needed to know how it was written'. She credits *Monkey Grip* with changing the way she read and how she saw the world. Its images 'made me feel somehow present, alert to the shifts in light and weather, to the look of a street, park or house…[Garner] looked around her with an eye like a torch, sweeping across everything, selecting and rejecting, illuminating'.

The quality of Garner's writing was never in doubt, though she herself remains embarrassed by what she has called this 'artless…naïve and appallingly revealing' book. Even Peter Corris couldn't help but praise Garner's style, albeit in somewhat patronising language:

> Ms Garner is a very good writer of English. Her prose,
> a few clichéd passages excepted, is attractive and acces-
> sible, a pleasure to read. She has the ability to capture

movement and stillness and light and sound with words
which belong to writers like E. M. Forster and, to give
a different but appropriate example, Kerouac.

Like Kerouac, Garner captured the voice of a generation
excited by dangerous freedom. Like Forster, she is attuned
to the physical world. Part of Garner's daily diarising ritual
has been to record the weather: the sun's warmth, the rain's
texture, how the breeze feels on her skin. Those tactile impressions infuse her prose:

> The kids begin to sing. We roll in unison…down the
> wide road and into the green tunnel, the cave of the
> Edinburgh Gardens…The hoses flick silver strings on to
> the drying grass. The cicadas beat a rhythm that comes
> in waves, like fainting or your own heartbeat. We sweep
> round the corner into the Belgium Lane, where the air
> is peppery with the scent of cut timber and even on this
> still day the poplars flutter over the ancient grey picket
> fence; they thrust up their sprouts through the cracking
> asphalt under our wheels.

Monkey Grip assumes a community of readers versed in rock
and literary culture. The narrative is suffused with music—Bob
Dylan, Joni Mitchell, Stevie Wonder, Elvis Costello, Aretha
Franklin, Bette Midler, Jo Jo Zep—that contributes to the
texture and tone of the prose. The careful reader is rewarded
if she brings to the story an understanding of the 'attenuated
weeping' of Stevie Wonder's 'They Won't Go When I Go', or
the fractured relationship of Joni Mitchell's 'Electricity'. Nora's
self-destructive behaviour takes on added pathos when one

appreciates that her mantra is Mitchell's 'giving it all away'.

Nora's reading practices also advance the narrative. In the early days of their relationship, she reads to Javo from Diane Wakoski's *The Motorcycle Betrayal Poems*: 'the one about the big snoring bikie who fell asleep beside her, drunk, and woke not knowing he carried her bullets in his back'. Nora understands that the poem is 'about love'. That is all Garner offers. In fact, the poem 'Love Letter Postmarked Van Beethoven' encapsulates Nora's—and Garner's—emotional state. It is infused with the speaker's repressed anger at not being loved enough by all the men who have been in her life, including 'my father who deserted me' and 'the bad husband who would drink late in bars/and not take me with him'.

Nora is a prolific reader, particularly of books portraying the lives of intelligent women trying to carve out a space for themselves as something more than simply daughter, wife or mistress. In *Washington Square*, Catherine Sloper struggles against, but eventually succumbs to, her father's powerful control. In *To the Lighthouse*, Lily Briscoe wrestles with the 'puerile' tediousness and 'beautiful necessity' of love before triumphantly choosing a life of art over marriage. Julia Martin, forced to live off men for survival, manages to regain a sliver of dignity in Jean Rhys' *After Leaving Mr MacKenzie*. Nora reads them all. She cites Anna Wulf in Doris Lessing's *The Golden Notebook* and lends Nina Bawden's *A Woman of My Age* to Claire. Both these novels are fiercely unsentimental about women's sexual and intellectual desires, and canvass ideas about infidelity, female orgasm, the pleasure of casual sex and the politics of family relationships. Lessing also explores how women might construct their lives through narrative.

Garner claims to have been surprised that *Monkey Grip* shocked some readers. She insists that she was living a 'sheltered' life surrounded by like-minded people and that it was hard for her 'to see what was going on then, outside that ghetto'. Clifton affirms that they were so immersed in their world that they had no idea how far from the mainstream they may have strayed. Garner's almost radical innocence, or ignorance, is underlined by her admission that she was extremely distressed that her father reacted badly to her lifestyle and continued to think of her as a 'bludger because I don't have a job and a wage'. She thinks her parents never read *Monkey Grip*. 'At 35,' she told Jan McGuinness, 'you'd think I'd be beyond caring what they thought. I wish to be in harmony with them but it's not possible and that's the ultimate contradiction of my life. I can't have both the things I value and my parents' approval and it makes me very sad.'

No one officially launched the novel. Eighty-four invitations were posted out: 'McPhee Gribble are about to publish *Monkey Grip* by Helen Garner. Can you come to a party on Friday 16 September at 5 o'clock?' Ponch Hawkes took a series of publicity photographs of a barefooted Garner in a floral dress and straw hat, dinking Alice around the streets of Carlton. People gathered in the McPhee Gribble office, now in Drummond Street in Carlton. The poet Vincent Buckley, who taught Garner at Melbourne University, bought ten copies of the book for Christmas presents.

Patrick White was one of a number of writers who listed *Monkey Grip* among his best books for 1977. In 1978 it won the National Book Council Book of the Year award; Garner was the first woman recipient of that prize. The judges were John McLaren, Joyce Nicholson and Anne Summers, author of *Damned Whores and God's Police: The Colonization of Women in Australia*. In their citation they remarked that *Monkey Grip* was neither an 'easy nor an early choice' and that its subject—'heroin addiction, inner-city communal living and obsessional love'—aroused 'some resistance among the judges'. They went on to say that the central character is 'superbly realised in her hesitancies and enthusiasms', that the book is 'beautifully constructed', and that Garner was 'utterly honest in facing the dilemmas of freedom, and particularly of social and sexual freedom for women trying to create for themselves a role which will recognise their full humanity'.

Monkey Grip was translated into French and Italian. Rights were sold to Virago in the United Kingdom and Seaview Books in the United States. Both published hardback editions with limited success. British reviewers, in particular, seemed perplexed by Garner's 'defiant' Australian voice. Meanwhile, in Australia, the book went from strength to strength. By the time Ken Cameron's film adaptation was released in 1982, *Monkey Grip* had sold over 100,000 copies. It is now recognised as a modern classic, and has been taught widely in schools. In 2016 *Monkey Grip* made its way to the Venice Architecture Biennale. The Australian pavilion was constructed as a swimming pool. The sign on the wall read: 'DANGER DEEP WATER/AQUA PROFONDA'.

3

Ruptures and Dislocations:
Honour & Other People's Children

…that mighty institution, the family, in all its unbearable pressures, its betrayals and abandonments and silent endurances, its rickety renovations of itself, and its unexpected explosions of compassion, pity and forgiveness.

HELEN GARNER, 'GOING THE BLOODY HARD WAY' (2016)

There is a fraught period, known all too well by authors, when the editorial work on a manuscript is complete and the publication date looms. During that time in 1977, while Garner waited for *Monkey Grip* to be released, she suffered a crisis of confidence. She was keen to write short stories but was not convinced she had anything to say. She decided to try for an Australia Council grant and reassured her concerned publishers: 'I finally dragged myself out of the doldrums I've been lurking in since I finished *Monkey Grip* and realized I'm not done for yet. I've written two short stories and am half way through a third.' She was also writing songs.

In April 1978 she sent McPhee Gribble the stories and the lyrics for ten songs, including 'White Eyes', of which she observed: 'I wrote this before I started *Monkey Grip*: someone suggested I could've saved myself the trouble.' Some of the songs had been written contemporaneously with *Monkey Grip*. The guitarist Andrew Bell was a member of the collective household in Scotchmer Street. Stiletto often rehearsed there in the front room. Clifton remembers Garner emerging from her room with song lyrics asking for an opinion. Bell would pick up his guitar and rehearsal would begin. In December 1977 Stiletto recorded 'Cream' for the Red Symons-produced *Debutantes* album. By the time Garner sent the sheaf of songs to her publishers, nine further songs had been performed by Melbourne bands. She wrote to them that 'people have started taking me seriously on that score, songs I mean, and I don't think I'm such a dog after all'. The songs were: 'Not Too Young for Joy', 'Look at That Sky' and 'Home' with Tony Burkys, 'Anything But That' with Sally Ford, 'Don't You Know What Love Is?' with Martin Armiger, 'Cream' and 'Second Home' with Andrew Bell and 'Run for My Money' and 'Charming Boy' with Jane Conway. Stiletto's *Licence to Rage* was released in 1978 and featured 'Not Too Young For Joy' and 'Second Home'.

In May 1978 Garner and eight-year-old Alice headed to Paris. The move was made possible by a one-year $6000 fellowship awarded by the Literature Board of the Australia Council. The timing was good. Garner felt the need to leave Melbourne and escape some of the fallout from *Monkey Grip*. But for much of the time she was lonely and homesick in Paris. Her French was improving but financial hardship plagued her and fed her anxieties. In her memoir, *The Student Cronicles*, Alice writes that her experience of walking to school 'through the streets of Paris's seventeenth arrondisement, wearing new knee-high red boots' generated for her a love of France, but at the time Garner felt it was a less than ideal place for a young child. Alice returned to Australia to live with Bill and his partner in January 1979. Bill had asked Garner for a divorce in order to remarry. Garner had by now met Jean-Jacques Portail, who was to become her second husband and who later translated *Monkey Grip* into French.

In October 1978 Garner wrote to McPhee and Gribble announcing that she was:

> nervously working on another story (novel comes later when I get into gear)…it is surprising to find that now when I put stuff on paper it is absolutely different in content & style, I feel as if I am writing in a dream. I would like the voice to remain the same but the tone & content and point of view to change radically.

She was also in detailed correspondence with Ken Cameron about writing the screenplay for what would become the 1982 film adaptation of *Monkey Grip*. Garner's letters to Cameron demonstrate her excitement about the project and her desire to be closely involved in the writing process. More importantly, they show an author, now at a certain distance from her text, reflecting upon her characters' motivations and development. Garner explained how essential it was to understand the gulf between Nora's actions and emotions. She stressed that the central connection between Nora and Javo was sexual. She suggested a rewrite of the first scene where they go to bed, insisting it be almost prudish, that the lovers be tentative, awkward and shy. There should be a 'weird sort of politeness' she wrote, 'in a way they are both a bit puritanical.' She explained what both Javo and Nora each want from their relationship, repeatedly asking 'Do you know what I mean?'. She was keen to see how film might be able to convey the weight of meaning she had sought to convey through verbal imagery.

Garner wondered also about casting. She did not want Javo to look like a 'clichéd Carlton type', and she was hoping Nora could be 'ORDINARY-LOOKING' rather than glamorous. In the end she was thrilled with Noni Hazlehurst's appearance and performance as Nora. She joked that, now she had seen *Palm Beach*, Bryan Brown was her 'current hero' but was too healthy to play Javo. Cameron had originally cast the singer Doc Neeson in the role, but The Angels began a lucrative tour two weeks before filming so Colin Friels stepped in. At the time Friels was playing Hamlet in the Sydney Theatre Company production. Jane Clifton hoped to play Angela. Cameron flew to Melbourne to watch her perform, then famously told her that she could not act or sing well enough for the part. Instead he cast Chrissy Amphlett, backed by the Divinyls. They were a Sydney band, but in casting them Cameron emphasised the central role music, pub bands and dancing played in the story. Also inspired was Cameron's casting of Alice Garner, then aged eleven, to play Gracie. Helen Garner attended the premiere with her mother, Gwen. She remembers being embarrassed during the sex scenes.

Garner told Cameron about the films she was seeing in Paris, including *La Femme qui pleure*, directed by Jacques Doillon:

> three main characters, a bloke, his wife and the Other Woman; also a child, about two years old…The bloke has started a scene with the other woman in Paris…His wife just can't cope, she cries all the time, is disgusted with herself, tries to get in control of her rage and sadness but can't…She goes to Paris, makes a rendezvous with the other woman in a café—HIGHPOINT OF FILM, I was tremendously impressed and moved by this scene, the mother says 'I can't stay long, I've got my daughter to pick up,' she says, 'I want to tell you I don't hate you, but it's so hard, I'm so unhappy'—begins to cry, runs from the table in shame, stops in the street outside, the other woman comes out, hesitates in front of her, impatient and yet moved in spite of herself, the wife is crying, ashamed, wanting to be brisk with herself, can't get control, the other woman hesitates, puts out her arm, the wife lets herself be comforted by this touch for a split second—goes soft against the other's shoulder, then stiffens again, too proud to give in to kindness—I wanted to stand up and cheer, it was SO TRUE…'

The point of all this, she wrote, is to do with structure and how it might work for the *Monkey Grip* film: 'Short stabs, very little explanatory stuff, between each stab a moment of blank screen so as to separate them firmly; almost no background of characters. In terms of classic structure—rising to climax, dénouement, slide to end—it took all sorts of liberties.' She was right. That unconventional structure was perfect for the film, precisely because it was the way she had structured her book.

More obviously, Garner's description of Doillon's film informs the narrative techniques employed in *Honour & Other People's Children*, *The Children's Bach* and *Postcards from Surfers*: short stabs, little explanation, textual silence. The importance of Garner's use of the fragment as a narrative device cannot be overstated. We also see it in 'Eight Scenes from a Friendship', 'Dreams of her Real Self' and her diary extracts. Garner crafts a series of intense moments or reflections and separates them. Meaning is generated and resonates across the space and time of the blank page.

Garner attended the 1979 Cannes Film Festival and was disgusted by the 'movie scene': 'another layer of the despised naivety goes down the drain'. She saw three Australian films there: *Dimboola*, *Palm Beach* and *Mad Max*. She loved *Dimboola* and found *Palm Beach* to be 'interesting technically but a bit empty in the human department'. *Mad Max* was 'indescribable': 'A giant, technically very competent male WANK. Fascist, even.' She walked out after an hour. Crucially, the film 'had the effect of forcing me further towards a political & moral & aesthetic POSITION, which I find an excruciating process though I know it MUST BE DONE'. She was adamant that *Monkey Grip* must not be 'another empty Australian STORY FILM'. The once naïve woman from the Fitzroy ghetto was beginning to take herself and her craft more seriously.

*

Garner had been trying to write her new novel but by June 1979 she admitted to McPhee and Gribble that she needed their 'stern advice' in order to progress. The publishers came to Paris and read the manuscript, titled *Honour*, sitting on the uncomfortable iron chairs in the Tuileries. It was not good. Garner's memory is of the two women, at her door, holding out a bottle of something. In *Other People's Words*, McPhee remembers: 'Helen came to the Hotel Esmerelda where we drank whisky and talked miserably for hours.'

One month later McPhee wrote encouragingly to Garner: 'We've both been feeling dreadful about our last heavy session with you in Paris. I only hope you didn't go away feeling cut off at the knees…needless to say we'd love to see the MS at the next stage.' Garner responded within the week:

> Of course I felt awful after the session but think it was still for the best and that you were right. I lost a few nights' sleep. Then I went away on holidays with Jean-Jacques and took it all out on him which he bore like the brick he is…I am rewriting massively.

It was Tim Winton who once suggested to Garner that she never really had an apprenticeship as an author. The manuscript of *Monkey Grip* had been accepted immediately by McPhee Gribble and with minor edits—Garner wrote a few bridging paragraphs to flesh out some characters—went on to be a publishing sensation. The pressure to produce an impressive second book was immense. Garner had tried to replicate the subject matter and style of *Monkey Grip*. It was never going to fly. She picked the novel apart and fashioned it into two long stories.

Garner returned to Australia in September 1979. In 1980 she married Jean-Jacques Portail and, on 17 November of that year, *Honour & Other People's Children* was published. The first print run was 6000, the second 1500.

Monkey Grip concludes with Nora reaching a point of some equanimity, knowing that it is '[t]ime to go home.' That home is the collective household that operated as a supportive family. The two stories in *Honour & Other People's Children* express, in different ways, the longing for, yet loss of, home. In both, home is located primarily in committed relationships between parents, children, lovers and friends. Characters face the painful possibility of being cast out of, or separated from, family. Both stories articulate the profound heartache brought about by losing contact with beloved children—a powerful theme that would re-emerge in Garner's later nonfiction works, *Joe Cinque's Consolation* and *This House of Grief.*

The book's epigraph:

> ...Things mattered
> and love, anxious love
> rose and put forth its flags.

is taken from the concluding lines of Chris Wallace-Crabbe's poem 'Genesis'. 'Genesis' speaks of a loss of innocence, and chastises Adam for being a weak man, before the poet goes on to celebrate what became the flawed everydayness of paradise; a place more real once it was energised by human love in all its anxious complexity. Eve learns 'the first lesson of humanity/

which is knowledge, pain and loss'. Garner's characters also learn that lesson. They become painfully aware of how much things matter: things like shared history, dignity in the face of loss, empathic understanding and a sense of belonging.

Honour is a polished, tightly structured story about the need for the formal dissolution of one marriage to make way for another. It opens with Garner's characteristic focus on the sensual world:

> On summer nights they walked through city gardens.
>
> The air stood thick in their nostrils, a damp warmth lay upon their shoulders. Water dripped somewhere, randomly, without rhythm…Jenny's head swam in heat: her pores opened for the sweat to break. She saw his face floating by the fleshy flowers, eager, sharp and gentle. She wanted to take him in through her skin.

Jenny and Frank are the newer couple, basking in a joyous period of openness and discovery. Frank was once married to Kathleen. They have been uncomplicatedly separated for five years. Their 'lack of interest in divorce had given them a certain bohemian status in both their families' and has kept them safe from making the mistake of marrying again. All that is about to change.

Kath is summoned to Frank's house. The front door is left open for her. It will not be again. Frank gathers 'himself into a bunch' and throws the news at Kath: Jenny, unused to their patterns of living, wants Frank to 'clean up' his past and get a divorce. Briefly, Kath is furious, but there is a connection between these two that extends even beyond their cherished daughter, Flo, a 'force-field' generated by a shared history: 'It was hatred, regret, pity; it was respect and the fiercest loyalty.' Frank and Kath had thought they would always go on being related to each other. Now Frank wants to settle down. And he wants Flo to live with him. Kath flounders: 'Some half-gagged splinter-self in the depths was twisting in protest: what about *me*?' To whom will she belong?

After another half-page of silence, Kath comes to collect Flo. She rushes in from the street only to be confronted by a closed screen door. She presses her nose against the wire that 'smelled coldly of rust' and 'rattled her fist against the wood'. It is Jenny, in some ways a more glamorous version of herself, who regulates entry into this new space of family. We begin to appreciate the actual and symbolic weight of the various houses in this story. Every discrete narrative section, with the exception of Frank's father's death and the family's journey to the funeral, opens with a house and Kath's exclusion from or welcome presence in it.

The third time Kath visits, Frank and Jenny have moved to their new home. Garner describes the house, particularly the kitchen, in exquisite detail. The real force of Kath's visit, however, takes place in the external 'wash-house' where she is transported back to the grey trough of her childhood baths, calling plaintively for her mother. Disturbed from her reverie by Flo's similarly intoned call, Kath moves to the edge of the yard, looks back at where this new family will live, and recognises 'the house of her childhood'. The spaces and memories of her childhood home rise unbidden. Kath longs to belong, but knows she cannot.

On Kath's penultimate arrival at Frank and Jenny's house, she breaks in through an unlocked window. The breach unleashes simmering tensions between the adults. Kath explains to Flo that Jenny is not used to the large communal households with their open doors and more fluid notions of family. Those days are gone. Propriety necessitates new rules, new boundaries. In a resonant passage, Garner describes the child's pain when told of her parents' planned divorce:

> She wept bitterly, in floods of grief: she did not touch her face, for she was sitting on her hands so that neither of her parents might seize one and sway her into partiality. The tears, unwiped, splashed off her cheeks and on to the table…

> They sat helplessly at the table, survivors of an attempt at a family, while the little girl wept aloud for the three of them, for things that had gone wrong before she was born and when she was only a baby, for the hard truth which they had thought to escape by running parallel with it instead of tackling it head on.

Most critics applauded *Honour*. Barbara Jefferis found it 'faultless in its structure and in the lightness of its touch'. Marion Halligan thought it 'a work of art'. Anne Summers and Geoffrey Dutton, on the other hand, each felt that Garner's canvas was too small. In different ways they suggested that Garner was treading water. Summers complained that Paris seemed to have made no mark on Garner's imagination: 'you would never know…she had ever left Fitzroy'. Compared to *Monkey*

Grip, however, Garner's structure in *Honour* was tighter, the narrative perspective was broadened and her characters were afforded more depth. The story addressed issues of birth, death, marriage and divorce with extreme economy. And Garner ventured more boldly into territory she had sought to avoid in *Monkey Grip*: jealousy between women.

Frank is a well-meaning, lovable man but he is largely ineffectual in the real drama of this narrative. *Honour* focuses on women's experiences of motherhood, belonging and purpose, across generations. Frank's newly widowed mother sits on the beach bracketed by Kath and Jenny. It is the first time we will see these younger women balanced in each other's company. The older woman is their fulcrum. Neither can answer her question: 'What am I going to do now?' Kath asks herself the same question when Flo goes to live with Jenny and Frank.

Midway through the story Jenny reaches out to a vulnerable Kath in a 'moment of blessing', a moment reminiscent of the scene described by Garner from Doillon's film. Significantly, they are again outside the house:

> Jenny felt a throb of almost sexual tenderness towards her: a hard spasm of the heart, a weakening in the pelvis. She darted out the gate and stopped in front of Kathleen, seized her wrist. With force of will she kept the other woman's hand, studied with a peculiar flux of love her sun-wrinkled eyes, the marks of her shrewd expressions. They could even smell each other: flower, oil, coffee, soap: and under these, warmed flesh, dotted tongue, glass of eye, glossy membrane, rope of hair, nail roughly clipped...

> Perhaps they would never dare again. They stepped out
> of each other, frightened.

This scene follows on immediately from Kath's sister's prolapsed uterus, reinforcing Garner's insistence that there can be a deep visceral connection between women, complexly related to their nurturing, life-giving potential.

Ultimately Kath comes to Jenny. She confesses her sense of failure as a mother and wife. Jenny is not disgusted. She aspires to friendship. At Flo's instigation they leave the domestic sphere of the house for the neutral territory of the park. There Flo positions them on a seesaw: 'They hung in the dark, airily balancing, motionless.'

It's possible to see why reviewers felt a sense of déjà vu when they read *Other People's Children*. The story returns to inner Melbourne communal households. There are familiar kitchen table discussions about ideology and music, there are house meetings and late night gigs. The central drama of the story is the breakdown of female companionship and the failure of the collective ideal. But in these early stories Garner is developing characters who will recur in later work. At times they are asked to deal with similar situations and fears. So Kath's abandonment of Frank and Flo, which features as a private confession to Jenny, later becomes a central plot device in *The Children's Bach*. In *Other People's Children*, Scotty and Ruth can find no common ground. Scotty is clever, articulate and officious. Beneath her tough, cynical exterior she is a wounded, loving woman. She foreshadows Janet, who will appear in *Cosmo Cosmolino*. Meanwhile, Ruth is a single mother weighed down by a 'harness of gloom'. The negative energy she generates, often due to her tense relationship with her children, calls to mind Nora's claustrophobia when living solely with Gracie, Rita and Rita's children.

Monkey Grip celebrates the collective responsibility of parenting in large share houses. In *Other People's Children* Scotty embraces that responsibility with Laurel, Ruth's daughter. Scotty has had two abortions and a tubal ligation. She is bossy and short-tempered, but she loves Laurel 'in the tentative way in which we love other people's children, fearful of rejection, even of mockery, loving without rights, thanklessly'. Ultimately, however, Scotty can never be part of Laurel's family. *Other People's Children* traverses familiar territory only to mark its passing. Nearly thirty years later, Garner will revisit the overriding bonds of family when Helen chooses her granddaughter over her friend in *The Spare Room*.

Much of *Honour & Other People's Children* was drawn from Garner's life, but this issue of biographical detail no longer obsessed the critics. Perhaps Garner's craft, particularly in *Honour*, silenced the dissenting voices. Personally, she was less satisfied with this book. The surprise success of *Monkey Grip* had made her 'self-consciously "a writer"'. As she explains in the *True Stories* essay 'The Art of the Dumb Question':

> I tried to apply what I thought of as 'fictional techniques'

to the mess of my experience. I got lost in the attempt and, like many writers, produced a second book which was poorer in spirit than its artless predecessor. The more I tried to disguise real people as 'characters', the more furious they got with me for writing about them at all...*Honour & Other People's Children*, in its clumsy and premature attempts to shape painful experience into 'stories', caused wounds in certain people which have not healed.

This issue of Garner offending friends and family by including them in her work has taken on something of a life of its own. She has said repeatedly over the years that she does not have a strong sense of the boundaries between public and private. Hilary McPhee and Garner's former agent and longtime friend, Barbara Mobbs, go further; each attests that when Garner is in full creative flight she has no filters or boundaries. Since she is interested primarily in investigating her lived realities rather than imagined ones, and since she does not make great attempts to disguise her characters, Garner provides both her detractors and friends with cause for complaint. She acknowledges that it is impossible to write intimately about her own life without revealing something of the lives of those close to her, but she believes that her methods are ethically justifiable because she examines her motivations ruthlessly and strives to apply to herself 'the same degree of analysis and revelation' as she does to others: 'I stress the unappealing, aggressive, unglamorous aspects of myself as a way of lessening my anxiety about portraying other people as they strike me.'

Garner is one writer among many—Updike, Knausgaard,

Tóibín, Didion, Kureishi, Tsiolkas—prepared to plunder her personal life for material. To a large extent, she is unapologetic. In her 1995 essay 'A World Apart', she admits to a certain detachment, and quotes Nadine Gordimer: 'Powers of observation heightened beyond the normal imply…the double process, excessive preoccupation and identification with the lives of others, and at the same time a monstrous detachment…The tension between standing apart and being fully involved: that is what makes a writer.' Garner also explains, in 'The Art of the Dumb Question':

> You may start from the 'real'—but in fiction you soon forget which bits are 'true' and which bits you made up. You get so engaged with the technical problems of making a story work that the connection between its characters and what exists outside the book becomes less and less visible to you, and of less and less interest.

4

A Blessing on this House:
The Children's Bach

*Yesterday I started to write my novel! and, quite unawares,
I found myself writing the first six or seven pages all about you, i.e.
about being in college in 1961 and having you pointed out to me.
How very extraordinary! I suppose I could say you had been the
biggest influence on my life.*

HELEN GARNER, LETTER TO AXEL CLARK (6 SEPTEMBER 1966)

*Whenever I hear Bach I am back again in your dining room
on a hot day at the beginning of 1963 when I never wore anything
but a grubby brown shift and was very happy.*

HELEN GARNER, LETTER TO AXEL CLARK (10 DECEMBER 1965)

Garner never did write a novel about meeting Axel Clark in 1961, but their friendship, forged in those university years, and the time she spent with the Clark family at Tasmania Circle in Forrest, ACT, informed her acclaimed 1984 novella, *The Children's Bach*. Helen Ford loved staying with the Clarks in Canberra. She was a great admirer of Manning and Dymphna Clark and felt welcomed and supported by them.

In his 2011 biography of Manning Clark, *An Eye for Eternity*, Mark McKenna writes that for 'a young woman from working-class Geelong, entering the Clark household was like passing into another world'. Garner told McKenna that she found the Clarks to be 'terribly impressive'. Manning introduced her to a broad range of classical music:

> Often after breakfast…he'd say to me…Listen to this Miss Ford. And he'd put on Bach's Partitas, or a Sibelius Symphony. He lent me the Mozart Piano Concertos… and for someone like myself who grew up in a house without an intellectual life, this music was a revelation—I think it is through music in particular that I can feel Manning's influence. It was heartening to see a man in his 40s learning to play the piano. I can still see him sitting at the piano, his feet crossed under the bench, picking away at Bach's Preludes.

McKenna suggests that, '[i]n Garner, Clark saw a person who was open to his brand of education'. He relates how Clark gave her Henry James' early novella *Madame de Mauves* to read:

> It was a typical Clark test. Garner, all too aware of the enormity of the task, nervously offered Clark her 'modern' interpretation—'I don't know why they didn't just go ahead and have an affair,' she told him. Clark gave a 'wry smile and turned away'. She felt he was 'disappointed' in her. Years later, Garner 'blushed with embarrassment at the thought of how shallow and unsophisticated' her response had been.

In *Madame de Mauves* a seemingly honourable American named Longmore believes himself to be in love with the lonely, sad Euphemia de Mauves. Euphemia is also American but has been educated in a French convent from the age of fourteen. As a seventeen-year-old innocent, she is seduced into accepting a marriage proposal from the manipulative philanderer Richard de Mauves. Misery ensues.

Longmore tells Euphemia, living virtuously and without complaint against her husband, that her life is a 'conscious compromise'. The drama of the narrative revolves around Longmore's moral wrestling about whether or not he and Euphemia should have an affair. Richard would welcome such a development and his sister puts the proposition to Longmore. Euphemia is appalled and begs Longmore, for the sake of friendship and decency, to leave her alone. Longmore returns to America and for two years, hears nothing more of Euphemia. The narrative, moments from conclusion, takes a dramatic turn. We discover that Richard, stunned by his wife's refusal to break her marriage vows, falls desperately in love with her. He repents and begs her forgiveness but the woman we have perceived up to this point to be a model of virtue and goodness, 'inexorably refused': 'She was stone, she was ice, she was outraged virtue.' In despair, Richard suicides.

Garner's 'shallow and unsophisticated' response suggests that she had not appreciated the questions James was investigating about innocence, compromise, duty, sex and power. It's also possible that James' narrative might seem a touch anachronistic to any nineteen-year-old living through a radical re-evaluation of social constraints regarding women, marriage, sexuality and freedom. *The Children's Bach* may be read as Garner's more nuanced response to Manning's 'test'.

The Children's Bach pays homage to both Manning and Axel Clark. Like Manning, and like Garner herself, Athena Fox is attempting to learn the piano. For much of the narrative her timidness impedes her ability to make much headway. Athena's husband, Dexter, shares many of Axel's idiosyncrasies. He is expansive, loving and opinionated. Like Axel, he shares 'an obsessive memory and faithfulness to the past' and fancies himself a dramatic baritone. Manning is identifiable in Dexter's father, Dr Fox, as he contemplates Elizabeth, Dexter's friend from university days:

> She must be nearly forty now…He saw her wide open eyes, her nervous nostrils, her desire to impress, something fancy and successful about her, and yet he felt sure she was the kind of woman who'd throw round terms like the *orthodox feminist position*…He remembered her at nineteen.

In her adult years Garner enjoyed staying in Sydney with Axel, his wife, Alison, and their three children. She wrote twice to Axel and Alison in 1985, thanking them for their hospitality, saying how much she loved being around their kids and remarking that 'after I've been with you I always feel I've been nourished'. Axel and Garner had exchanged a number of letters discussing their children when she was in Paris. An idea began to form: a book about a family in which 'there would be a little boy who had something wrong with him, so you could only reach him through music'. *The Children's Bach* is a clear example of how Garner's imagination works. She drew inspiration from some aspects of the Clarks' family life, but she interwove her own life, her own family, and her creative impulses into the narrative. As she later explained, writing a novel was 'like trying to make a patchwork quilt look seamless. A novel is made up of scraps of our own lives and bits of other people's, and things we think in the middle of the night and whole notebooks full of randomly collected details.'

In *Monkey Grip* Garner stressed how the new patterns of communal living offered, particularly for women, a sense of liberating possibility beyond marriage and childrearing. In *Honour & Other People's Children* she explored how those hard-won freedoms were coupled with compromise and painful loss. In *The Children's Bach*, she shifts her focus to the suburban household of a married couple, and the burdens and benefits of responsibility and commitment. She burrows into the domestic space of the Fox family's home, before throwing the doors open to the destabilising influences of the world beyond. The house itself becomes almost porous, a membrane through which various characters pass. Yet something solid remains at its core.

Dexter is a principled, gregarious man. He and Athena are lovers and friends. They live a contented life in Bunker Street caring for their two sons, Arthur and Billy. Billy is autistic, which affects the family dynamics. Until Elizabeth and her lover Philip come into their life, the Foxes remain quarantined from the world of nightclubs, drugs and extramarital sex. Athena runs a peaceful household. She washes, cleans, irons and gossips with friends, but she is suffocating in a house whose doors are never locked. She fantasises about escape, about her children dematerialising and her husband dying painlessly, yet even in those fantasies she dreams of the fabulous curtains she would sew and the 'order she would establish and maintain!'

The novella's extraordinary opening paragraph describes a photograph of Alfred Tennyson and his family. Garner had found this photograph well into her research, and was struck by the body language of the subjects. Here was a confident patriarch, with his seemingly subservient wife and two sons, one with a distant, contrary perspective. Dexter has stuck this photograph to the kitchen wall. It is tattered and grease-stained, but every time it threatens to slip off the wall, 'someone saves it, someone sticks it back'. From the outset, therefore, Garner suggests that the Fox family, though it may be battered and bruised, will survive. In musical terms the photograph operates as the statement of the theme.

It was Tennyson who wrote 'The Lady of Shalott', the great Victorian poem about female entrapment and the sacrifice required of women artists. So, at a time when second-wave feminism was enjoying a healthy ascendancy in Australian life, Garner invites her reader to consider how far women have progressed since Victorian times. Like Tennyson's 'Lady', Athena tinkers with her art, removed from the outside world. Like Tennyson's 'Lady', she too will be tempted from her sequestered existence into a world of risk and uncertainty.

Athena operates as a modern-day 'Angel in the House', a term coined by the nineteenth-century poet Coventry Patmore to describe women in the Victorian era:

Confined to the home, women were expected to be

domestic, innocent, and utterly helpless when matters outside the home were concerned. Not only was the home where women would be protected from the dangers of the outside world, it was also where they could keep their innocence and be a beacon of morality for their husbands.

Dexter insists that Athena is a 'saint'. Philip's daughter Poppy thinks she is 'perfect.' To Elizabeth's younger sister Vicki, she seems 'contained, without needs, never restless'. Meanwhile, Athena's shoulders 'tremble with holding back'.

Music infuses this narrative as language, metaphor and lived experience. Each character has a unique approach to music, in its various forms, which reflects their personality, their openness to the world and their relationships with each other. Garner rates music as 'probably the greatest pleasure and interest of [her] life, apart from books and people'. She had her first piano lesson when she was forty, a few years before she wrote *The Children's Bach*. Learning the piano made her aware of 'the almost *moral* struggle that playing music entails'. Like Athena, Garner struggled with the piano keys, striving 'to perceive form, to establish order'. So too in her writing, she pares back, edits and shapes her narrative so that it reads seamlessly, offering a textured consideration of ethical relations. Philip makes this link between writing and music obvious when he advises the young songwriter: 'Take out the clichés…Just leave in the images…Make gaps…Don't explain everything. Leave holes. The music will do the rest.'

The novella's title is taken from a primer of keyboard music, edited in 1933 by E. Harold Davies, in whose opening pages we read: 'Polyphony: which is the combining together of many melodies—requires, first and foremost, a sure instinct for each individual part.' Through short vignettes, Garner simultaneously provides access to each character's thoughts and voice. As Don Anderson suggested, Garner 'weaves her characters' loves and lives together through her many unnumbered subsections in a way that Papa Bach would have recognised as contrapuntal'. This moving in and out of each character's thoughts marks a significant progression in Garner's style and is reminiscent of Virginia Woolf's narrative method in *The Waves*, where she interweaves six interior soliloquies into a wavelike rhythm. Woolf was also influenced by music. On 22 December 1930 she recorded in her diary: 'It occurred to me last night while listening to a Beethoven quartet that I would merge all the interjected passages into Bernard's final speech, & end with the words O solitude; thus making him absorb all those scenes, & having no further break.'

Garner has credited the women's movement for giving her the licence to write about 'what happens in people's houses' rather than politics or history: 'The War or that kind of thing: huge subjects, mighty things.' The politics of gendered relations informs the drama of *The Children's Bach*. Athena, Vicki, Elizabeth, Poppy and old Mrs Fox represent, in various ways, female experience, opportunity and expectation across three generations. They exist in a world where 'men fuck girls without loving them', a world where women are sexually harassed, and denigrated through obscene humour. But they also exist in a world—unknown and abhorrent to Dexter—where the 'rules' of 'modern life' allow them sexual freedom and personal liberty.

Dexter, for all his old-fashioned ideas and domineering style, is a likeable character. Indeed, Garner has commented that *The Children's Bach* demonstrated a significant change in her writing about men and women, 'because there is a male character capable of love, which I hadn't been able to think about before'. She received a lot of mail from readers, mostly women, who loved Dexter. In August 1984 she wrote to Axel from Perth, where she was writer-in-residence at the University of Western Australia:

> I have a young friend over here, a writer called Tim Winton, who's just read *The Children's Bach*. He rang up yesterday and said, 'I <u>love</u> Dexter. He's <u>wonderful</u>. He's so <u>deep</u> & <u>warm</u> & <u>human</u>. He's the best thing that's happened for <u>ages</u>.' This made me laugh very much. I love Dexter, too. Dexter is my rehabilitation of the male.

Garner sets up a powerful contrast between the solid, righteous Dexter and the amoral, unreliable Philip. Significantly, both men are caring fathers, but Dexter's commitment to his wife and children, particularly Billy, contrasts with Philip's casual availability to Poppy and to women generally. Both men are desirable in different ways. Ultimately, Athena's sexual attraction to Philip, and the world he represents, cannot be repressed.

In a spare and moving scene, Elizabeth offers Philip to

Athena: 'Their fingers met formally at the high corners of the sheet. Elizabeth's relinquished, Athena's accepted. As they folded, as they spoke, the light left the garden.' With Philip, Athena thinks: 'Perhaps there was a world where people could act on whims, where deeds could detach themselves cleanly from all notion of consequences.' And so she abandons Dexter, her sons and her home, to go with Philip to Sydney. Yet in her freedom there is loss. She walks the city feeling like a tourist, aware 'that the day without duty passes with the slowness of a dream'.

Sydney is represented as a nightmare landscape. Athena cannot survive, or does not wish to survive, in the wider world. Dexter follows her and pleads for her to come home, but she is not yet ready. Shattered, he returns to Melbourne alone and at the end of a drunken evening makes love to Vicki, only to wake up in a blaze of self-disgust. No one, in Garner's world, is beyond reproach. But neither are they judged.

Marriage, life, playing music: all are complex tasks requiring dedication and hard work. In an early scene where Athena is patronised and humiliated by Dexter and Vicki for her lack of musical talent, Elizabeth remarks: '*The Children's Bach*. God, listen to this—how pompous. "Bach is never simple, but that is one reason why we should all try to master him."' We might substitute 'life' or 'marriage' for 'Bach' in that sentence.

At a time of her choosing, Athena returns to her husband, children and messy home. It is a conscious choice and is a cause for celebration. Her return, says Garner, makes this novel a 'moral' book. In response to suggestions that she was being too conservative in affirming the family unit, Garner explained to Eleanor Wachtel that she had never been much of a 'tough-talking radical':

> I've always loved children, and I've always thought that children have redemptive power. I think that having children can open people in a way that's quite miraculous. I don't mean that everyone should have children, nor do I mean that everyone should stay married, but I do think that there are some marriages that are good. Marriage is an institution that is not set up with the welfare of women in mind…it's a very, very powerful urge in people, the urge to marry, and I think that to remain 'a tough-talking radical' in the face of deep human needs and huge sacrifices that people are knowingly willing to make would be blind.

In Greek mythology Athena, the goddess of war and needlework, is born from the head of Zeus. Garner's Athena is a strong, thinking, self-contained woman. On her return she sets about restoring domestic order before she sits down at the kitchen table and waits for her family to come home. Garner concludes the novella with an exceptional sentence in the future continuous tense, a sentence that sweeps up the many fragmentary strands of the narrative into a vision of hope. Hope does not, however, translate to facile romanticism. Athena will be reconciled to Dexter, and to life with Dexter, but she will also 'dream again and again, against her will, of Philip, or rather of not-Philip'. Female desire cannot and should not be quashed. Somehow, Garner suggests, that desire can be reconciled within a marriage.

The Children's Bach, the keyboard primer, opens with 'A Song of Resignation' and closes with 'A Song of Love'. So too Garner concludes her novella with a song of love, a song about the complexity of married love and the conscious compromises it might entail: both the steady left hand of duty and the soaring right hand of joyous potential: 'and Athena will play Bach on the piano, in the empty house, and her left hand will keep up the steady rocking beat, and her right hand will run the arpeggios, will send them flying, will toss handfuls of notes high into the sparkling air!'

The Children's Bach, launched by Joan Grant on 6 December 1984, was a resounding critical success. The grumblings about Garner's choice of subject matter and creativity seemed to be put to rest. There was, however, still some controversy. Prior to publication Garner had shown the manuscript to Axel and Alison Clark. Axel seemed unfazed. Alison was less sanguine, but they both respected Garner's right to publish the novella and raised no public objections. McPhee notes:

> One or two people, who knew the family, were outraged on their behalf and attempted to talk us out of publishing the book, not, I think, because of what was *said*, but because they were offended by the blurring of the boundaries between the real and the imagined. The couple depicted behaved with dignity and their friendship with Helen survived.

Critics now began to take more note of Garner's prose than of any borrowings from life. In his review for the *National Times*, Don Anderson wrote about the carefully chosen adjective and the perfectly placed adverbial phrase in the novella's opening sentence, before concluding: 'There are four perfect short novels in the English language. They are, in chronological order, Ford Madox Ford's *The Good Soldier*, Scott Fitzgerald's *The Great Gatsby*, Hemingway's *The Sun Also Rises* and Helen Garner's *The Children's Bach*.' From further afield, Raymond Carver wrote to Peter Craven: 'Please give my regards to Helen Garner…I'm a fan of her work.'

In 1993, when Sue Woolfe and Kate Grenville invited Garner to contribute to *Making Stories*, she agreed to be interviewed and gave them the notebook she had used in the early days of writing *The Children's Bach*. It is divided into five sections under the names of the major characters. In each section, handwritten entries are interspersed with pasted fragments of typed and scribbled notes. The order appears to be random. Ideas for character and plot development jostle with snippets of dialogue, overheard conversation and descriptions of people and events. The notebook confirms the truth of Garner's insistence that in writing there comes a point where she loses the demarcation line between what has been found and what invented. It also demonstrates Garner's meticulous work crafting the novella. When Peter Craven invited her to submit an excerpt for publication in *Scripsi* she declined. 'It is so painstakingly stitched together,' she wrote, 'that it causes me actual <u>pain</u> to think of bits of it being cut out and asked to stand on their own, out of context'.

Soon after the novella's publication there had been talk about film and script options, which came to nothing. In 2008, however, a chamber opera, based on *The Children's Bach*, composed by Andrew Schultz to a libretto by Glenn Perry played for fifteen days at the Merlyn Theatre in Melbourne. Garner attended one rehearsal expecting to feel little more than intellectual interest in the adaptation of her book, but when Dexter stood up and sang she was powerfully moved: 'this rush of emotion came over me and it plunged me into the past, because people that you've written about die. The idea that Dexter, that character I wrote, that a young man who's young enough to be the real Dexter's son, is now getting up and singing...that's very thrilling to me.'

5

Boundary Riding:
Postcards from Surfers

I think Surfers is a wonderful book and Helen a wonderful writer.
I heard her read two stories up here last week and was bowled over, as
I always am, by the courage with which she takes on pain in her writing,
and the way, without any visible fuss, she makes the writing itself a kind of
moral activity, so that if you want to ask what she stands for you have only
to look at the writing itself—its cleanness, its strictness, the distinctions it
makes, her unwillingness to create easy effects, the savagery with which
she cuts away everything that is not absolutely essential.

DAVID MALOUF, LETTER TO HILARY MCPHEE (28 NOVEMBER 1985)

From the early eighties Garner entered into a productive relationship with the prestigious literary journal *Scripsi* and its founding editors, Michael Heyward and Peter Craven. Heyward and Craven commissioned pieces from Garner, including reviews of work by Elizabeth Jolley, Germaine Greer and Christina Stead. Over the course of a decade they edited the fiction she submitted, became sounding boards for ideas, and each became her friend.

In 1983 Garner was writer-in-residence at Griffith University. She worked primarily on *The Children's Bach*, but she was also writing stories experimenting with dialogue, breathless monologues, condensed sketches and allegory. Her range of style and voice marked her increasing confidence as a writer and her readiness to move outside her comfort zone. She sent Heyward and Craven an enigmatic, intensely visual story titled 'La Chance Existe'. The story is invested deeply in questions of seeing and knowing and, through its use of an initially androgynous narrator and a series of associative images, suggests an exciting possibility that the boundaries of sexuality and gender may be dissolved. The thrill of anonymous sex is linked to the thrill of being free from prescribed expectations. Opportunities exist when one is prepared to take risks and play games, particularly when outside one's linguistic or cultural space. In such places, the senses are on heightened alert. The story concludes with the narrator's welcome embrace of a voyeur's gaze as he and his friend melt ecstatically into one another's bodies. Garner originally intended this story to be the opening chapter of a novel. Heyward and Craven cautioned against it, largely because the story was so polished and complete. It was published that year in *Scripsi* and subsequently in *Postcards from Surfers*.

Postcards from Surfers is a collection about crossing borders, most often the border between a female's innocence and experience in matters of love and sexuality. In a number of stories, the narrator is a woman at a transitional period in her life, either en route towards, or recovering from, a lover in a distant location. Repeatedly these vulnerable women are betrayed or belittled by men. But Garner is not unsympathetic to her male characters. Through loving awareness and friendly satire, she captures a certain masculine fragility, even a sense that men are floundering, almost unaware of the complexities of heterosexual relationships.

Postcards are liminal, fragmentary modes of communication. Neither completely private nor openly public, they rely often on implication. Garner is an avid maker, collector and writer of postcards. The condensed, fragmentary form works brilliantly for her literary purposes. In 'Tutto Sereno' she writes that a postcard brings 'an urgent sense of reality': 'It challenges you to get straight to the point, to fill its tiny oblong with energy…the struggle with the constraints of form ignites the imagination, rouses the sluggish mind from its torpor.' In *Postcards from Surfers* Garner combines that condensed form with allegory to great effect. Private pain and inner conflict are palpable beneath the characters' public façades.

The title of *Postcards* can be read in different ways. Each story, with its ironic, shaped and often fragmentary forms, is a kind of postcard from its characters who are riding the waves of desire, dislocation and experience. One of the book's central themes is learning to live alone, or trying to step off the treadmill of desire. Garner sets the tone of the collection with her epigraph from Colette: 'One night I dreamed that I did not love, and that night, released from all bonds, I lay as though in a kind of soothing death.' Garner's stories build towards the ambitious goal of a single woman living a full creative life, without the pain of love.

In the opening titular story, there is a certain camaraderie between the adult daughter and her father, but a sense of menace begins to build around him. His 'big blunt' hands 'looked as if they had no feeling in them but they teased out the wool, judged it…He came home with thorns embedded deep in the flesh of his palms'. Allegory and realism blend. When the narrator was a child the father called her 'Fordie' and held her hand in his. Truth and fiction blend. Through the narrator's postcards to her ex-lover, Philip, we discover that those hands turned violent; he twice hit his fourteen-year-old daughter across the head. Years later he read her mail, found her contraceptive pills and humiliated her. The lover and the father become aligned through this act of writing. Even though she eventually throws the postcards away, the daughter achieves some form of reconciliation with Philip; she forgives him for everything. Does she also forgive her father?

These stories revolve around emotion, implied most often by Garner's manipulation of detail. In 'In Paris', a couple's incompatibility becomes evident through an argument about pairing brussels sprouts with fish. In 'A Thousand Miles from the Ocean', the random, abandoned details of a man's starkly white apartment confirm there was never any relationship with, or space for, the woman who mistakenly crossed the world to be with him. When, in 'Little Helen's Sunday Afternoon', a child called 'Little Helen' falls through a red plastic bucket, she crashes into, and is crippled by, knowledge that involves injury, pain, embarrassment and bleeding. Throughout the collection, women bleed on their lovers' sheets, signifying their displacement while also affirming that every aspect of women's lives can be worthy of aesthetic consideration. As we read *Postcards*, however, we realise that Garner is also charting a feminine anxiety about ageing and childbirth.

Through a series of vignettes, 'The Life of Art' maps out the territory before and after feminism. Before feminism, women were enslaved to their bodies, shattered by unwanted pregnancies, subjected to painful abortions. Before feminism, women were passed from father to husband. Before feminism, women tolerated sad and humiliating marriages. After feminism, women were freer to choose a more spontaneous life of creativity. Their art could be about self-expression. They were allowed to put themselves first. Yet, in crossing that boundary, they paid an enormous price. The narrator's friend is forty, broke and lonely. She wants a man 'who's not going to think my ideas are crazy…a man who'll see the part of me that no-one ever sees…a man who'll look after me and love me'. In a moment of ironic deflation, the ukulele-playing narrator toys with putting this lament to music. Instead she delivers the killer blow: 'Women like us…don't have men like that…We've done something to ourselves so that men won't do it. Well—there are men who will. But we despise them.'

This devastating conclusion operates as a subliminal mantra through much of Garner's work around this time and persists into *Cosmo Cosmolino*. When she first published 'The Life of Art' Garner was forty-three years old and her second marriage had just ended. Years later she described to Craig McGregor this period of her life:

> I was all over the map. I was crawling, I had a year by
> myself, it was terribly painful; like, one marriage break-
> up seems to be standard, but two, you begin to wonder

> what it is about you that's not kosher…it seemed to me
> that I was sort of finished in some way.

'Philip' characters populate Garner's fiction. The first Philip appears on the periphery of the *Monkey Grip* crowd. Then there is the desirable, amoral Philip in *The Children's Bach*. The narrator in 'Postcards' writes to a seductive, but lost, Philip. Yet another Philip commands the narrator's love in 'Civilisation and its Discontents'. As Garner explained to Ray Willbanks in 1991: 'Philip has turned into an archetype in my work now. He's the sort of man who is very attractive to women for the reason he is unreliable…He's charming, talented, kind of seductively independent, a sort that women find irresistible.'

In 'Civilisation and its Discontents', the narrator is Philip's mistress. She wants to break some boundaries. She wants to be a boy so she and Philip can have a homosexual affair. Philip wants her to be both male and female. He also wants her to remain his lover when he reconciles with his wife. The narrator wonders aloud whether women and men make love in order to 'bend the bars a little, just for a little; to let the bars dissolve'. Here we are returned to the territory explored in 'La Chance Existe'. The idea of that perfectly crafted story being the opening chapter of a novel begins to make more sense. Perhaps Garner intended to exploit the scope of the novel's form to dramatise the various ways in which sexual, moral and philosophical boundaries operate within individuals and between lovers to open up or thwart new possibilities of desire and expression.

Freud's book *Civilization and Its Discontents* not only underpins this story, it informs the entire collection. Like Freud, Garner examines the fault lines between the individual's desire for freedom, sexual gratification and self-fulfilment and the restrictions imposed by society's mores and expectations.

In 'A Happy Story', which concludes the collection, the narrative strands of ageing, settling scores with parents, menstruation, childbirth and surviving alone, coalesce: 'I turn forty-one.' A joyous Helen, having dropped her daughter and her saxophone-playing younger sister at a Talking Heads concert, heads home listening to Elisabeth Schwarzkopf singing Richard Strauss' 'Zueignung'. Helen rejoices: '"I am finally on the far side of the line." *Habe Dank*!'

David Malouf launched *Postcards from Surfers* on 8 November 1985. It went on to win the NSW Premier's Literary Award for fiction the following year. Garner's reputation at home and abroad was growing. In Australia, Katherine England wrote of Garner's 'almost dazzlingly confident manipulation of different styles and personae'. The *Age Monthly Review* spoke of 'the fine sense of scale' and the book's 'intriguing' play with autobiography, concluding that 'the stories are far too carefully crafted to be read as raw testimony'. In 1985 Bloomsbury produced a combined edition in the UK of *The Children's Bach* and *Postcards from Surfers*. In her memoir, McPhee identifies this publication as the moment when Garner's 'position as one of the best stylists of her generation was finally secure in the UK'. The *Guardian* called it 'an exceptional, triumphant collection...which climbs with easy fluent precision to an eagle's eye view of life'. Kathryn Kramer in the *New York Times Book Review* wrote that Garner's 'idiosyncratic vision, her controlled lyricism, and a goodly variety of feisty characters who insist on having their say' make her fiction 'compelling'. It is hard to gauge the reach of *Postcards from Surfers* because so many of the stories, and translations of the stories, have been reprinted in diverse collections, newspapers and journals in Australia and around the world. 'The Life of Art' was broadcast on London's Radio 3, the World Service and BBC radio. 'The Dark and the Light' was read on ABC 'Readings'; 'A Happy Story' was broadcast on 2BL.

6

Relinquishing Control:
Two Friends and *The Last Days of Chez Nous*

*My method of work is a kind of blind scrub-bashing, a blundering
through a trackless forest. But now...I had to turn my old, organic,
secretive, privileged, hyper-sensitive work process inside out.*

HELEN GARNER, INTRODUCTION TO
The Last Days Of Chez Nous & Two Friends (1992)

Midway through my research for this portrait, Michael
Heyward asked me what I considered to be *the* most important
book in Garner's oeuvre. To my surprise, I answered *Monkey
Grip*, not because I consider it Garner's most impressive work,
but because of the ways in which that book and its reception influenced Garner's writing life. Garner shaped *Monkey
Grip* intuitively. Free from expectations that she was a writer,
she was able to experiment and to flounder. *Monkey Grip*, as
Peter Craven described it, is a 'rough, obsessive, unstoppable'
book. Therein lies part of its power, but the tightly structured
and highly polished three books that followed were arguably

Garner's response to the patronising implication that she was not a *real* writer. In these books she demonstrated that she was a brilliant stylist who could shape language to great effect. Yet something began to shift after *Postcards*. Perhaps it was a growing confidence in her ability. Perhaps it was something more fundamental in her personal relationships. Maybe it related to her burgeoning spiritual interest. Most likely, it was a combination of all these things. Garner began to experiment even further with form and style. Her sentences lengthened and her subject matter broadened. Before all that, however, she ventured into film.

Jan Chapman had suggested to Garner that she would be open to producing her work if she ever decided to write for film. In desperate need of money, Garner thought she would give screenwriting a go. Her first step was to devise a strict structure. From there the writing happened at an alarmingly fast rate. It seemed too easy.

Her screenplay for *Two Friends* was directed by Jane Campion and produced by Chapman. The telemovie was first screened on ABC television in 1986. As Craven noted in his *Age* review, the match of Campion and Garner 'seemed exact'; Campion understood that 'in Garner small is always beautiful: never over-emphasise, never emote even when the emotion to be registered is violent'. Both the script and film are divided into five self-contained sections that trace the relationship of two fourteen-year-old girls back in time from July 1985 to October 1984. This reverse timeline operates simultaneously to control emotion through dramatic irony and to intensify, particularly at the film's conclusion, a bitter and haunting sense of lost opportunity.

Malouf had cautioned Garner that after *The Children's Bach* she had exhausted the theme of teenage girls. She proved him wrong. In *Two Friends* she captures the intensity of the girls' relationship as well as their innocence, confusion, vulnerability and burgeoning sexuality. Louise and Kelly are poised between childhood and adolescence. Louise is studious and uncool. The more physically developed and sexually curious Kelly is less uptight. The greatest difference between her and Louise is that she suffers cruelly from parental neglect.

It is possible yet again to overlay biographical details onto this story, and Garner admits that when she came to write the screenplay she 'saw a little story, a little shape' in some of her recent experiences. She thought she was basing the story on her daughter's relationship with a friend some years earlier. Partly Garner was driven by a sense that she had failed the friend by not intervening in her difficult family circumstances. Partly she was interrogating her own actions as a single mother who had 'dragged' her daughter through her personal life. More interestingly, she discovered, when she saw the film, that it was 'really, in a funny sort of way, about me'. Garner had read that the 'behaviour of delinquent adolescent girls was often a kind of wild protest against the weakness of their mothers…to stand up for them'. She realised that in Kelly she had crafted a character psychologically similar to herself.

When I mention *Two Friends*, Garner exclaims: 'Ah, I LOVE *Two Friends*. Tonally it is *exactly* what I wanted.'

She was thrilled by what Campion did with the screenplay: 'She got hold of it and flew away.' In the introduction to *The Last Days of Chez Nous & Two Friends*, published in 1992, Garner writes of the terror she experienced on surrendering her novelist's independence, compelled to hand over a script that was less than perfect. Yet she did relinquish control. She learned about outlines and treatments. She had to plan the territory to be covered ahead of the actual writing process, rather than rely on the act of writing to make sense of experience. Alarmingly, she could no longer work alone: 'I had to learn to walk into someone else's room, whack down my idea like a lump of raw meat, and watch it quiver while it was rolled and prodded on the table.' She enjoyed it. While she still clung to her need for 'long spells of obsessive loneliness' writing fiction, she enjoyed the pleasure of collaboration and watching her characters come to life on the screen. *Two Friends* screened at the Cannes Film Festival in 1986. In 1987 it won the Australian Film Institute Award for best telefeature and the NSW Premier's Literary Award for television writing.

Garner's next foray into film was her screenplay for Gillian Armstrong's *The Last Days of Chez Nous*, which was released on 8 October 1992. The film draws its story from Garner's 1985 marriage break-up with Jean-Jacques Portail, who fell in love with and later married Garner's youngest sister. Obviously this subject matter, with its attendant hurt and intricate family dynamics, was potentially explosive. While she may not have seen it this way, I would suggest that Garner's decision to write a screenplay rather than a novel was apposite, precisely because she would not be able to maintain total control of the script or its dramatisation.

Back in June 1987, Garner had written to Craven declaring that she had just finished the draft of a telemovie that was funnier than *Two Friends*. By the time she delivered a series of scenes, roughly in filmic order, to her publishers, she explained to them that her aim was 'to write "a gay comedy, almost a farce"—(Chekov's description of <u>The Cherry Orchard</u>)—beneath the noisy surface of which lies a rather painful story about the necessity for emotional violence at times when people are resisting change'. Garner outlined the 'bones of the plot':

> BETH and JP are in disarray. Their marriage is cracking seriously under the strains of its history and of being cross-cultural; various painful infidelities on both sides have taken place; JP is fed up and not even trying to hide it, but BETH is hanging on like grim death. VICKI comes back from another country and rejoins the household. While BETH is on a ridiculous, comical and sad trip into the desert with her domineering FATHER, JP and VICKI begin an involvement which explodes the household out of existence.

The combined screenplays of *Two Friends* and *The Last Days of Chez Nous* were published to coincide with the latter film's release. With their acute dialogue and wry observations, they read like Garner's fiction. *Chez Nous* develops many of the themes of Garner's earlier writing: a woman in her forties anxious about fertility, motherhood, being desirable and sustaining a committed relationship; that same woman trying to make peace with an intransigent father; adolescents negotiating a complicated adult world; and questions about God, spirituality and death.

Unfortunately, much of Garner's direction for *Chez Nous* has been edited out of the published script, and in the translation from page to screen some of her vision was lost. She was disappointed by a number of aspects of the finished film, particularly its tone. She hoped for a 'dense crazy little movie, without melancholy or correct line on anything'. Armstrong got the second part of that suggestion right; no one is judged or blamed, except perhaps Beth. Because she is Garner's 'me' character it is possible to say that Garner mercilessly represents herself. In a tortured scene with J.P., Beth cries: 'Do you think I need to be *told* I'm not lovable? I *know* that! I know what I'm like! I'm bossy, impatient, too motherly, ill-mannered, unfaithful, greedy, a spend-thrift.' Later, when she has humiliated J.P. and is reprimanded, she hides her discomfort by trying to joke that she is not good at being a couple, only to be struck down by a familiar Garner line: 'What have you women *done* to yourselves? You're like husks.'

Armstrong was concerned that Beth appeared too strong on the page, so she softened her through her direction and her casting of Lisa Harrow, a New Zealand actress who had worked extensively with the Royal Shakespeare Company and was best known on Australian screens for her role as Claire Jeffries in *Come in Spinner*. Craven was scathing. He acknowledged that Harrow's was 'not a bad performance'—she won an AFI award for best actress—before laying the blame squarely at

Armstrong's feet: 'it's simply a pity that Armstrong's direction has encouraged Harrow to give a performance that is essentially external to this portrait of a woman shuffling among lovers and fathers, intent on preserving the myth of a family while being constricted by the myth that her various "families" lay upon her.' He continued: '[Judy] Davis (or Helen Morse) would have captured the shrewd intelligence in this woman, as well as the spoilt hippie still searching for the meaning of it all and for her father's love.' It is a fair, but tough, assessment. In softening Beth and overplaying the emotional potential of the material, Armstrong delivered a more sentimental film than the ironic, understated feature Garner had intended.

The Last Days of Chez Nous has considerable merit. I doubt Garner could ever have been entirely happy with the finished product, given the painful circumstances at its heart. In her introduction to the screenplays, she zeroes in on the replacement of her preferred row of pencil cypress trees with a church spire as one of two core disappointments. Garner had specified some essential characteristics for the house. When Armstrong found the close-to-perfect house in Glebe, she took Garner to see it. They sat on the back steps and rewrote scenes around its physical limitations. When they saw the spire that seemed to be floating in the middle distance, 'it seemed a gift, and we persuaded ourselves that the spire would do'. Yet Garner insists that the compromise was too great: 'A spire, no matter how indistinct and beautiful, is literal. It represents a known religion, a particular theology, with all the sectarian and social meanings that this entails. The mystery of the image is lost.'

Garner's second major complaint related to geography. *The Last Days of Chez Nous* was imagined in Melbourne, yet filmed in Sydney, as was *Monkey Grip* before it. For a writer so acutely attuned to her environment, this relocation was problematic. Both movies demonstrated that the 'qualities of air and light in a certain place…are more than purely aesthetic. They form the tone of people's lives, the way people move about and behave towards each other and feel about themselves.' In her original notes Garner had wanted the atmosphere in the house to be 'inbred and claustrophobic'. Armstrong achieves that sense at times, but, as Garner discovered, 'The very image of *a house,* on which both films heavily depend, bears one sort of psychological emphasis in warm, open Sydney, and a completely different one in Melbourne, where dwellings are enclosing, curtained, cold-weather-resisting; more like burrows.'

Arguably Garner's filmic imagination was asking too much. Her insistence on the theatrical and screen images of the house and the extent and character of the games she wanted played were ambitious. Of central importance was her desire that the script 'be played with exaggerated realism' and that the 'peculiarities should intensify the potential emotionalism of the plot…way past the point of sociological realism'. Needless to say, some viewers interpreted the film as a slice of life dramatising simply the breakdown of Garner's second marriage and subsequent family tensions. After Craven wrote his review slamming what he perceived to be the movie's sentimentality, Garner dropped him a postcard:

> Dear Peter, I suppose this is unethical or something but thanks so much for the piece you did in the Age abt <u>Chez Nous</u>…I think that the wild swings of reaction people display probably show that <u>I</u> hadn't digested the subject matter as well as I thought I had—people react to it as if it were a piece of gossip they'd been told—they gasp & TAKE SIDES between the characters. So your piece is a place for me to stand—thankyou—Helen.

The Last Days of Chez Nous screened at twenty-one film festivals in Australia and around the world. Garner was particularly pleased by the positive reception it received at the 1992 Berlin Film Festival; not only did the audience laugh, they laughed in all the right places.

7

The House of the Spirit:
Cosmo Cosmolino and Other Stories

I feel as if I've got more nerve than I have ever had before. Now I can write about death, suicide, murder and mysterious characters that might be angels…Realism takes you only so far.

HELEN GARNER, *Writers in Action* (1990)

Helen Garner turned fifty in 1992. She began the year with the publication of her fifth book, *Cosmo Cosmolino*, a triptych of stories involving angels, death, uncertain symbolism and dreams. A raft of essays followed, many of which illuminate various preoccupations in *Cosmo Cosmolino*. In October *The Last Days of Chez Nous* was released. In 1992 Garner also began following the sexual harassment case that would inform *The First Stone*. And she married the acclaimed novelist and short-story writer, Murray Bail.

Much had been made of Garner's so-called silence over the previous seven years since *Postcards from Surfers* was published. While she gave some explanations for her reduced output—that she had nothing to say and that she was too shattered by personal events to be able to write—she had in fact written, in addition to her screenplays, a number of stories and reviews, many of which signalled her increasing preoccupation with death and its relationship to spiritual awareness. In her review of Germaine Greer's *The Change*, she was energised by Greer's insistence that a woman can learn 'to shift the focus of her attention away from her body ego towards her soul', and was struck by the idea that menopause is an 'essential stage in a woman's journey towards death'. She explained in 'On Turning Fifty', that she wanted to 'learn the language with which to speak of death'.

In the midst of the emotional turmoil that followed the end of her second marriage in 1985, Garner had felt 'an obscure longing for something nameless and inexpressible'. She started going to church and decided to undergo psychoanalysis. Garner had always recorded her vivid and often disturbing dreams but she did not know what to make of them beyond some amateurish Freudian interpretation. For nine months she went to a Jungian psychoanalyst in Melbourne. He taught her how to better appreciate and interpret her dreams. She learned to take seriously the emblematic objects that appeared in them and she set about trying to bring that 'strange, crazy dream-richness' into the texture of her writing.

In 1987 Garner moved to Sydney and rented a room at Drusilla Modjeska's house in Enmore. It was a sociable, vibrant writers' house with 'the doors open and music playing and people coming in, and meals around the table'. Garner and Modjeska lunched together most days, and talked writers and writing. Modjeska was writing *Poppy,* her biography of her mother. Garner had a two-year Literature Board grant but the novel she planned to write just wasn't happening, so she took the opportunity to read three versions of the Bible: the King James, the Jerusalem and the modern J. B. Phillips translation of the New Testament. She was shaken yet thrilled by the violent physicality of some stories, and inspired by various narrative techniques of others. She felt morally challenged reading the New Testament and imaginatively liberated reading the Old.

In 'Dreams, the Bible and *Cosmo Cosmolino*', collected in *True Stories*, she describes the kind of writing she was capable of when her filtering consciousness was switched off. It was this kind of writing, and this texture of writing, that she wished to command:

> This style was urgent, direct, simple; stripped of ornament yet rich in imagery, correct in syntax and grammar, and graceful in its movement; muscular in its verbs; laconic without being dessicated; capable of fine distinctions without nit-picking or pedantry; able to move easily between high diction and blunt serviceable everyday speech.

Dreams and the Bible were two major influences in her life and work at this time. The third was Murray Bail. As Garner told Susan Wyndham some years later: 'I was very influenced by Murray...He always liked reading these tortured Viennese modernists and I started reading that stuff, too, and I began to think differently about writing. I maybe lost my natural voice for a while there.' Perhaps, or perhaps she needed a different voice if she wanted to explore and articulate questions about spiritual longing and the soul. Bail's conviction that fiction of any real significance was sustained by myth would have resonated with Garner's imaginative project. Around this time Garner was also reading Proust and Christina Stead. Both authors, in different ways, inspired her to take risks.

Three important stories written in 1987 and 1988 signalled a major shift in Garner's work: 'What We Say', 'What the Soul Wants', and 'The Psychological Effect of Wearing Stripes'. All three stories explore issues to do with female creativity, woundedness, dreams and the soul.

In 'What We Say', Natalie—whom we meet again in *Cosmo Cosmolino*'s 'Recording Angel'—and the narrator discuss their experience of *Rigoletto* with two men. When one of the men wonders if women have a fundamental fear, and if it might not be of violation, the narrator toys with citing Yeats: 'Nothing can be sole or whole/That has not been rent.' She is besieged by unspoken thoughts of rape and powerlessness. In the tense silence, 'Words which people use and pretend to understand floated…and bumped among our heads. Virgin. Treasure. Perfect. Clean. My darling, Anima. Soul.' Garner wants to understand these words. In various manifestations, as images, metaphors and myths, they flow through all the stories she writes in these years.

The kernel for 'What We Say' grew out of a time at the end of 1985 when Garner stayed with David Malouf for six weeks. As theatre critic for the *Australian*, Malouf could not keep up with the volume of performances he needed to cover for the Sydney Festival, so with the paper's permission he and Garner shared the load. He recalls a wonderfully interesting time attending and reviewing theatre together. Malouf and Bail were regular lunch companions. It was at one such lunch, in Malouf's kitchen, that Garner met Bail. None of these facts need be known in order to appreciate 'What We Say', but it is fascinating to re-read the story with this history in mind. Here we have a defensive, opinionated narrator who exposes a raw wound on her hand to a man she has instantly assessed as 'one of those', a man who has earlier made a quip about feminist theoreticians. When he offers to help dress her wound, the narrator draws an 'independent breath' to 'say *what we say*…I can do it for myself', but she stays silent: 'I gave him my hand.' The story's conclusion is intensely sensual and erotically charged. The man, focused on examining the narrator's deep, festering cut, remarks, 'You've made a mess of yourself, haven't you', before closing the wound with his thumbs, applying a bandaid and letting go of her hand.

In 'The Psychological Effect of Wearing Stripes', Garner interrogates the notions and ethics of beauty and representation, particularly as they entrap and construct the female artist. Philip has returned, as both remembered lover and photographic image. He appreciates the power of beauty. He likes to look and be looked at. The female artist won't play his games. She wants to be 'the one doing the looking', rather than the object of the gaze. Alone in her hotel room she attempts to create, but is distracted by her displeasing reflection. Her self-portrait, constructed through a doubly refracted image, is distorted. The story wants to interrogate the fractured relationship between the beautiful, vain Philip and the ageing narrator, but it veers away. The narrator tells us that the point of what she is trying to convey recedes from her as she writes. Through the layers of obfuscation, a painful story of lost love and lost youth emerges.

The third story, 'What the Soul Wants', is like nothing else Garner has ever written. As Kerryn Goldsworthy has noted, the story 'is perhaps closer to the lyric poem, closer even to allegory, than to any modern prose form'. Goldsworthy illuminates Garner's narrative style through an apt citation from A. S. Byatt's *Imagining Characters*. Arguing that the story has 'no realist framework at all', she suggests it is much more like what A. S. Byatt calls 'a kind of dream…which is most deeply to do with myself as a writer—a dream which is experienced more like a poem—where all the images fuse into a kind of intense symbolic knot or painting'. In 'What the Soul Wants', Garner refashions the Eros and Psyche myth, itself often interpreted as an allegory for the soul's journey through life and its final union with the divine after suffering and death. In Garner's world Philip, as the Eros figure, is present and absent, he is love and loss, beautiful and ugly. It is Philip who has been to the underworld; he has suffered beyond comprehension. Is it the female narrator's fault? And what of the suffering he causes her? There can be no happy ending, no embrace, no eternal bliss. The soul wants comfort, presence and love, but in Garner's prose poem there is only desire, absence and pain. Garner wrote to McPhee saying that she wanted this story to be 'laid out with <u>huge</u> gaps between the sections so they will float like scraps of dream or thought. Maybe only about twelve lines per page.' By visually fragmenting the dense, fluid prose she sought to refuse concrete meaning.

By mid-1990 the story 'Cosmo Cosmolino' was taking shape. Garner envisaged it as the centrepiece of a collection of stories. It is, but not in the way it was originally intended. I found a manuscript for *Cosmo Cosmolino* among McPhee's papers in the National Library of Australia and was surprised to see that in the year before publication the manuscript consisted of seven stories: 'The Psychological Effect of Wearing Stripes', 'What the Soul Wants', 'Recording Angel', 'A Vigil', 'A Visitation', 'Cosmo Cosmolino' and 'My Hard Heart'. Neither Garner nor McPhee remembered this original arrangement, and neither could explain why it was changed.

The most surprising thing about this discovery was the story 'A Visitation', which has never been published (though a severely edited and reworked version appears as 'My First Baby' in *Everywhere I Look*). I emailed a query to Garner. She did not remember the original story and thought it was the middle story in *Cosmo Cosmolino*. When she recalled that the middle story is in fact 'A Vigil', she asked what this other story was about. I gave a brief outline, and she responded:

'Oh yes now I remember. Gosh it sounds so overblown and gothic. Which would be why I never published it. Don't even remember showing it to anybody, except (I think) Alison Clark… Who liked it, as I recall.' I asked if she would like me to get one of the library staff to copy it for her but she declined the offer. She remained unconvinced about the story and did not want to look at it: 'I couldn't face it…I remember how I felt when I was writing it—an awful sense of strain that scared me.'

'A Visitation' runs to thirty-seven single-spaced typed A4 pages. A demure young girl, on the cusp of sexual awakening, works in the basement toy section of a department store. She never has any customers, so passes her days curled up reading and sleeping. At home she is stifled by the attitudes and nearness of her parents. She falls asleep reading Petrach's *The Triumph of Death*, dreams vividly, and knows she is too young for such dreams.

Garner was worried about what she saw as the increasing weirdness of the stories she was writing, but explained in a letter to McPhee that she hoped 'the way the stories develop out of each other will make their varying degrees of skill, syntactic complexity & weirdness seem an interesting aspect of the whole'. She sought to link the stories through a ukulele, a boat, a certain mythic element where various characters visit the underworld, and '<u>waiting</u> (the world's most demoralizing state)'. All these elements feature in 'A Visitation'. Replacing the boat with trams, they also inform *Cosmo Cosmolino*.

Garner has commented frequently that with *Cosmo Cosmolino* she threw off her 'tight-arsed perfectionism' and enjoyed throwing syntax around. I'm not convinced that she surrendered the perfectionism, but she was certainly having linguistic fun. In 'My First Baby', she writes that her feet 'ached rhythmically, like string quartets of pain, and by the end of each day, like a great screaming Wagnerian orchestra'. In the earlier 'A Visitation', her description of the shop assistant's sore feet is positively baroque:

> They hurt with a perseverance that had its own moral value, with such inexhaustibly clever variations on the theme of hurting that she pictured them as a pair of bony vaults whose padding of muscle and meat had been helpless to prevent them from shattering into fan-shaped arpeggios of fracture: for the form of this pain was musical, orchestral—even, by the end of the afternoon, symphonic, underscored as it was by a perpetual shifting from one foot to the other, one, two, one, two, a rhythm occasionally syncopated by a small flutter of despair but more often regular; established first as a pulse and taken up immediately by the groaning of the double basses, their unwieldy tramping; then by whole string sections in a suave and swooning middle register; then electrified by stabs of brass, embellished by flutes that trilled a warning, and screwed tightly into a climax by the dry shrieking of the piccolos: and at its intensest point, which she interpreted with the fixed, mad stare of a sight-reader at speed, it became soundless, theoretical, nothing but signs: the little flagships, the fluttering towers, the thronging forests of rests and semi-quavers that comprised its final excruciating bars.

'A Visitation' is punctuated by three sightings of a Chinese sailor who stirs a thrilling yet terrifying subconscious sexual desire in the girl. In the early afternoon, an imperious older woman—perhaps Petrarch's old woman—arrives to buy a farewell gift. The girl wakes (possibly) and offers various options; nothing is deemed suitable until she presents a ukulele: 'It lay on its back across her palms, naked, cheeky, weighing nothing…A tiny odour emanated from the hole in its belly, a perfume of something wooden, virgin, shaped by steam.' The woman is momentarily stilled. She speaks of how large stringed instruments laid on their sides appear to be human. The girl is at a loss, humiliated by her lack of musical expertise. Curiously the woman concedes that even the ukulele, left alone on its side, 'looks like a baby'. We begin to have an inkling of the shifting symbolic nature of Garner's imagery. Wooden creations, a baby, a ukulele and a Madonna figure all feature in 'Cosmo Cosmolino'. What might they signify other than themselves?

Just as the woman discovers a sand-filled, naked baby doll and insists on buying it, the girl's father appears. The girl knows 'she was his chosen one. He had come to watch her…working like a real person in a real world. He wants to see what I look like as a grown-up, she thought; he is proud of me.' She is keen to impress, but she cannot serve this woman. A violent physical and psychological struggle erupts when the girl, who must have the doll for herself, refuses to sell it. While a cataclysmic storm rages overhead, the doll is torn asunder. The sand bleeds onto the floor. The father disappears. The powerless young shop assistant is forced to sweep up the detritus, wrap and tie it neatly in a parcel 'not much bigger than a large grapefruit or perhaps an unripe melon', and surrender it to the woman.

In 'My First Baby', Garner writes:

> I don't remember what happened to the doll. Within
> three years I'd had two abortions, and within eight
> years, a child. The abortions I went into briskly, without
> conscious regret. But now I'm in my fifties, they've come
> back to haunt me. I've had to grieve for them, and mourn
> them. I never expected this to happen. It was awful, and
> it took a long time.

Garner was baptised in 1962. I asked her about it. I wanted to know if this decision had anything to do with her first abortion. She replied that she would have to check the date but that she 'would not be at all surprised if I went to church looking for something at that time. I wrote a story about it once.' Her epigraph for 'A Visitation', taken from J. E. Cirlot's *A Dictionary of Symbols*, is instructive: 'One dreams of a child when some great spiritual change is about to take place under favourable circumstances.' My truncated exegesis cannot do justice to this complex story. It can be read as the traumatic reimagining of the psychological consequences of a young girl's abortion. It also offers another example of how Garner interweaves real and abstract images, symbols and dreams to probe her personal history and her larger anxiety about female autonomy and creativity.

Garner had a tubal ligation not long after *Monkey Grip* was published. She was thirty-five years old. Bill Garner was the only person who urged her to reconsider what she was planning. It was some years later—when she made a slip in speaking to her therapist and said, 'after I <u>had</u> *Monkey Grip*'—that Garner realised that her decision to have the procedure had been an unconscious choice between writing books and further motherhood. In February 1990 she wrote to McPhee:

> I feel gloomy & sad, not sure why. Something to do with Ali's having shown me a page of George Steiner's new book <u>Real Presences</u>, in which he suggests, with a kind of courteous regretfulness, that there are few (or no) 'great' women dramatists, painters & composers because women, being able (symbolically & actually) to produce from their bodies a living creature, do not experience that fierce drive to challenge the Creator which male artists feel & which pushes some of them to tremendous creative heights. I feel the ground drop away when I read this kind of thing.

In 'Cosmo Cosmolino' the childless Janet is a writer, but she has had a tubal ligation. It is the eccentric carpenter Maxine who is driven to conceive. It is Maxine, in all her ambiguity, who embodies the hope for a creative, female future.

Neither of Garner's parents was religious. Through her education she was exposed to Anglican teachings and ritual. While she writes flippantly that within two weeks of her baptism she reverted to her 'wicked ways', her spirituality has remained vitally important to her. Around the time of her baptism she discussed her beliefs with Axel. She had tried 'to think things out about God', but she could not understand religion and felt that she never would because her 'depth of thought and understanding is not great'. She added, 'I don't know why I believe in God; I suppose in this way I seem naïve but I find it comforting to believe in him and so I do.'

Decades later, when she was living in Sydney and writing the stories that would become *Cosmo Cosmolino*, she discussed her beliefs with Ed Campion and wrote about her preoccupations to Peter Craven who became, for a short time, an interlocutor on matters spiritual. Garner told him that Jesus did not seem at all real to her and that she did not understand religion intellectually. She had a sense of a presence that had appeared to her, but was now absent, and she wondered if its failure to reappear was due to her 'cowardice' in refusing to acknowledge it. A form of this presence makes itself felt to various characters throughout *Cosmo Cosmolino*. Garner experienced it as a 'mighty force'. Tim Winton thought it was the Holy Spirit.

Garner and Winton had first met at a writers' weekend in Fremantle in the summer of 1982. Winton remembers being somewhat 'star-struck'. *Monkey Grip* had made a huge impression on him and he felt honoured that Garner, whom he considered to be 'cool', 'grown-up and quite worldly', took the time to review his first novel, *Open Swimmer*, in the *National Times*. He drove to Fremantle to hear her read and was impressed by her lack of literary affectation, her warmth and the interest she took in his life and writing. They exchanged addresses and so began a long and fruitful conversation.

Winton comes from a fairly strict evangelical background, and has explored throughout his writing the physical manifestations of the sacred in everyday life, always seeking to put 'the bodies and the creatures and the blood and water and shit back into the picture'. It is unsurprising that, when Garner was searching for a language with which to speak of her mystical encounters and spiritual yearning, she turned to him.

Winton tells me he is not sure that he was much help to Garner beyond being a trustworthy friend who was open to talking about 'matters of transcendence' without 'ridicule or judgement'. In fact, he believes he was the major beneficiary from their conversations:

> I remember a card Helen sent, and a photo of a wounded gum tree and sap was boiling out of it in whorls and wens, and her caption—'The Mighty Force'. I wish I'd had an ikon made from it. She probably never knew it, but that image, and that little aside moved me on in my thinking; it confirmed and clarified some things I'd been grasping at for years. A gentle bump in the road that finally unhitched this little trailer from the big old roadtrain of evangelicalism.

The published version of *Cosmo Cosmolino* consists of three interlinked stories from the proposed seven: 'Recording Angel', 'A Vigil' and 'Cosmo Cosmolino'. All three stories concern transformation. They are connected through recurring characters and through the presence in each story of various forms of angels. The book's structure mirrors that of a Christian pilgrimage: 'Recording Angel' confronts the physicality of the suffering body, 'A Vigil' enters the underworld to witness death head-on and 'Cosmo Cosmolino' offers a sense of possible redemption, perhaps even resurrection. The structure can also be read as a meditation on the past, the present and the future.

With the opening sentence of 'Recording Angel' we are in familiar Garner territory: 'Soon after the collapse of my last attempt at marriage,' the narrator begins. She goes to Sydney to visit Patrick, her *oldest… most loyal friend*. Over the years she has served up all the successes and failures of her life to Patrick. He does not need the many postcards he has kept; he has catalogued the narrator in a way she can never change: 'sad girl; problem with her father; full of anger; nympho; self-destructive; unstable; hyper-sensitive; a failure at marriage; unfeminine; man-hater; lost soul'. Patrick seems to know more about the narrator than she remembers herself. Now she wants a clean slate, a new narrative.

Patrick has a brain tumour and all that history may be wiped away. But much more is at stake. The narrator, although welcomed into the household, exists on the periphery of this family. Her love and concern for Patrick pales in comparison with his wife's commitment to him. On the eve of his surgery, Patrick asks her to photograph himself and Natalie with their two children. She is to be their recording angel, but only on Patrick's terms. She is to use his camera, not her own; this family portrait will not be captured through her viewfinder.

A quartet is playing on the radio. Natalie likens it to a family or a four-way conversation. The narrator's outsider status is palpable. When Patrick realises it is in truth a quintet, the narrator understands the 'point' of the frightening extra cello:

It dropped through a rent in the net and plunged away into the darkness, crying out. It groaned a warning: it prowled, it ranged, it lay in wait. It was the bad dream of the quartet, brooding, ravening outside the fold, and its argument was doubt and panic, a desolation as yet unlived.

Does the cello represent the narrator, terrified for her friend's wellbeing? Or is it death that prowls, and lies in wait?

As the narrator walks towards the hospital next morning, she is attuned to the 'sharply shimmering' world. The first of this book's many presences becomes manifest: 'Something in soft soles was keeping pace with me wherever I walked, padding along silently behind my left shoulder.' In the waiting room she confronts Natalie with a breathtaking question. '"Have you ever," I blurted, "wished that someone you loved would die? So that the record of all your crimes and failures would be obliterated?"'

The narrator continues, expressing her terror for Patrick in language about her own needs. Natalie is appalled and exasperated. She is powerless to stop the self-indulgent sentimentalism. Garner ensures there is a witness. She has a teenage girl drag a chair across the room towards the women and fix them 'like a judge or witness'. The story veers into a Dantesque hell as the women enter intensive care. Garner graphically describes Patrick's post-operative body in its abject distress. She contrasts the narrator's panicky fear for Patrick with Natalie's dignified self-control. Natalie can bear neither her husband's suffering nor the narrator's perceived treachery. She flees from both.

Alone, the narrator encounters a boy in a cape standing in the liminal space of the hospital's entrance porch. She knows him. He has come for her: 'He was a small, serious, stone-eyed angel of mercy.' What does he signify? He is not the angel of death that Patrick has earlier dreamt about, yet he transmits a message through his raised gun arm. His name suggests the possibility of compassion and forgiveness. In Jewish and Christian traditions, the angel of mercy is a messenger from God sent to end earthly pain and suffering. Is he there to wipe *her* slate clean? Has Patrick's suffering been for *her* sins? Or is he on his way to Patrick?

'Recording Angel' was another example of Garner crossing the porous boundary between private and public lives. By 1989 Axel Clark had undergone a series of operations to remove a brain tumour. This story hurt him deeply. He wrote Garner a long, angry letter and told her to stop writing about him. She sent a curt reply. 'I was very defensive,' she told me. 'If I was honest I would have admitted that I had gone over the top.' In 1995, while discussing the topic of writers' responsibilities to their subjects, Garner admitted further details of the circumstances surrounding this story and her friendship with Axel. Without naming him, she spoke of the stand-off between them, of her insistence that her interpretation of the story as being filled with a 'complicated, angry, frightened sort of love' was more correct than his reading of it. She said that a year or so later, she began to appreciate more of the story's intent and effect. She wrote an apology to Axel and asked for his forgiveness. He replied that forgiveness was neither appropriate, nor required. 'He said he had realized that my story was only another phase in a very long, deep and complicated friendship.'

In truth, Garner knew she had crossed the line before the story was published. Writing to McPhee in April 1990, she admitted that she was becoming 'panicky' about *Cosmo Cosmolino*. She had sent the second story, 'A Vigil', to Winton who had responded saying he thought it was too gruesome and did not understand what she was trying to say. Garner saw a way to loosen the texture of that story by slowing down its pace and toning down some of its unrelenting horror. As for 'Recording Angel', she acknowledged, it was 'clearly unpublishable'. She knew it would cause too much hurt. An increasingly anxious Garner wrote: 'I can't quite imagine what sort of collection these stories can make. I feel as if I'm in some kind of ghastly transition stage: as if I'm technically much more competent than I've ever been, but that the matter on which I'm exercising this technique is still murky & uncertain.'

Back in 1986, Garner had written two stories for the *Age*: 'Marriage' and 'Death'. In 'Death' she ventures into the huge chambers of ovens at Melbourne's Springvale crematorium. Garner gives an extraordinarily detailed description of the cremation process, from chapel service to raking out the ashes. Her conclusion demonstrates the profound influence that the experience had on her spiritual enquiry:

> I didn't start shaking and crying till two days later.
> And on my way home, I had, for the first time in my

> life, a conviction —…not a thought but knowledge—that
> life can't possibly end at death. I had the punctuation
> wrong. I thought it was a full stop, but it's only a comma,
> or a dash—or better still, a colon: I don't believe in
> heaven or hell, or punishment or reward, or the survival
> of the ego; but what about energy, spirit, soul, imagina-
> tion, love? The force for which we have no word? How
> preposterous, to think that it could die!

Writing 'Death' did not exhaust her response to this experience. She revisited the material through fiction. In 'A Vigil', Ray's girlfriend Kim dies of loneliness, passivity and neglect. Ray has no qualms using Kim's barely conscious body for his sexual gratification, although when he does a bird trills outside the window. On the day Ray turns up for sex and finds Kim's corpse, the bird is at its loudest. He runs away. Kim's mother, Ursula, tracks him down and drags him to Kim's funeral service.

Three times Ray is asked if he was Kim's boyfriend; three times he denies the relationship and, therefore, his culpability. With his final denial 'a bird uttered three notes of a mounting song, and fell silent'. The biblical narrative underpinning this story of cowardice and betrayal is undeniable.

Ray is shanghaied by two Cuban-heeled men, or angels, and taken underground to the ovens. Forced to watch the process of Kim's cremation, he sees her feet as tongues of fire: 'In the passion of their transfiguration they loosened. They opened. They fell apart.' Everything falls apart for Ray. Phil, one of the angels, turns his 'calm stone gaze' on Ray and sends him on his way. As he ascends towards the 'unbearable diamond of evening sky' he is engulfed by 'a vast and infinitesimal cacophony of insects living, living, living'. We leave Ray expelled from the underworld 'out on to the staggering lawn'. Garner's adjective sends us reeling.

In 'Cosmo Cosmolino' we are introduced to Janet, whom we discover to be the narrator from 'Recording Angel'. Janet is, as Moya Costello humorously asserts, one of Garner's 'head girls'. Along with Kath, Scotty and Elizabeth from Garner's earlier fiction, she is an intelligent, jaded, acerbic woman. She is also wounded, lonely and kind. Childless by choice and recently separated, Janet is a journalist living alone in her dilapidating house, Sweetpea Mansions. Into Janet's house and life come Maxine the new-age carpenter and Ray, now an evangelical Christian.

The gormless Maxine is the driving force of positive energy in the story. She inhabits a world of feeling and heightened perception. Maxine can see the huge, shadowy column behind Janet's left shoulder. She is obsessed with the idea that she is to conceive a child, so when Ray, in his reflective sunglasses and bathed in sunlight, arrives on the doorstep announcing he has been sent, we recognise Garner's orchestration of a modern-day Annunciation.

Cosmo Cosmolino dramatises the desolation of an existence without intimacy. For much of this final story, Janet is in mourning: for her marriage, for the once bustling collective household, for the person she might once have been. Through disappointment, hurt and betrayal she has become a brittle cynic. In opening her house, and therefore herself, up to the company of others, she begins a kind of spiritual rebirth.

Sweetpea Mansions is more than a house. Garner was searching for ways to explore the numinous. Her solution was to complicate any sense of the real by incorporating symbolic images and allusions into the narrative. Dark columns hover, birds sing, wind gusts and an alarm clock ticks for years in a sealed room. The rooms of the house, becoming decrepit and marking time, are also the rooms of Janet's heart and soul. Some she cannot bear to enter. Sweetpea Mansions is 'bruised'; the 'heart of the house was broken'. Ray experiences the lounge room as 'a white-washed tomb, a whited sepulchre'. Janet has had her hair cut, and looks like a 'skull'. There is 'nothing but bones' to be found in the kitchen. Even the discarded mattress has a 'ribcage'.

Janet has no language with which to speak of death. At thirty, she'd had a tubal ligation. She is now forty-five. When she hurts for the child she will never have, the dark column moves into position: 'Behind her left shoulder a fissure opened in the room's density. I will die. I will die and leave nothing behind: I will be forgotten.' But Janet's generosity will save her. She invites Maxine and Ray to stay.

The three inhabitants orbit each other in a swirl of crossed purposes, resentment and missed opportunity. Ray and Janet fight about religious belief. The failure bird trills. Tempers fray. Maxine sculpts a trembling, tiny cradle out of 'tortured willow' and places it in rooms where peace is most needed. Finally, the absence of food causes a showdown between Ray and Janet. Their fight ends, miraculously, in laughter. Janet recognises what she has truly lost: spiritual contact with others and 'the pleasure of serving'. To make reparations, she prepares a sacramental meal of roasted rabbit as an invitation to table. Neither Ray nor Maxine attend.

Garner has explained her need for, and love of, the Eucharist, particularly in times of crisis. In her essay 'Sighs Too Deep for Words', she says:

> It's quite simple. You examine yourself, formally, in calm and serious words, together; with everyone else in the building; you acknowledge that you have, well, basically stuffed things up again; in the name of Christ you are formally forgiven; and then they say to you, formally, 'Come up here now, and we'll give you something to eat and drink.'

In August 1991 she sent an excerpt from 'Cosmo Cosmolino' to *Scripsi*. In the accompanying letter she noted that 'of course the failure bird is the Holy Spirit':

> when writing this I went to church at Pentecost and nearly keeled over to realise that I had unconsciously, & in my abysmal ignorance, incorporated many of the images of the Holy Spirit—bird, wind, fire—the Comforter etc—in this story, <u>innocently (almost) dragging them in out of daily life, I mean domestic life</u>.

Ray's brother Alby finally arrives at Sweetpea Mansions, armed with nostalgic memories of happy times past. His joyous optimism suggests a possible future for this fragile collection of people. Maxine prepares breakfast. A communal meal is shared. Janet's column reappears with renewed intensity, but something has shifted. Behind her lids are 'tears of bliss'.

At the story's conclusion Maxine, carrying another little world inside her, ascends into the cosmos and looks down benevolently on the house and its new configuration of lodgers. In what Garner describes as a moment of grace, Janet invites Alby inside to choose a room. *Cosmo Cosmolino* charts the re-emergence of Janet, one of Garner's 'me' characters, back into the world of love and feeling. Yet it can never be simply a happy ever after. In 'Recording Angel' the Melbourne tram is an agent of death. In the closing lines of 'Cosmo Cosmolino', a tram goes 'shattering through the intersection'.

Garner's use of symbolism in *Cosmo Cosmolino* perplexed some commentators. John Nieuwenhuizen, for example, penned a scathing review. He was unconvinced by the characters' 'grapplings with spirituality and the meaning of faith'; 'their dilemmas treated simplistically' were 'gathered about in a rush of meaningless hyperprose'. In the *Australian Magazine* Susan Chenery reported that members of the literary establishment who had received advance copies of the book were unimpressed by Garner's 'move into religion and fantasy'. Anonymously, one critic stated that the book was 'insubstantial', another that it was 'just the same old stuff with magic realism thrown in', a third that as 'soon as writers discover religion, their work goes downhill'. These comments confirmed Garner's private anxiety that readers might be embarrassed by her focus on the metaphysical. In any case, she felt that there was a perception that Brand Garner had let the side down. In her essay 'Dreams, the Bible and *Cosmo Cosmolino*', Garner explained she was trying to write of 'a more wondrous world that would still stubbornly be this world'; she set out to 'write something that had all the squalid panic, the wild swerves of narrative, the radiant emblematic objects and the passages of swooning bliss that [she] had found in dream'. She insisted that she was mature enough to weather any disparaging reviews. In truth, she was stung deeply by the negative criticism.

Over time, Garner internalised the less favourable responses to *Cosmo Cosmolino*. She adopted the language of critics such as Jenna Mead and Fiona Capp, who argued that she had veered into 'purple' prose. She later said it was her clumsiest work, that the book somehow got away from her and that she did not quite know what she was doing. Yet it was never going to be possible for this spare, exacting stylist to pin language down precisely enough to express her ideas about the inexpressible.

At the heart of her struggle was her need to articulate the complex nature of life; the banal realities of individual existence and the mysterious beauty of the numinous world. Garner hoped that readers would appreciate the different modes operating in the book and look beyond a simple realist approach. Janet discovers the limitations of such an approach when she has Maxine's drawing of her shadowy column mounted and framed: 'the framing had not worked out satisfactorily at all, for the picture was so dark and so densely layered that once enclosed behind the sheet of glass, it vanished. It completely disappeared.'

Tim Winton judges *Cosmo Cosmolino* to be Garner's best work. He remembers telling Garner: '*The Children's Bach* was like a perfectly built cottage, all squared away, a lovely thing and an achievement to envy, but *Cosmo* was like a big sunny shack with all the windows and doors open to the light and breeze…I love its raggedness, its waywardness, its openness.' Praising the book's 'grounded mysticism', Winton said to me that *Cosmo Cosmolino* marks 'the point at which Helen really goes her own way, where you can see she's not quite of her people…from here on in she's…well, unreliable in the finest sense.'

Garner has often recounted the time she wrote to Manning Clark complaining that she was sick of her style. He replied that her style would not change until she did. *Cosmo Cosmolino* marked a significant change in her style, but there were even greater changes afoot in her life at this time. *Cosmo Cosmolino* would be the last work of fiction Garner would publish for sixteen years.

PART II:

Questions of Judgment

*The characters of nonfiction, no less than those of fiction,
derive from the writer's most idiosyncratic desires and
deepest anxieties, they are what the writer wishes he was
and worries that he is.*

JANET MALCOLM,
The Journalist and the Murderer (1990)

8

The First Stone:
Some Questions About Sex and Power

*In a work of nonfiction we almost never know the truth
of what happened…Only in nonfiction does the question of what
happened and how people thought and felt remain open.*

JANET MALCOLM, *The Silent Woman* (1994)

There is no correct line.

HELEN GARNER, PROCESS JOURNAL FOR *The First Stone* (1993)

The truth of events surrounding the Ormond Smoko on
16 October 1991 may never be fully known. The undisputed
facts are that following the valedictory dinner at Melbourne
University's prestigious Ormond College, there was a party—
the Smoko—which was attended by about 250 staff and
students. Two female students later reported that they were
sexually harassed during the evening by the Master, Dr Alan
Gregory. One student, known in *The First Stone* as Nicole
Stewart, alleged that Gregory had twice placed his hand on her
breast while they were dancing. A second student, given the
name Elizabeth Rosen, alleged that around 11 p.m. the Master

123

invited her into his office whereupon he locked the door, made sexually suggestive remarks and touched her breasts.

Nicole Stewart first spoke to Dr Jenna Mead, a live-in tutor, director of studies for arts students and elected member of the Ormond College Council, the day after the Smoko. Mead advised her to wait until after her exams to lodge a complaint. In November a student acting as an emissary gave Sir Daryl Dawson, Chair of the College Council and serving High Court judge, two unsigned statements alleging misconduct by the Master. Dawson asked to meet the complainants. A few hours later he was told by their representative, and the Vice Master, that the students wished to withdraw the allegations and that they wanted the statements destroyed. Dawson phoned the Master and told him allegations had been made. He did not divulge the nature of the allegations, but he cautioned him against attending student functions and being alone with students in his office. He did not destroy the statements.

On the weekend of 22–23 February 1992, two additional signed statements were delivered to Dawson. The first was an elaboration of one of the previous statements, the second, from Elizabeth Rosen, was new and it outlined her allegations against the Master. Within forty-eight hours Dawson appointed a subcommittee of three Council members, Bill Rogers, Sarah Stephen and George Gaze, to enquire into the allegations and formalise the statements. The complainants gave evidence to the committee. They also attended two conciliation sessions with Suzy Nixon, the director of the Melbourne University counselling service. When the subcommittee submitted their findings to the Ormond Council, which subsequently found that the students acted in 'good faith' yet expressed full confidence in the Master, the young women were aghast. They had thought, in leaving their statements unsigned, that they could seek advice and redress within the College rather than involve the legal system. They had expected the College to find against the Master. Now, feeling dismissed and silenced, they took their allegations to the police.

Alan Gregory knew nothing of the specifics of the allegations against him until March 1992. When questioned by CIB officers at Carlton Police Station on 9 April, he denied all the allegations 'totally and emphatically'.

On 25 August 1992 Garner opened the *Age* and was jolted by an item recounting that Gregory was to appear before a magistrate on an indecent assault charge. She called her friends, 'feminists pushing fifty', all of whom were apparently 'unsettled' by the article. In the second paragraph of what went on to become one of the most explosively controversial books of the decade, Garner wrote: 'He touched her breast and she went to the *cops*? My God—why didn't she get her mother or her friends to help her sort him out later, if she couldn't deal with it herself at the time?' By the book's conclusion she was no closer to an answer, although after nearly three years of research and writing she was more aware of the radical complexity of the question that she posed.

On the day she read the *Age* article Garner dashed off a letter of sympathy to the Master. It is 'heartbreaking,' she wrote, 'for a feminist of nearly fifty, like me, to see our ideals of so many years distorted into this ghastly punitiveness'. She labelled the girls' actions as 'appallingly destructive, priggish and pitiless'. She assured him that 'there are plenty of women out here…who still hope that men and women…can behave towards each other with kindness rather than being engaged in this kind of warfare'. And she signed off by sending Gregory and his family her 'sincere sympathy and warmest good wishes'.

David Malouf thinks that Garner's letter to Gregory goes to the core of who she is. It represents, he says, a 'moment of irrational, irrepressible generosity of feeling'. Garner's agent at that time, Barbara Mobbs, agrees. She calls Garner 'the thoroughbred'. 'She charges ahead towards a barbed-wire fence. She will either clear the fence or come crashing down tearing her fetlocks.' Some critics have argued that Garner wrote to Gregory as a way of writing herself into the story. She insists that she had no agenda. She didn't think, she asserts: 'I just galloped onwards'. In her essay 'The Art of the Dumb Question: Forethought and Hindthought about *The First Stone*', published in 1997, she notes that the letter was 'quite dumb' in its 'ignorance, and…naïve spontaneity'. Only later did she come to realise that she could not 'write letters to strangers any more, without their having a meaning—and a *use*—beyond what I intended—because Helen Garner is not just me any longer: there's no simple link between the words "Helen Garner" and this person I feel myself to be'. She conceded that: 'Awareness of that fateful initial letter moves through the text of *The First Stone* like a tidal wave.'

*

Gregory was found guilty of indecent assault while dancing with Nicole Stewart. No conviction was recorded. He appealed. When the second set of allegations was reported in some detail, Garner's interest was whetted. On 2 September she was in the Magistrates' Court to hear judgment delivered in Elizabeth Rosen's case. Gregory was acquitted. A few weeks later she fronted up to the County Court for Gregory's appeal. She took her notebook. Like the judge, Garner was impressed by Nicole Stewart's poise, honesty and integrity. Yet she also believed, and felt sorry for, the Master. After Gregory won his appeal, the students' solicitor announced that they would be taking their complaints to the Victorian Equal Opportunity Commission. Garner was perplexed. Surely it was too late for confidential conciliation? She 'felt the first stab of real, businesslike curiosity'. She was hooked. And she was hamstrung.

With the intention of writing an extended piece of journalism, incorporating multiple points of view, she began to contact those involved in the events. Gregory was keen to talk, and keen to please. Garner wrote polite letters to both young women and to Jenna Mead, dismissing rumours that she was writing a 'pro-Gregory' book, admitting she had 'shot her mouth off', and appreciating the hurt and distress they had endured. From the complainants there was silence. She phoned Mead, with whom she had been cordially acquainted, and was taken aback by her response: 'Helen, you have been incredibly *stupid*. You have been amazingly, *unbelievably* stupid.'

By March 1993 Garner knew she was writing a book,

though she refused Hilary McPhee's offer of a contract at that stage. In her journal she recorded that she was hesitant because she was 'afraid of the power I would have to hurt and damage people'. She wrote a second time to the complainants and to Mead. There was silence from the young women. From Mead, she received a stern written response, accusing her of intimidation, provocation and harassment. Battle lines were being drawn and Garner was rising with relish to the challenge. Yet, as Malcolm would later note in her review of *The First Stone*, Garner had 'shot herself in the foot' with her letter to Gregory: 'She did what a journalist must never do—she showed her hand too early.' Without Garner's knowledge or consent, Gregory copied and circulated her letter widely. Her impartiality could not be restored. Despite appeals to the complainants and their supporters, despite reassurances that she wanted to write a 'truthful, calm and balanced account of what happened', and 'to unpick the knots of the story & make more complex sense of it than the press' had been able to do, doors slammed in Garner's face.

That first court notebook grew to a series of five process journals, kept over the two years of her research. The journals are archived among Garner's papers in the National Library of Australia. They are embargoed until January 2022 and thereafter require permission for research during Garner's lifetime and that of her daughter. Garner authorised my access to these and other files in the NLA. She has meticulously erased any identifiable trace of the complainants' identity.

Never intended for publication, these journals became a form of diary, a daily account of Garner's thoughts, emotions, and discoveries along with contact details and appointment times for interviews, transcribed interviews and, fascinatingly, her dreams. By recording her dreams—and nightmares—Garner was able to reflect on their relevance and to understand more of the subconscious forces informing her thinking. Garner signposts most of those forces—her attraction to some of the crusty Ormond men, her sense of intellectual inadequacy, her sympathy for and identification with the Master, her concerns about becoming invisible as a woman—in her book. Others she only begins to understand years after publication. In 'The Art of the Dumb Question: Forethought and Hindthought about *The First Stone*' she interprets her response to Mead's accusation of her supposed stupidity:

> In my psyche, this was *my father* speaking. On the very next page you can see a faint tinge of my semi-awareness of this: 'Nobody had taken that tone to me *since I was a teenager*.' But the penny didn't drop till years later, that the rage and pigheadedness which her tone provoked in me was a throwback to my struggles against my father's disapproval. This phone call planted in me the seed of a hostility which…took root and began to flourish in me…and grew, I think, into the unconscious or semi-conscious force that drove that book.

The First Stone is, to a large extent, driven by an impassioned battle between Garner and Mead, a battle whose boundaries became blurred and whose reporting was fatally compromised due to defamation laws. Another driving factor is Garner's fluctuating responses to the complainants' silence. Without their input she did not have a story that could be fully developed or resolved. Gregory was acquitted of all charges. Neither he nor the complainants were found by the courts to be lying. The most solid material Garner had to work with was her own intense reaction to the events and her puzzlement as to why she was so 'haunted' by them.

Garner had always used writing to make sense of the world. Why would she change now? She could not let this story go. As she explained in her first letter to Mead, she had 'continued to be extremely distressed by the story, but in increasingly complex & confusing ways, & I've got a strong desire to get some kind of a handle on it, as much for my own peace of mind as for any other reason'. She set about interviewing key players: Dr and Mrs Gregory, Sir Daryl Dawson, past and present members of the Ormond College Council—George Gaze, Sir George Lush, Bill Rogers and Sarah Stephen—and the university counsellor Suzy Nixon. She read the minutes of Ormond meetings—the College Council, the General Committee of the Students' Club and the Equal Opportunity Committee. She expanded her focus to include people with knowledge of Ormond, the Uniting Church and Melbourne University. She interviewed dozens of people; many insisted on anonymity. This was a Melbourne story; everyone seemed to be either connected to, or to know something about, the central people involved. On the other hand, of course, it was a universal story about the fraught terrain of sexual harassment and the tangled nexus between power and desire.

Throughout the writing process Garner sought close counsel from members of her French reading class, her daughter, Drusilla Modjeska and Hilary McPhee. In May 1993 when Garner's 3a.m. uncertainties were mounting, it was McPhee who suggested she insert herself as a character into the narrative and write a book that charted the effects of each person's statement on her own point of view. That strategy allowed her to explore the issues with which she was grappling, despite the absence of the complainants' perspective, yet it later infuriated some commentators. Mead and the complainants' solicitor chastised Garner in almost identical prose. 'Helen,' they told her, 'this story is *not* being played out for the benefit of *your* finer feelings'.

While writing her book, and in a number of academic articles, reviews and books written in response to it, Garner was lambasted for constructing herself as a victim of a feminist conspiracy, thereby aligning herself with Gregory. She never credited the conspiracy theories put to her by a number of people interviewed; her decision to centre the book around her intuitive responses was a conscious strategy. In the manuscript drafts she breaks up blocks of interview transcripts with notes, 'more me here', 'weave me in and out', and with irony, 'poor me here'. This would be a radically unstable narrative of personal anguish and ambivalence that mirrored her psychological and intellectual turmoil. Just as she could not find a correct line, just as she fluctuated between fury at and respect for the complainants' silence, so too her narrative refuses the reader a place to settle. Garner persistently changes her position and her allegiances, she charges forward, she digresses, she retreats, she comes back for more. 'Again and again' she feels 'sharp flashes of empathy with the girls; but something in me, every time, slams on the brakes'. It is not surprising that when Shirley Hazzard wrote to congratulate Garner on *The First Stone*, she noted that the book 'seems to engage much, much of inner and outward life—so much that one mentally gets up and walks around while reading it, trying to sort out the unsortable from the sortable'.

Garner has spoken often of the ways in which her own psychotherapy, and her reading of Janet Malcolm—in particular *The Silent Woman*—contributed to her approach in *The First Stone*. She realised that sketching character and situation through imagery and attributing meaning through body language were not techniques reserved for fiction; they were aspects of good writing. So she used the inefficient, demanding fireplace in the Gregory's lounge room as an image of Mrs Gregory's generosity: 'her uneconomical, exhausting, undiscriminating, selfless good will'. She appreciated that when, during their interview, Sir George Lush put the lid back on the biscuit jar, he was, despite saying otherwise, refusing to give her any more information. She came to understand that the smell of the moss outside his house rekindled childhood memories of her grandparents' home, and lulled her into a more subservient, accommodating frame of mind.

Garner was drawn to the psychological dimensions of the narratives she was uncovering about people involved in the

Ormond events. In May 1993, swamped with information and troubled by how to give it shape, she spoke to her friend, Jungian psychoanalyst Peter O'Connor. O'Connor saw a series of interlocking unconscious motivations at work. He suggested she shift the story from the literal to the mythological, believing the material would best be suited to the novel form. Garner agreed. On the same day, her publisher contacted her with a breakthrough. The student who had taken the unsigned statements to Dawson had telephoned from Canada and wanted to talk. A novel seemed out of the question. As late as May 1994, however, she recorded in her journal: 'Ooh I wish I were writing a novel instead.'

One third of the way through *The First Stone*, Garner identifies the moment when she knew she should 'put the whole thing down and walk away'. She also admits that for 'some obscure reason' she could not do so. What was that reason? Why was she 'haunted' by this story? Why was she so afraid of 'finding out things that would cause an upheaval in [her] whole belief-structure, particularly where men and women were concerned, and the way power shifts between them'? These questions can be partially answered by pursuing more deeply Garner's psychological motivations because, as Kerryn Goldsworthy noted in her monograph, 'The Ormond drama was played out on what was, for her, a complex site of psychic unease.'

Like many Carlton residents, Garner used to ride her bike

through the grounds of Ormond College. Now she parks her bike and re-enters the places of her formative undergraduate experiences. For the first time in thirty years, she returns to the Master's house and to the neighbouring Janet Clarke Hall. She wanders the corridors of Ormond, where she notices the sexist, class-based nature of the photographs, and appreciates the weird allure of Ormond's rarefied atmosphere of privilege. From Janet Clarke Hall she looks over to Trinity College, remembering the time she spent there with her former history tutor who was her lover when she was an undergraduate. All these years later she can state calmly that the tutor broke her heart, that she felt herself 'tragically bereft'. From this distance, Garner can classify that relationship as 'a relatively minor episode', which she values for what it taught her about the world. It was not, she insists, 'sexual harassment' or 'abuse of power'.

As she goes about the campus interviewing academics and brilliant young women, a nagging sense of intellectual inadequacy returns. Garner's 'old fear of professors and people with PhDs, a leftover from [her] undistinguished and almost totally silent university career', is rekindled. She feels out of her depth, not because she is lacking in intelligence, but because she has little understanding of the historical development of feminist theory. The current academic discourse of feminism is completely foreign to her more pragmatic and intuitive understanding of feminist politics. She admits in the book:

> I functioned from day to day on a set of assumptions
> that I was rarely forced to examine: the adjustments I
> made under pressure of events were semiconscious and

usually motivated by a desire to avoid taxing mental
activity. I was still skating along on ice that had frozen
in the early seventies.

There had been no discourse of sexual harassment in
Garner's seventies' world of 'free love' and women's liberation.
She remembers the hard-drinking, leftist men at the Pram
Factory and APG who dictated a so-called correct line that
everyone was supposed to tread. She had never been able or
willing to toe that line and had internalised her inability to do
so as a fault that made her anxious and ashamed. She could not
see that the new language with which women could speak of
unequal power and their refusal to be coerced validated their
feelings just as Lionel Trilling's suggestion that 'one might live
in doubt' had validated hers.

Garner would not be drawn into the academic discourse
on feminism. She felt alienated by it; a feeling that seemed to
confirm her belief that the gulf between contemporary academic
feminism and the lived experiences of many women remained
immense.

In her productive discussion with the law lecturer known in
the book as 'Dr M', Garner demonstrates that she is not oblivi-
ous to arguments about the abuse of power. She acknowledges
that the persistence of sexual harassment is real. She agrees that
women should have recourse to mechanisms that protect them
from abuse, and that students need to understand that they are
not in an equal power relationship with their lecturers. She is
impressed that Dr M could disagree with her arguments about
allowing flirtation and consensual relations without having to

'hate' her or deny her a voice. In contrast, when the Women's Officer of the Student Union insists that in cases of sexual harassment an apology and the cessation of inappropriate behaviour can never be sufficient, that 'retribution' is required, Garner is thrown. She feels 'out of date, irrelevant', 'terrifically at a disadvantage'. She does not understand this new form of feminism, which she interprets as vindictive, 'priggish, disingenuous, unforgiving'. She rails against what she sees as victim feminism with its 'constant stress on passivity and weakness'.

In June 1993 Garner read Dr Marion Tapper's paper '*Ressentiment* and Power: Some Reflections on Feminist Practices'. Her response was immediate, dramatic, and visceral; her nose bled and she burst into tears. She remembers a feeling of relief that an academic philosopher had articulated a similar sense of dismay about the direction of feminism within the academy. Tapper argued that *ressentiment* was 'both a backward looking spirit—it needs to keep remembering past injustices—and an expansive spirit—it needs to find new injustices everywhere'. Garner heard echoes of the call for retribution. She highlighted much of this paper, including the following passage, and filed it with her research notes:

> What began as an attempt to reclaim female sexuality
> and bodily pleasure from its denunciation and denial
> has been transformed into a radical rejection of sexual
> desire and pleasure as nothing but a social construct
> of male power. And what began as a necessary and
> legitimate struggle against sexual harassment and abuse
> of women and children has extended into a suspicion

Helen Garner and Axel Clark at Drummond Street, Carlton, in the early 1980s. In her story 'My Hard Heart' Garner writes: 'The front of the house was festooned with great twining loops of wisteria.'

2. not even a sensible word about my grievous sickness. I had five (5) letters, a card and a nanny from my first form kids while I was away. School is marvellous, I can't remember ever having a job that I enjoyed so much. I am finally learning how to make the kids laugh <u>and</u> work; the lessons turn out to be tremendous fun. I am form mistress of 3A, and one of the other teachers reported to me that the 3A girls are collecting to buy me an Easter present....! Happy happy Jordie.

Lots of love,
Miss Jord.

July 31, 1985

Dear Ali, dear Axel,

Thanks for putting me up once more. I always love staying with you & in fact don't know how I'd manage without a couple of visits a year! David Malouf rang up just now from Brisbane & says he's coming down to Melbourne for the Premier's Award dinner on August 14; he's going to stay the night here & on the morrow we'll fly together

back to Sydney – I'll go to the Lit Board meeting & he says I can stay at his place in Cremorne Point on the night between the 2 meetings. Tom Shapcott lives nearby & will drive me to work each day. How terribly convenient. I must confess

On 4 December 1975 Garner writes to Axel that, in rewriting her 'junkie poem', 'White Eyes', as a song, it became 'a lot cruder in one way', but she was pleased there was 'a nice tight feeling about it—no extra words'.

In 1995 James Kilby, then owner of 259 Scotchmer Street, Fitzroy North, invited past residents to paint a mural on the house's side wall. Sally Ford and Alice Garner captured the spirit of their time in that house.

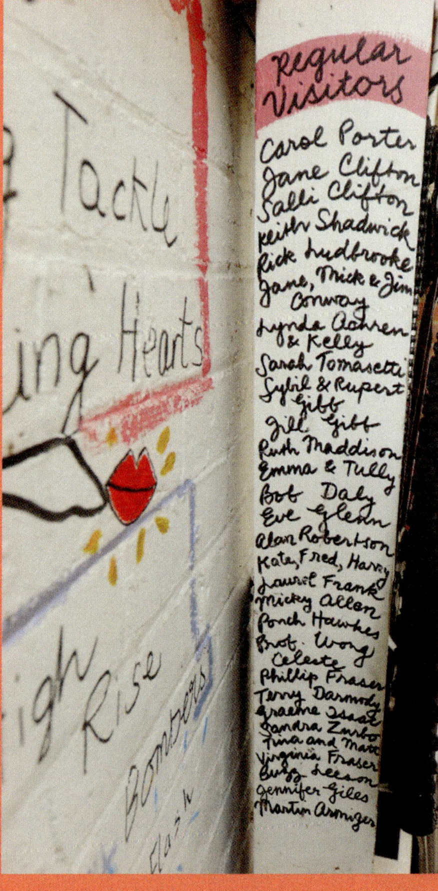

28/12/07

<u>cf 16 Dec 07 home diary</u>
(a house)
↓

Jack K:

'Is a person like this? In one
room someone is crouching in
fear. In another room someone
else is screaming w unspeakable
madness. In another someone
is laughing. In another
someone weeping. While all
the time the domestic goes
about her work. We think
we're the domestic, just
tidying things up here &
there.'

ABOVE: Jack Kirszenblat's suggestion that a person may be like a many-roomed house resonates throughout Garner's writing. While researching *This House of Grief*, Garner transcribed this passage into her process journal and private diary.

RIGHT: Soon after publishing 'The Insults of Age', which described her controversial hair-pulling incident, Garner sent this postcard to the author with the note: 'So my attack had a literary precedent!'

June 1998

An Open Letter to Helen Garner

Dear Helen,
        We have read Rosi Braidotti's contribution, Remembering Fizroy High, in Gemma Mead's *Bodyjamming*. As your former colleagues we feel outraged at the attack on your professional expertise as a teacher. We are also keenly aware that you are unable to defend yourself. You can claim all you like that you were a responsible and responsive teacher and people can just write it off as defensive rubbish.

Braidotti vilifies you for diminishing the standing of the school just when it was raising its profile with student achievement and cultural activities. She also claims that you had a patronising attitude towards the migrant families attending the school. There are many other references about you which seem to have more to do with her preoccupations rather than really touch on what you did at Fitzroy High School. We will deliberately ignore them because they are so far off beam as to be ridiculous.

Our memories of you are of someone who cared passionately about her students and valued them for who they were. You were constantly talking about how honest they were. How Braidotti can write "she despises their broken English and their general ignorance" (p.135) is beyond us. You were in fact teaching about Ancient Greece when confronted by the graffiti which initiated the lessons on sexual matters. You were acutely aware that their backgrounds were diverse and they were taken into account in your teaching. We would be amazed if you actually thought they were ignorant, different yes. But your teaching was definitely not based on a deficit theory; that they were empty vessels waiting to be filled with your wisdom.

You knew them extremely well, one does if one teaches the same class for ten periods a week for a year. There was a feeling of trust in your classroom; that is why they could ask you such intimate questions. Braidotti referred to you appealing "to the complicity of her first formers, in letting them lock the doors of the classroom and in asking them NOT to repeat their class discussion" (p.136). In fact you talked to them directly to allay their fears and inform them and this was reciprocated by their wish to protect you from the authorities of the time. She also refers to the fact that "A climate of erotic complicity has set in between her and the boys in the class; as for the girls, that's another matter" (p.136). This is pure smear and is not justified in any way. We can only imagine the fury you felt when you read this passage. We know that it is without foundation.

There are many emotional undercurrents running through Braidotti's writing and you appear to be the victim she has chosen to focus on. Regardless of all the statements made in this article and the book in general, our memories of you are of a vibrant, reponsible and creative teacher who valued her students for what they were.

With very best wishes,
Caroline Hogg
Liz Aird.

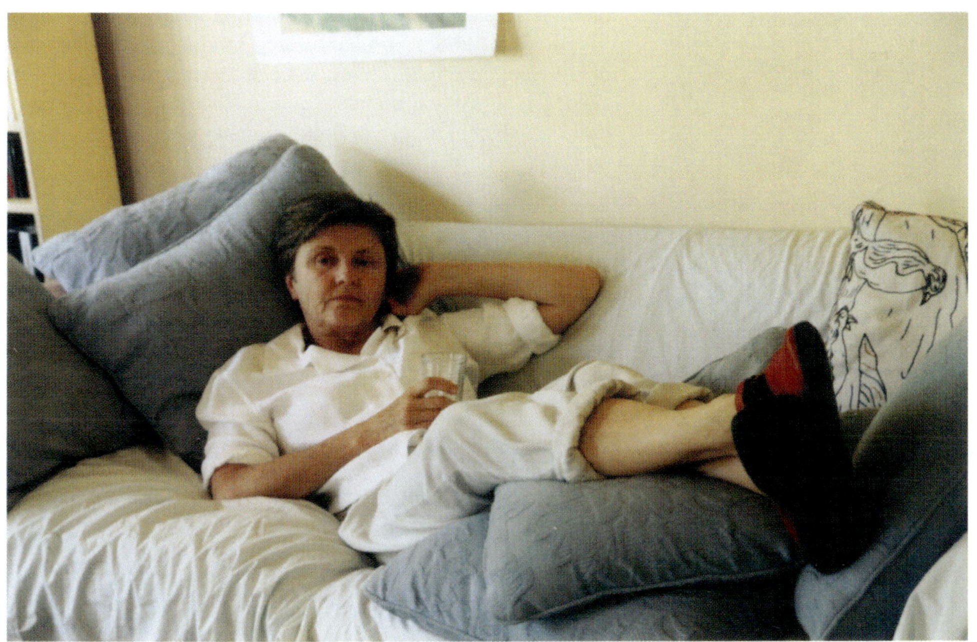

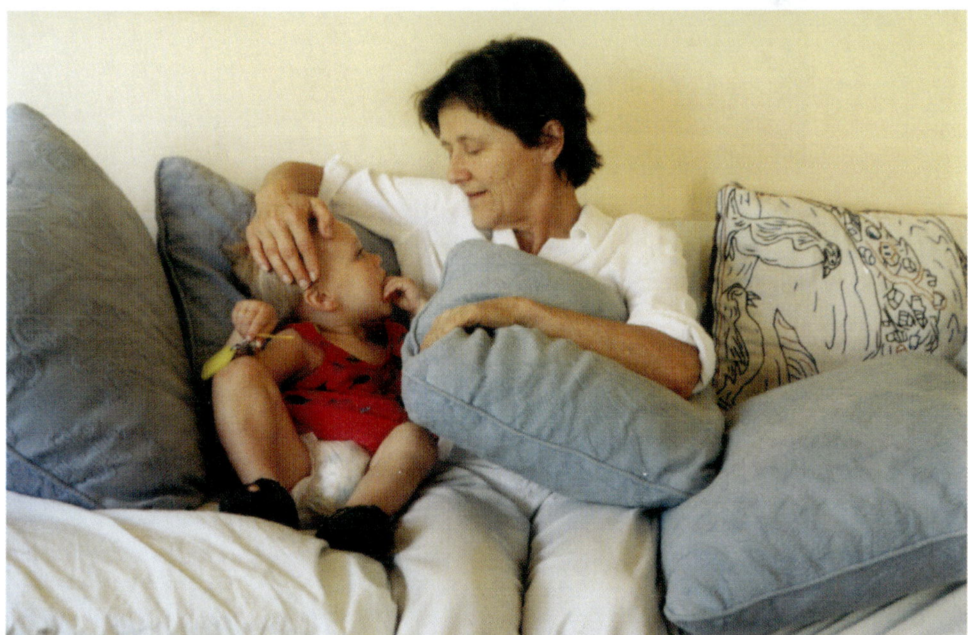

TOP: In 2002 Jenny Sages photographed Garner in her Fitzroy North home. Garner remembers the occasion warmly: 'Jenny Sages never tried to make me smile. I felt very relaxed in her company.'

BOTTOM: Helen and her granddaughter, Olive. In her essay 'The Nanna-Mobile', Garner writes about their relationship: 'I was pole-axed by an emotion unlike any I have ever felt before. The word *love* hardly touches the sides.'

LEFT: Helen as a baby with her mother in January 1943. Garner writes about this photograph in the essay 'Dreams of Her Real Self': 'I am six months old. I am still an only child. She is carrying me in her arms...She is my mother, and I am content to rest my head upon her breast.'

BELOW: Garner with her parents, Gwen and Bruce Ford, at their home in Melbourne, December 1998.

Helen Garner and Tim Winton at the 1986 Adelaide Arts Festival. Winton says this is one of his favourite photographs of them together. He describes Garner as 'laughing like a pirate's parrot'.

of all bodily contact, gesture and movement as possibly expressive of male power.

It was Nietzsche who first wrote about the concept of *ressentiment*. In *On the Genealogy of Morals*, he defined it as the 'revenge of the powerless', and the triumph of the 'slave' morality. Garner wanted women to feel empowered. In her journal she cited Mary Wollstonecraft's declaration from *A Vindication of the Rights of Woman*: 'I do not wish them to have power over men; but over themselves.' When a friend told her about a bright, confident young woman who took years to tell her parents that she withdrew from university and retreated from social contact because she was sexually harassed, Garner acknowledged that she might not have given enough credence to young women who were not strong enough to defend themselves. She noted: 'I see that I am often too <u>breezy</u>—arguing on the basis of strong people's experience—as James Button says, leaving out the fact that some girls haven't <u>got</u> whatever is required in order to snarl "Crawl back to the barnyard where you belong."'

In September 1992 Garner had accepted a job with *Time Australia* to cover what turned out to be two trials of Paul Aiton, a thirty-two-year-old man accused of beating to death his girlfriend's two-year-old son, Daniel Valerio. Day after day she sat in the Victorian Supreme Court listening to evidence about the horrific violence inflicted on Daniel. Although the toddler had been seen by twenty-one professionals, no one intervened to save him. His postmortem revealed partially healed fractures and at least 104 'bruises upon bruises'. Bearing witness to Aiton's sadistic violence reinforced Garner's belief in what constituted 'real' abuse. Having classified Gregory's alleged offence as no more than a drunken pass at a party, she was incensed by the argument that the complainants had every right to call in the police 'right from the start…[as] a response to violence against women'. Garner refused to accept what she heard repeatedly, 'the slide from *harassment* to *violence*'. She was adamant that there were gradations of offence and that the 'ability to discriminate *must be maintained*'. She insisted that to deny the difference between 'being made to feel uncomfortable' and 'violence against women' was to 'insult the suffering of women who have met real violence, and…distort the subtleties of human interaction into caricatures that can serve only as propaganda for war'. It is no coincidence that 'Killing Daniel', for which she won a Walkley Award, immediately precedes 'The Fate of *The First Stone*' in *True Stories*.

Apart from observing Nicole Stewart give evidence in court, Garner's knowledge of the complainants was largely limited to Elizabeth Rosen's statement to the Equal Opportunity Board at Ormond and a photograph of each girl. Nicole Stewart appeared to her as intelligent, 'pretty' and 'conservative'. She described Elizabeth Rosen as a 'daring beauty', 'a woman in the full glory of her youth, as joyful as a goddess, elated by her own careless authority and power'. Critics seized upon this description as evidence of Garner's envy of the younger woman. Elspeth Probyn, for example, writing about the role of *ressentiment* in intergenerational feminist debates, identified Garner's question 'What's wrong with young feminists?' as evidence of the older woman's 'resentful "I want" their youth, the privileges that they have because of me/my generation'. For her part, Garner not only interrogated herself about precisely those emotions, she charts her doubts and responses in the book:

> I thought…at fifty, I might have forgotten what it was like to be a young woman out in the world, constantly the focus of men's sexual attention. Or maybe I was cranky that my friends and sisters and I had got ourselves through decades of being wolf-whistled, propositioned, pestered, insulted, touched, attacked and worse, without the big guns of sexual harassment legislation to back us up.

She writes about telling her friend of her 'pathetic bravado' when faced with the ferocity of the young Women's Officer:

> I practically pleaded for her respect…I talked about abortion law reform, demos and police and so on—I said, '"We put our bodies on the line"—but she just looked at me coldly—she didn't give a shit about our *magnificent heroism*.'
>
> We sat at the table howling with laughter. 'It's a dialogue between generations,' said Angela Z—, wiping away the tears.
>
> 'It's not a dialogue,' I said, blowing my nose. 'It's a fucking *war*.'

Garner draws attention to actual and metaphorical mother–daughter relationships throughout *The First Stone*. Yet she is also interested in father–daughter dynamics. She links her supposed generational envy to her relationship with the Ormond men:

'So this is about middle-aged mothers and daughters, then, just as the old council members and I (with my sudden pity, my reluctance to condemn) are about fathers and middle-aged daughters.' Her response to the Ormond men is complex and shifting. She describes those in the college photographs as wealthy men whose insolent stance draws attention to their genitals. Their very existence seems dependent on the invisible, subservient maids. On her first encounter with Ormond men she is dismissed and humiliated. While waiting in court for the verdict on Gregory's appeal, two 'grim-faced Presbyterians' push past her 'into the row, shoving hard against my legs although I tried to turn aside to allow passage'. She speaks to them and moves her bag to facilitate their passing. 'They did not answer, but stood in the row and waited, blank-faced, staring into the distance, without the slightest acknowledgement that a fifty-year-old woman was down on her hands and knees among their legs.' As Goldsworthy observes, these passages 'say more to a larger number of people about the nature of institutional power…and about the place of women in the structures and histories of such institutions, than any paragraph of sexual harassment legislation, any graffito, any new book on feminist theory'.

Significantly, the Ormond men come to operate as father figures for Garner. In her journal she wondered if she was attracted to them because they flattered and showed interest in her. She is 'putty in the hands of these old stagers, with their racy turns of phrase, their imagery drawn from sports and war, their confident bandying of biblical and Shakespearean references'. She enjoys the banter, the laughter. Her need for their approval is deep and revealing. A decade earlier she had confessed to Candida Baker that she broke into a 'nervous sweat' whenever she approached a university because she felt 'inferior and despised and frowned upon' by academics. She equated universities with 'the negative father', explaining: 'I desperately want them to approve of me but I behave in such a way that they won't.'

In Gregory's ignorance of both the charges against him and the behind-the-scenes machinations at Ormond that led to his forced resignation, Garner heard echoes of her sacking from Fitzroy High in 1972. Then she swallowed her rage and went quietly. Now she commands an audience. She will speak in his defence. Of most interest in this identification is the idea put forward by Goldsworthy that, in labelling the complainants, their supporters and their attitudes as 'priggish', 'puritan', 'punitive' and 'prissy', Garner was possibly 'conflating the genuinely "puritan" motivation behind her own sacking…with the much more subtle and complex forces in play around the Gregory accusations'. Understanding Garner's history as an undergraduate and young teacher goes some way to explaining her sympathies in this story, her inability to 'put it down and walk away', and some of the intensity of her emotional responses.

Another significant factor in Garner's approach was her marriage to Murray Bail, which rates only a passing direct reference in the text: 'I dreaded discovering that I had become cold-hearted; that a happy marriage, after all these years of fighting men, might have undermined my sympathy for my own sex, and weakened my moral imagination.' Bail is an old-fashioned, reserved man of letters. Garner says the sixties and seventies, and their revolutionary ideals and practices, largely passed him by. In fact, he spent part of the sixties fixing and racing cars in Adelaide. In contrast to Garner's unsettled adult life, Bail had enjoyed a long, traditional marriage with his first wife. They had no children. His primary interests were reading and writing. It was Bail who, having read Robert Craft's *Stravinsky: Chronicle of a Friendship 1948–1971*, delighted in the story that while Stravinsky was composing he insisted that his wife and children eat lunch in silence. It was a story about male genius and the sacrifices others needed to make for the cause of great art. Garner was appalled by the tale. She relayed it, and Bail's approbation of it, to Modjeska and McPhee. 'Stravinsky's lunch' became a kind of comic shorthand between the women to signify the unreasonable egos and demands of male artists. Modjeska picked up on this theme and titled her 1999 study of Stella Bowen and Grace Cossington-Smith *Stravinsky's Lunch*.

Garner and Bail's relationship was intellectually enriching. Garner readily admits that Bail influenced her intellectual life for many years. He created a quiet world of thinking and reading which she enjoyed sharing and from which she learned much. With Bail, her horizons were greatly expanded. Friends talk about their obvious joy in each other and their shared intellectual vigour. But there was a tension at the heart of the relationship. They were very different writers operating on the same turf of Australian fiction. Where Bail was financially secure and therefore able to be focused on whatever project he was undertaking, Garner always needed to juggle various kinds of work. For four years of their time together she was a film critic, in addition to writing feature journalism, essays and longer works of nonfiction. For many years of their marriage Bail was writing *Eucalyptus*, a novel in which men attempt to classify and contain both unruly nature and the life and love of a young woman.

Bail insisted there was no rivalry between them: 'We should be better than that.' But Garner sensed that there was rivalry and it flowed both ways. Only years after they separated did she appreciate that by moving to nonfiction she had abandoned the disputed turf. Bail, a high modernist, had a personal hierarchy of literary forms; the novel was established in top position, journalism close to the bottom. He made clear to Garner that he was not all that interested in the book she was writing about feminism and attitudes to it. In her journal Garner asked herself how much of her new anti-feminist feeling was due to Bail's influence. She noted that in the middle of an argument about the need for her to 'be nicer & less assertive', Bail 'slid sideways and continued', 'Also—I think in this book you're writing, you've got to look beyond sociology & examine it from the angle of the sexual attraction blokes feel towards girls who get themselves up like that…even if the bloke's a poor bastard. I think you've really got to examine that.' In brackets Garner wrote: 'The fact that he imagines I'm not going to—that I wdn't—shows me how dumbly and blindly feminist he thinks I am.'

Garner was torn. As a feminist she feared that 'she was about to discover something that upset her whole ethical thinking' and become disillusioned with the movement that had transformed her life as a young single mother. As a fifty-one-year-old married woman, perhaps she needed to be 'nicer & less assertive', not so much a woman who appeared to be 'grim and dull and wowserish and self-righteous, struggling against men in the name of boring old justice'.

When *The First Stone* was published, Garner was savaged for resorting to personal stories and anecdotes as a form of evidence. Cassandra Pybus refused to review the book for *Australian Book Review*, publishing instead a bitter three-page assault on 'the famous novelist' who got it so wrong and refused to fulfill her 'author's responsibility to seek answers to the questions she poses'. Pybus concluded:

> talking to your friends, listening to hearsay and reading Jung may be useful for grappling with 'one of the most difficult and confounding issues of our time'. But it is no substitute for rigorous engagement with the multifaceted context of the issue, especially when you are feeding off the devastation and distress of your fellow citizens.

The anecdotes in *The First Stone* functioned on a number of levels. Many were blended or paraphrased comments from interviewees that introduced and developed ideas without revealing identities, or painful or libellous details. Garner's journals and early drafts are dotted with notes: 'can't use this—too hurtful', 'must never mention this', 'how can I include this?'. In their conversational, somewhat tentative tone, they also invited the reader into the discussion. Ihab Hassan, in stark contrast to Pybus, praised the text's 'implacable ambiguities, ambivalences, lacunae'. He argued that the 'integrity of the work derives, paradoxically, from its fragmentary form', from the 'series of vignettes, portraits, meditations'.

In the book Garner recalls the experience of being harassed. One instance of particular note was the time she was kissed by a masseur while naked on his table. Despite being 'thunderstruck', *'embarrassed'* and awkward, she said nothing, smiled, scuttled out of the room and paid: 'I behaved like a child. *I kept my eyes shut.* That is, I declined to take responsibility in the situation.' In her journal she wrote: 'If I can grasp the meaning of this, I will be on my way to understanding the question at the heart of this whole issue.' This question, why women feel so vulnerable and become passive in the face of abuse or offence, runs through the book. It also resounds through the hundreds of readers' letters Garner later received. 'What *is* this fear women have of our own power?' Garner asks. In the closing pages she admits how she again 'felt intensely foolish, like a child...*ashamed*' after failing to stand up to an Ormond man on the telephone: 'Stupidest of all...I actually *thanked* him and said goodbye. Then I sat here at my desk like an idiot, flushed with astonished fury.' It is one of Garner's 'flashes of empathy': 'Was I, like the girls at the Smoko, doing everything I could to spare his ego?' Yes, a little, but unlike the girls, Garner had a public voice and, therefore, the power to articulate how that passivity made her feel.

Sexual harassment was a prime topic for public discussion. In December 1992 the federal parliament, in response to the Report of the Inquiry into Equal Opportunity and Equal Status for Women in Australia, passed the *Sexual Discrimination and Other Legislation Amendment Act 1992*. One of the five amendments reads: 'Strengthen the sex harassment provisions by including harassment of staff by students and sexual harassment in the provision of goods and services.' In 1993 Cassandra Pybus published *Gross Moral Turpitude: The Orr Case Reconsidered,* which examined events from the 1950s when Sydney Sparkes Orr, a professor of philosophy at the University of Tasmania, formed a relationship with his undergraduate student Suzanne Kemp. Also at this time George Miller's film *Gross Misconduct,* shot at Ormond in 1992 and based loosely on the Orr scandal, was released. In June 1993 Jane Gallop, a leading American feminist scholar, was the keynote speaker at a University of Sydney symposium entitled 'Erotics and Pedagogy'. Gallop decried the recent introduction at a number of North American universities of a blanket ban on all consensual student–teacher relations. She railed against the taboo on any discussion of the issue about desire between teachers and students in universities, and, even more alarmingly, the extension of institutional harassment policies into the lecture theatres.

In an interview with Geraldine Doogue, Gallop warned that the laws designed to battle harassment were reactionary against women and puritanical in their view of sex. 'What is disappearing from the sexual harassment agenda,' she noted, 'is the original feminist idea that the problem is not sex but sexism. The problem is discrimination against women, but I feel as if we're going back to the image of women as victims.'

Gallop described to Doogue the erotic frisson that could be generated in teaching and learning environments. Garner defines it, in an academic context, in *The First Stone*:

> The erotic will always dance between people who teach and learn, and our attempts to manage its shocking charge are often flat-footed, literal, destructive, rigid with fear and the need to control. For good or ill, Eros is always two steps ahead of us, exploding the constraints of dogma, turning back on us our carefully worked out *positions* and *lines*, showing us that the world is richer and scarier and more fluid and many-fold than we dare to think.

Garner may have been remembering her early relationship with her history tutor. Gallop, an academic who boasted that she consciously sexualised the learning environment, was far more invested in this debate. As a graduate student in the mid-seventies she had seduced two of the professors on her dissertation committee. She insisted she felt valued, respected and powerful as a result. Ironically, only months before the 1993 symposium, she was accused of sexually harassing two graduate female students at the University of Wisconsin. She denied the charges and was cleared of them but she was found guilty of breaking the rule forbidding 'consensual amorous relations' between teachers and students.

Throughout 1993, Garner's working title for the book was *The Ormond Coathanger*. That title emphasises her intention to use the events at Ormond as a stepping-off point for a larger discussion about sexual harassment, sexual miscommunication and feminism. Her exploration of the Jungian concept of Eros in the teaching and learning environment was an essential line of enquiry. She was not equating the alleged events at the Smoko with her affirmation of Eros as a generative force of desire and play. The lines of demarcation were less stark, however, when she wrote:

> But feminism too is a conduit for Eros. Women's struggle for fairness is a breathing force, always adapting and changing. It is not the exclusive property of a priggish, literal-minded vengeance squad that gets Eros in its sights, gives him both barrels, and marches away in its Blundstones, leaving the gods' messenger sprawled in the mud with his wings all bloody and torn.

It is possible to see how some commentators concluded that, in her celebration of Eros, Garner was taking direct and unfair aim at the complainants.

The complainants were swept up into Garner's rage, which was itself inspired largely by Mead, the complainants' solicitor, the Women's Officer and those responsible for smear campaigns against Gregory and Nixon. These people were the core of her 'priggish, literal-minded vengeance squad'. They were associated in her mind with writers like Andrea Dworkin and Mary Daly. In her journal she recorded reading Dworkin's *Mercy* and being aghast at Dworkin's 'horror about sex', and appalled by the 'grinding, gnarlish, brutish ugliness of her world picture'. In August 1993 Zoë Heller published a review, in the *Times Literary Supplement*, of Helen Benedict's *Virgin or Vamp* and Helen Birch's edited collection *Moving Targets*. Garner underlined and copied out much of this review, including the line: 'willingness to acknowledge facts which may embarrass or even contradict feminist ideals is crucial'. The review supplied a new epigraph for the second draft of her manuscript. In place of Marion Milner's 'Everything one thinks one understands has to be understood over and over again in its different aspects, each time with the same shock of discovery'—a quote she continues to return to today—she substituted these lines by Heller: 'The struggle for women's rights is…not a matter of gender loyalty. It is a matter of ethical principle, and as such, it does not dictate automatic allegiance to the women's side in any given argument.'

Garner was troubled by the fraught position in which she found herself, but she was determined to act ethically, which for her meant risking the wrath of feminists by challenging what she saw as errors in a prevailing orthodoxy. She was also adamant that it was not ethical to make Gregory the sacrificial victim for the greater sins of other men. She voiced her concerns to McPhee, who affirmed that she would need to be brave, that the book was vitally important and that she would be lonely.

*

In September 1993 Garner and Bail headed to New York for Garner to take up a position teaching creative writing at New York University. She took her process journals with her and wrote the first draft of the book over three months. Garner's journals reveal not only the extraordinary amount of material that she needed to distil and shape, but also the emotional turmoil she was experiencing. She wrote the draft in a kind of fury. Years later she said that some of the 'craziness' in the story had rubbed off on her. Living in a small apartment, where Bail worked during the day, was less than ideal, but Garner had an office and typewriter at NYU in its Institute for the Humanities. She was inspired by the openness of vigorous debate among her NYU colleagues. Bail introduced her to the writers Shirley Hazzard, Robert Hughes and Mark Strand. She briefly met Janet Malcolm at a party when she walked into a room and found her on a couch with her grandchild on her knee.

Sexual harassment was a dominant topic of conversation in the United States. Anita Hill's testimony against Clarence Thomas at the Supreme Court confirmation hearings in 1991 had inspired a national debate. David Mamet's divisive *Oleanna* had been playing off-Broadway for nearly a year. *Oleanna* is a two-character, two-act play in which a female student accuses her university professor of sexual misconduct and destroys his chance at tenure. Frank Rich in the *New York Times* suggested that Mamet 'rips open what might be society's most virulent scab'.

Garner's clipping file was expanding exponentially with

stories about sexual harassment. Professors, school teachers and students were being accused of sexual harassment; while many were found innocent or had the charges withdrawn, all recounted the personal cost. Academics, editors and writers wrote articles and letters decrying the moves by university policymakers who, in Margaret Talbot's words, ran 'the risk of sanitizing all the life out of pedagogy' by trying 'to eliminate the possibility of injured feelings or misunderstandings or erotic currency between teachers and students'.

There was a remarkable similarity between Garner's perspective and the article she read by Erica Jong in *The Washington Post* about the multiple charges of sexual harassment brought against Senator Bob Packwood. Jong admitted to loathing the 'Packwoods and Woody Allens of this world'. In 'Fear of Flirting: Let Sense Prevail', she argued that men 'like that' were confused about the line between flirtation and harassment. She labelled so-called 'sexual harassment commandos' as puritans, noting that 'they want to rule out even the possibilities of the messiness of sex'. She asked, 'So how should we treat these old guys—as antiques or as rapists?' Jong, also a successful fifty-year-old writer, continued:

> I am working to change the system, but I am also for mercy and rehabilitation… shall we allow feminism to become a reign of terror?… how can we eradicate sexism without eradicating sex?
>
> In some curious way, I feel more able to deal with old goats chasing me around the desk than with the ideology commandos who want to scrutinize my writing to make sure I never say a non-P.C. thing as long as I live.

> I can trip the old goat or I can call his wife, but the
> P.C. brigade will never be satisfied with anything as
> ambivalent or murky as human nature.

And then there were books such as Katie Roiphe's *The Morning After: Sex, Fear, and Feminism on Campus* and Naomi Wolf's *Fire with Fire: The New Female Power and How It Will Change the 21st Century*, both published in 1993. These books were very different in their method and perspective, but both argued against 'victimhood' and championed 'power feminism'. Roiphe's work was of particular relevance to Garner's project. In a provocative attack, she zeroed in on academic feminists, asserting that the discourse of sexual harassment had moved beyond the relatively clear area of abuse of power into a pervasive anxiety about sex itself. She argued that the incidence of sexual harassment and date rape on campus was highly exaggerated and that the climate of fear encouraging women to see all men as aggressors was doing women a great disservice. Roiphe insisted that sexual harassment and rape were being reinterpreted and redefined as part of a fierce ideological debate.

Amid Garner's many clippings, however, there was also a heavily underscored letter to an unidentifiable magazine. Written by Steven S. Berizzi from Connecticut, it read: 'The sexist premise of your article—that there is a distinction between "illegal harassment" and "an awkward and boorish pass"—is precisely the type of faulty reasoning that permits longtime harassers like Senator Packwood to prey on women.'

*

The First Stone ends on a bitter note: 'If only the whole gang of them hadn't been so afraid of life.' The suggestion that the complainants were 'afraid of life' is harsh and unfounded. It signals Garner's fury and frustration and undermines much of the moral authority she had sought to establish in her important theses about female passivity and the nexus between power and sexual desire. She had drafted a number of different endings. In one draft she wrote about how, in refusing to speak to her, the complainants did her a favour: 'They forced me to abandon dreams of objectivity and to get personal, to range more broadly over my own experiences and those of the people I met more than I would have if the story had been a simple detective yarn, a comparing of versions.' Then she wrote of how she had imagined the two women:

> People have told me things about them which I have kept to myself; some of these I believed, others doubted…The girls exist now in my imagination with all the challenging reality of characters in a novel. Sometimes they endear themselves to me. Sometimes I find them disingenuous, vengeful, naïve, boring. At times, as a novelist is with her characters, I am at their mercy. In one of them I recognise myself when young. Towards her I feel both disgust and tenderness. The other arouses my pity, and my respect, but rarely my liking.

She continued in pencil: 'I want to round it off in this vein.' McPhee commented on these drafts and agreed she had hit 'the right note on the girls'.

In the end Garner drew the many threads of her story

together in a paragraph of 'if only' scenarios—scenarios which affirmed the institutional failure of the Ormond Council to deal with the alleged harassment, but which also emphasised the various agendas, conscious and otherwise, at play. Garner was searching for 'a less cruel and more *useful* ending' to the whole destructive saga. Her emphasis is important. Those party to the allegations had sought to avoid legal proceedings. Those involved in the alleged events, and their resolution or otherwise, were traumatised. Most people involved agreed that there was disproportionate anger and response. Surely a more constructive approach could have been taken.

In *The Silent Woman* Janet Malcolm writes: 'The freedom to be cruel is one of journalism's uncontested privileges, and the rendering of subjects as if they were characters in bad novels is one of its widely accepted conventions.' Garner is not so much cruel as hostile towards the complainants. Throughout her research she was worried that she was too empathetic towards those interviewees she came to know well. And she was. Her sympathies are weighted in Gregory's favour. There is no point speculating on the kind of book she might have written had she gained access to the complainants. It is worth considering, however, what Malcolm says about a writer's supposed impartiality:

> Writing cannot be done in a state of desirelessness. The
> pose of fair-mindedness, the charade of evenhandedness,
> the striking of an attitude of detachment can never

154

be more than rhetorical ruses; if they were genuine, if the writer *actually* didn't care one way or the other how things came out, he would not bestir himself to represent them.

Though Garner suggests at the outset that neither she nor her friends thought for a moment that 'a man accused of such an act might be innocent', she feels deeply Gregory's humiliation and pain. She constructs him as an outsider to the Melbourne establishment; a well-meaning loser who tries too hard to belong to a club that will never accept him. The ferocity of her allegiance to the character she comes to know best drives the direction of this narrative, as it would in her next major nonfiction book, *Joe Cinque's Consolation*.

The real intergenerational divide was less about jealousy of younger women's beauty and opportunities and more to do with being old enough, and secure enough, to see the pathos of older men allegedly making sexual overtures to younger, unknowingly powerful women. At fifty, and as an outsider to institutional power dynamics, Garner could not see how Gregory might be seen as threatening. He, and men who behaved as he was accused of doing, were to her mind 'just poor bastards'. The feminist historian Marilyn Lake argued that this 'sympathetic rendering' of Gregory as 'that central Australian icon, the "poor bastard"', contributed to the power and success of *The First Stone*. Gregory 'joins the line of defeated men—Ned Kelly, Henry Lawson, Burke and Wills, the Gallipoli diggers, men on the track, the blokes on susso—who embody our national mythologies', she wrote, adding: 'The narrative is all the more powerful as his doom is engineered by that other archetypal figure, the vengeful woman. It is a narrative that taps deep into cultural anxieties about women's power and capacity for revenge.'

Lake is correct to observe these cultural anxieties. Much to Garner's horror, conservative commentators such as P. P. McGuiness, Terry Lane and John Laws applauded the approach she had taken. Their response lent support to Lake's argument. But there is another 'poor bastard' in this book: Gregory's wife, Beryl, for whom Garner feels great compassion. Here, and in her later nonfiction books, Garner asks: Who are the true victims? Decades after *The First Stone*, Garner would further destabilise Lake's and other feminist academics' reading of her so-called manipulative construction of Gregory by describing another 'poor bastard': Robert Farquharson, a man convicted of murdering his three young sons.

Garner's 'shifting speculations' throughout her process journals revolved around strategies for forgiveness, understanding and compassion. In her choice of second epigraph and title, she invokes the biblical narrative in which the Pharisees are asked to pause and examine their hearts and consciences before rushing to condemnation and punishment. In her journal Garner wrote out three versions of John 8:7, from the *New Jerusalem*, the *King James* and the *Revised Standard Version* Bibles. She chose the *New Jerusalem*; it was gender neutral and did not speak of guilt or sin. 'Let the one among you who has done no wrong cast the first stone.' Of course, she would not be able to convince some critics who argued that Garner's parable was yet another example of men in power punishing a woman for her sexuality. And in her final furious attack on the 'whole gang of them', she too succumbed to judgmentalism.

By the time Garner returned to Australia in early 1994 with a completed draft of what was now titled *The Ormond Overcoat,* her relationship with Hilary McPhee was strained. McPhee was the publisher at Picador, an imprint of Pan Macmillan, and was Chair of the Australia Council. Her husband, Don Watson, was Prime Minister Paul Keating's speechwriter. Garner remembers them as being something of the 'golden couple', jetting around the country. She felt that McPhee was sometimes too busy to discuss her book. McPhee remembers running two phones, being frantically over-worked and mostly exhausted. McPhee and Garner had nurtured their personal friendship and professional relation-ship for close on twenty years. Their friendship had made the editorial process a delight. Now, however, things were begin-ning to come unstuck.

Threats of defamation proceedings stalked the research and writing of *The First Stone.* Garner had to negotiate a path between what she knew and wanted to write, and what was legally permissible. In March 1994 the first of what would be three lawyers' opinions was delivered. It recommended a massive rewrite of the manuscript as a safeguard against litigation. McPhee thinks it might have been she who suggested, as a desperate measure, splitting Jenna Mead's character into six different people. She remembers Garner being vehemently opposed to the idea.

Garner understood well the contract between the nonfiction author and the reader. She had also paid close attention to Janet Malcolm being found liable in June 1993. In October 1982 Malcolm began a year-long series of interviews with Jeffrey Masson, a psychoanalyst who had been dismissed from his position as projects director of the Sigmund Freud Archives. When the first of her *New Yorker* articles, 'Trouble in the Archives', appeared in December 1983, Masson was outraged. In November 1984 he sued Malcolm, the *New Yorker* and Knopf, claiming that Malcolm had quoted him out of context and fabricated conversations.

At the time of that trial Malcolm could not locate her handwritten notes of the interviews. It transpired that her husband, who was also her editor, had reorganised disparate conversations into one simple monologue. In her copy of the *Australian*'s report of the trial, Garner highlighted the comment by Wallace Shawn, the late editor of the *New Yorker*: 'We do not permit composites.'

But Garner had little choice. Reluctantly she capitulated. She worked through the manuscript, changing singular pronouns to plural and inserting her mix of names for Mead. She stated in her draft Author's Note that Australian defamation laws had led to a device that 'distorted core truths of the story'. In the published Author's Note she mentions 'obstacles' to her research that forced her to 'write a broader, less "objective", more personal book'. She hoped to keep faith with the expectations for nonfiction by explaining obliquely about legal compliance: 'They also obliged me to raise the story on to a level where, instead of its being just an incident specific to one institution at one historical moment, its archetypal features have become visible. This is why I have felt free to invent names for all the characters.'

The crucial change did not impress Mead or many critics. Garner's strategy made the book an easy target for those who argued it could not possibly be taken seriously as nonfiction. Ten years after publication, Garner would tell Sara Dowse that she had no regrets whatsoever about writing *The First Stone*, except that she had lacked the courage to keep Mead as one character.

In May 1994 Garner completed the necessary legal emendations. She retitled the manuscript *The First Stone*. On 5 July she sent the manuscript to Alan Gregory with a letter that drew attention to the 'hoops' she had had to go through to minimise the book's defamatory potential. She noted: 'I know you will not agree with some of my opinions & interpretations. There is also plenty of material here which you will find painful.' She identified some of the difficulties of writing the book including the 'harsh' treatment suffered by him and his wife, and some 'less than heroic things I have had to confront in myself'. Gregory was shattered. He felt the book was slanted against him. He produced a list of corrections and objections that ran to fifteen pages. Garner invited him to her home to discuss his concerns. She remembers him arriving looking sad and defeated. She listened to him and worked her way through his document. She made changes where possible without compromising the integrity of her story.

McPhee and Garner worked on completing the edits in the Pan Macmillan Port Melbourne offices. On 18 and 20 July McPhee suffered two serious heart attacks, at exactly the time that Garner was signing off on what she hoped would be the final draft. Garner had committed to a three-week trip to Europe in August with her parents and her recently widowed sister. She did not want to go. It was a terrible time for her to be away with McPhee hospitalised and the manuscript in the hands of the lawyers. In her absence there was a serious falling out between Bail and a group of mutual friends from Melbourne's artistic community. McPhee and Watson were very critical of Bail. On her return Garner, with mixed emotions, supported Bail's position.

As the tensions surrounding the publication of *The First Stone* escalated, Garner was convinced that her fears for one side of her relationship with McPhee would make frankness on the other impossible. On her arrival home, a series of misunderstandings, through the confused emotions of friendship and business coupled with the hostility directed towards Bail, added to Garner's distress. She became increasingly anxious that the book seemed to be going nowhere.

On 15 September McPhee's second husband, the father of her youngest son, died of Alzheimer's. Garner wrote her a note of condolence. She also informed her that she could no longer offer her the support of a friend and that all correspondence should henceforth be carried out through her agent, Barbara Mobbs. Ten days later Garner wrote to James Fraser, the publishing director at Pan Macmillan, asking that the subtitle be changed from 'an argument about sex and power' to 'some questions about sex and power'; a significant change brought about by a conversation she had had with Tim Winton.

At the end of September 1994 Pan Macmillan obtained further legal advice that substantial parts of the revised manuscript were defamatory. Around the same time the board was notified by Gregory's solicitors that, having read the draft, they were reconsidering their previous position and were of the view that there was an actionable claim that could result in aggravated damages. Pan Macmillan briefed Peter Bartlett, a senior defamation lawyer at Minter Ellison. In response to Bartlett's lengthy and detailed advice, Garner made further substantial emendations. On 28 October, McPhee met with Bartlett to work systematically through the manuscript. That night Brian Stonier, chairman of the Macmillan Group, telephoned McPhee at home to express his concerns about the book.

Pan Macmillan was being pressured on a number of fronts. In addition to the threats from Gregory's solicitors, lawyers representing the complainants had notified Stonier that Pan Macmillan was under strict legal obligations under statute law. If the identity of the girls as victims of alleged sexual assault was revealed in any way they had instructions to sue. They also threatened Pan Macmillan's printers, McPherson's, with legal action. Meanwhile, there was talk in the Melbourne Club about the complainants needing to be protected. The father of one of the girls was a member, so too was Stonier.

On 14 November, having worked through another round of emendations, Garner sent Bartlett the final manuscript. Three days later Fraser rang McPhee to alert her that Stonier was minded to stop publication because, as she recorded in her diary, he felt the book was 'too harsh on Gregory and unfair to the girls'. Ross Gibb, managing director at Pan Macmillan, sent Bartlett a list of fourteen key questions. On 21 November he flew to Melbourne and met with Bartlett, McPhee and Garner. Bartlett eased some of Gibb's concerns.

One week later, McPhee had a heated discussion with Gibb and Fraser over the delays in publication. Gibb informed her that the board, well aware of her position, would make the decision about publication without her say. She tendered her resignation. She found untenable the extended delays and the manner in which the Sydney office had sought to interfere with her editorial autonomy. In early December the board, after what Gibb remembers to be a 'robust discussion', voted to go ahead with publication of *The First Stone* in March. They also accepted McPhee's resignation.

Bail and Garner had moved back to Sydney in October. Garner was relieved to be away from the stresses of the Melbourne scene. When she heard of McPhee's departure from Picador she wrote to her, thanking her for her attention and help. 'You were a wonderfully subtle, perceptive and imaginative editor,' she said. 'You poured energy and encouragement into this aspect of our relationship'. McPhee would never be Garner's publisher again, but their long and rocky friendship would be re-established the following year.

The opening print run of *The First Stone* was 20,000 copies. After an ABC journalist, ahead of publication, pinpointed a sentence where it remained possible to identify the source of the complainants' photographs, the entire run was pulped. In addition to threats of defamation actions, Garner was also subject to court applications seeking to gain access to all her diaries, notes, interview transcripts and manuscript drafts.

On 14 March 1995 the complainants made another application to the Victorian Supreme Court seeking an injunction against publication because they claimed the book would be defamatory of them. The judge rejected the injunction and *The First Stone* was published on 27 March 1995.

At this time Garner was advised by her gynaecologist that she would need surgery. The timing could not have been worse. In early May she was admitted to King George V hospital for a hysterectomy. The operation was of enormous physical, emotional and metaphorical consequence, and it coincided with the many public assertions that Garner was envious of young women and their sexual allure. Significantly, she has never written about the operation, save a mention in 'Dreams of Her

Real Self'. When I asked why, she responded that she did not want people thinking she was using illness as a defence. She remembers thinking at the time that she was being punished for having somehow betrayed women.

The book was an instant sensation. It sold 70,000 copies in the first few months and more than 100,000 copies overall. Every major newspaper in the country ran columns about it. Scores of academic articles were published, many of which decried Garner's vengeful attack on young women who had exercised their legal right of protection against a powerful, patriarchal institution. Some academics made their case through vicious personal criticism. Pybus described Garner in language more appropriate to a parasite or a bird of prey, 'feeding off' the complainants' distress. Mead accused her of being motivated by 'envy...hatred and a desire for revenge'.

As Marilyn Lake observed, the 'charges and counter-charges unleashed by the publication of *The First Stone*...polarized debate in unhelpful ways'. Rather than engage with the complex relationship between sex and power, critics fell into one of two camps: for the book or against it. More troubling was the tendency to be for Garner or against her. She was pilloried for writing of her personal difficulties, of constructing herself as a victim. On 16 and 17 August 1995 Michael Leunig's 'Helen Garner Dolls' cartoon was published in the *Age* and *Sydney Morning Herald* respectively. The doll-seller's caption reads: 'Twist her into all sorts of amazing positions! Relieves tension. Hours of creative fun.'

Garner found the unrelenting publicity confronting. She was unnerved by the many representations of herself. She was equally uncomfortable whether publicly attacked or defended. From March through August 1995 she kept her own counsel, refusing multiple offers to deliver speeches and give interviews. On 8 August she delivered the Larry Adler lecture to the Sydney Institute. She said she was astonished by the 'primal' nature of the response to the book. She stated clearly the things she did not say, but had been accused of saying, she took aim at her critics and she pleaded for a careful reading. Her language of doubt and ambivalence gave way to an invitation to 'these young idealists to get real—to grow up...to get conscious'. She encouraged young women to be aware of, and take responsibility for, their effect on men. She naïvely hoped this speech would put an end to the fighting. In fact, it fuelled the flames.

Just over a week later Mead announced in the *Sydney Morning Herald* that she had been fictionalised into six or seven different characters. Garner was relieved. Yet the revelation had the potential to destroy the book's credibility. Immediately Garner and *The First Stone* became erroneously linked with the furore surrounding Helen Demidenko/Darville's *The Hand That Signed the Paper*. When Mead addressed the Sydney Institute on 20 September, she attributed Garner's strategy to an attempt to create the impression of a feminist conspiracy. She belittled Garner's understanding of events, attributing her 'confusion' to 'ignorance'. Garner made no comment, but noted privately: 'Our deep disagreements must not be disciplined as unseemly...

These conflicts are legitimate, necessary & honourable. I hope they will also be fruitful.'

In addition to the raft of articles, newspaper columns and letters to the editor, five books were published as a direct response to *The First Stone* (and possibly Summers' challenge to young feminists in her polemical 'Shockwaves at the Revolution'): Virginia Trioli's *Generation F: Sex, Power and the Young Feminist*, Kathy Bail's (ed.) *DIY Feminism*, Catherine Lumby's *Bad Girls: The Media, Sex and Feminism in the 90s*, Mead's edited collection of essays, *bodyjamming: Sexual Harassment, Feminism and Public Life*, and Rosamund Else-Mitchell and Naomi Flutter's (eds.) *Talking Up: Young Women's Take on Feminism*. Mark Davis' *Gangland: Cultural Elites and the New Generationalism* also had much to say about *The First Stone*, although Davis' focus was not exclusively on feminism.

Trioli wrote twice to Garner asking to interview her for the book. In *Generation F* she states that she wanted to tell the complainants' story and was both frustrated and pleased that they remained silent. She then writes: 'More perplexing, however, was Helen Garner's refusal to speak to me…Garner refused both requests.' Trioli paraphrases a little of Garner's first letter and cites a phrase from the second, before concluding: 'She wished me well with the book.' In fact, Garner responded to Trioli with great encouragement. She also made her reasons for not wanting to be interviewed very clear. In December 1995 she wrote that she was glad Trioli was writing a book about Australia's younger feminists and continued:

> It would be an excellent thing for a woman of your generation to compose a broader & more accurate picture. I wish you the greatest success with your book. However, I don't want to do an interview. Enough is enough. I'm sick of talking about these things & everybody is sick of hearing me. I am not going to become one of those professional feminist mouth-pieces… Feminism is part of what has formed me & enriched my life but as I get older I find it insufficient as a basis for a whole attitude to life.

In January 1996, after Trioli's next entreaty, Garner replied that she did not want to return to the 'horror of what happened last year' but that she wished her 'every encouragement'. 'Don't link your book to mine,' she advised, 'Move on out and see where it takes you—it would be exciting & I'd love to read it.'

Mead's *bodyjamming* is an uneven collection of essays, stories and an interview with Meaghan Morris. In the context of this literary portrait, I need only to engage briefly with one contribution, Rosi Braidotti's emotional tirade against Garner. For Garner, this essay marked the lowest point in the fallout from *The First Stone.* 'Remembering Fitzroy High' harks back to Garner's time as a teacher at the school in 1972, when Braidotti was a gifted Year 12 student. Braidotti writes her version of the events and emotions surrounding Garner's dismissal. Garner was devastated by the piece, largely because it cast doubt on her fierce loyalty and love for her students. Publicly, she said nothing. She wrote to Braidotti, but never posted the letter. In the top corner she scrawled: 'not sent—written for relief only'.

In her letter Garner corrects five factual errors, including Braidotti's accusation that Garner was notably absent from the 'extra efforts to train [the senior] migrant students to pass the examinations', presumably because she 'simply had other interests'. Garner, who taught junior students, and coached them in reading and writing English out of class hours, wonders if Braidotti, as a feminist, might agree that as a part-time teacher and single mother of a two-year-old Garner did indeed have other responsibilities. Deeply wounding was Braidotti's assertion that Garner 'despised [her students'] broken English and their general ignorance'.

bodyjamming was pulped after the university counsellor, Suzy Nixon, won a defamation suit against the publishers, but it is still available in libraries. Amid the many letters Garner received about *The First Stone* and its aftermath, there is one that warrants particular attention after all these years. It is from some old colleagues at Fitzroy High who felt outraged by Braidotti's essay. They remember Garner as a 'vibrant, responsible and creative teacher' who 'cared passionately about her students and valued them for who they were'.

There are over five hundred letters in response to *The First Stone* in Garner's files. Eight are from readers who took objection to various aspects of the book. Garner replied to each of them. There are moving, congratulatory letters from something of a who's who of feminist Australian writers: Elizabeth Jolley, Amy Witting, Kate Grenville, Hazel Rowley, Rosemary Dobson, Joanna Murray-Smith, Anna Maria dell'Oso, Jane Campion, Gillian Armstrong, Elisabeth Kirkby, Beatrice Faust, the list goes on. And then there are letters from readers whose most common response is simply gratitude. One after another the correspondents say they read through the night, that they could not put the book down, that it exorcised their feelings of guilt for their passivity in past experiences. Many said they have never written to an author before but felt compelled to contact Garner. Some began by noting they too were firing off a letter in quick response to reading. One woman wrote: 'The book clarified a number of issues for me which have nothing to do with its overt subject matter.'

Obviously Garner's strategy to make the text porous and invite the reader into a conversation worked because so many letters, extending anywhere up to eight foolscap pages, sought to continue a conversation with Garner and indeed to answer many of the questions posed in the text.

A decade later, Garner received letters from people who had been enraged by the book at the time of publication, but now had a different perspective. That response also works in reverse, as the feminist historian Zora Simic demonstrates in her essay 'On Reading "The First Stone" Ten Years Later'. Simic relates how as a young undergraduate from the suburbs she was initially 'persuaded by Garner's argument that surely feminism had evolved enough for young women to deal with the usual repertoire of unwanted sexual interest directly'. She was 'attracted' to 'a more empowering feminist position'. She enjoyed the 'exposé of college life' and was irritated by 'middle-class privilege'. Simic read the book in the context of Garner's fiction, with its shifting perspectives and less than politically correct protagonists. She thought that Garner was harsh on younger feminists but she was also harsh on herself. Ten years on, having completed a doctoral thesis on the historical representation of Australian feminism, Simic finds the book's content 'difficult to defend'. Teaching at the University of Melbourne, she acknowledges that her response is 'indelibly refracted' by her duty of care towards her students, including those at Ormond College. She draws attention to what she sees as Garner's 'barely restrained contempt for the young women and their so-called sexual power', the idea that for 'seventies feminists… sexual harassment' was 'almost a rite of passage' and Garner's rejection rather than analysis of 'responses to sexual harassment that are legislative, rather than personal or conciliatory'. Despite these criticisms, Simic concludes that *The First Stone* offered 'a way of speaking about sex and feminism that could be very empowering indeed'. She affirms that the public debate engendered by this book was both vigorous and essential.

In 2015, twenty years on, I spoke to Drusilla Modjeska about *The First Stone* and the debates surrounding its publication. Modjeska, who was working in a university environment during the early nineties, and discussing concepts with Garner and commenting on her drafts, did not anticipate the attacks the book inspired. We discussed the historical development of sexual harassment legislation and structures with which

170

complaints can now be addressed. The timeline, Modjeska stressed, is important to remember. It was not such a long time before the Ormond allegations, she mused, that we were living in shared households where naked people arrived uninvited into your bedroom, and where suggestive hands on the legs, even in the university setting, were simply brushed off.

On further consideration, Modjeska suggested that Garner's response might have had something to do with having sisters. In an email she explained: 'a kind of robustness among girls, the rough and tumble of sisters, which doesn't let you droop around too much. get up. fight back, etc.' Modjeska's reasoning makes sense. As 'A Scrapbook, An Album' demonstrates, so much of Garner's identity is tied up with being one of five sisters. In that essay she writes: 'The spirit of our family is "Pick up your lip before you trip over it." Is that sisterly?'

In the 1997 essay 'The Art of the Dumb Question: Forethought and Hindsight about *The First Stone*', Garner admits that during the years spent researching and writing *The First Stone* she was, at times, driven by 'vanity and pride... mixed with fear, anger and competitiveness'. Soon after its publication she read Norman Mailer's *The Executioner's Song*. She was impressed by the way Mailer kept himself outside the text, featuring only as an organising intelligence that drew a massive amount of interview material together to weave a gripping story. Garner thought that if she ever wrote another extended piece of nonfiction that she would try to emulate his method. She never has. And she could not have used such an approach for *The First Stone*. Yes, she was battling feminist orthodoxy. Yes, she was asking important and difficult questions about heterosexual relations and power. At the centre of it all, however, she was interrogating herself: her past, her passivity and her shifting political and ethical allegiances.

9

Asserting Her Credentials:
True Stories and *The Feel of Steel*

*Opposite me sits a blind woman…She is one of those strangers
you sometimes see in a public place who have something in their
demeanour that makes you want to go up to them and say:
'Please tell me your life story. Tell me what you know that I don't.'*

HELEN GARNER, 'FIVE TRAIN TRIPS' (1982)

As early as October 1986, Hilary McPhee and Di Gribble had
suggested to Garner that she publish a book of her essays. She
declined, believing she had not done enough quality journalism
to make a strong book. The only piece she felt good about, she
wrote, was 'the death one'. By the time Michael Heyward at
Text Publishing approached her with a similar offer, in 1995,
she had a wealth of material. The timing suited. Apart from
a film review column for the *Independent Monthly*, Garner
was not writing. She set about organising her best pieces of
journalism into what became the carefully structured *True
Stories: Selected Non-Fiction*. 'Death' became part of the

book's powerful closing trilogy.

Heyward suggested the book's title. With the fallout from *The First Stone* raging, it was an ironic, indeed mischievous, statement about the fluid yet fraught relationship between fiction and nonfiction. Garner took the opportunity to address the festering accusation that she had breached the implied contract with her nonfiction readers by splitting Mead's character into multiple personas. In the opening essay she articulates her understanding of that contract in no uncertain terms. She also explains that writing fiction had got her into trouble with friends and family. She admits that she threw herself into journalism as a defence mechanism against further transgressions, but also because she was not confidently inventive.

The arc of *True Stories* spans nearly twenty-five years and offers a fascinating study of Garner's persistent yet deepening ethical and moral imagination. Garner sets 'The Art of the Dumb Question' as her foreword, giving an overview of the salient events of her life from primary school through to the present. Here we meet the terrifying Mrs Dunkley, queen of grammar and syntax. Garner dreams of Mrs Dunkley transformed into a version of her 'favourite character in all fiction': Thackeray's Fairy Blackstick. In *The Rose and the Ring*, the Fairy Blackstick is an active and officious fairy. She bestows wondrous gifts on her royal godchildren until she realises that she is contributing to them becoming 'capricious, lazy, ill-humoured [and] absurdly vain creatures'. At consequent christenings she wishes the infants 'a little misfortune'. The reality of painful, lived experience is, in Garner's world, a gift—for herself, her subjects and her work. At times in this collection, she manifests as the Fairy Blackstick, weaving her way in and out of people's lives, probing, feeling and analysing moments of profound personal importance.

Garner positions 'Mr Tiarapu', a story about a bewildered and frightened French-speaking patient in a Sydney hospital, as her prologue. The story gestures towards some of the central themes of the collection: family, friendship, fear and death.

'At the Morgue' affirms the vitality of human life and the dignity of the body in death. Given licence by her journalist's notebook, Garner spends days at the city morgue attending autopsies and talking with the staff. Initially overwhelmed, she goes on to record with graphic intimacy the physical process of bodies being sliced open and organs being excised, weighed and recorded. Through her language of familiar domestic routine, confronting procedures become bearable, almost sacred.

In a triptych of essays Garner tries to understand what fuels masculine aggression and articulates what we will discover to be her enduring concern about our society's culpability for violence. The story of Daniel Valerio's abuse and neglect is a 'bleak story of moral paralysis and missed opportunities'. So too, Garner will later argue, is the story of Joe Cinque's death. The closing paragraph of 'Killing Daniel' resonates powerfully with the final lines of *This House of Grief*:

> What happened to Daniel Valerio reflects on us all, on
> our private and public natures. It stirs up deep fears
> about ourselves, and makes us frightened and ashamed.
> I don't see how it is possible to contemplate Daniel's

story without acknowledging the existence of evil; of something savage that persists in people despite all our enlightenment and our social engineering and our safety nets, something that only philosophy, religion or art can handle.

True Stories concludes with 'Marriage', 'Death' and 'Labour Ward, Penrith'. In 'Marriage', the 'sceptical, ironic but still… benevolent' Fairy Blackstick, recently separated from her second husband, revels in the array of emotions, personalities and 'tiny human dramas' on display during a variety of civil wedding ceremonies.

In 'Death', as in 'At the Morgue', Garner's intense observation bestows dignity on the deceased and respectfully records the care with which their bodies are handled. Garner explained in an interview with Ramona Koval for *Australian Book Review* that watching the cremations 'changed her way of looking at life and thinking what it meant'. In the essay, she writes about her 'conviction' that life could not possibly end at death. In conversation, she stresses that she *felt* rather than thought or believed in this possibility:

> If you watch a body being consumed by fire, the thing you notice about it is this tremendous concentration of force and energy that's around that process. It doesn't seem to have anything to do with death. I felt in some way cracked open by that experience of seeing the body burn. I'm not interested in talking about what I believe in this area, because that always seems so intellectual. The whole thing opened up some tremendous metaphorical realm to my imagination.

Not long after *The First Stone* was published, Garner received a letter from an obstetrician working at Penrith Hospital. She suggested that some of those who took offence at Garner's stance might like to see what transpired in her hospital. Garner wrote back and asked if she could come. She spent five days there. In 'Labour Ward, Penrith', she stalks the wards, corridors, delivery rooms and cafeteria of a maternity hospital, recording the complex emotions and almost unbearable stress of patients, their partners and the attendant medical staff, as they labour together towards giving life. Told in the continuous present, the story takes readers in and out of delivery suites, capturing in extraordinary detail the drama and power of childbirth. We feel the exhaustion of the mothers and the doctors. Like them, we hold our breath waiting for the baby's first wail.

While Garner is everywhere in the action, there is no authorial 'I' in this piece. It is one of only a few stories in this collection written in the third person. Perhaps she chose this voice as a protective mechanism. She explained to Koval:

> I saw a woman giving birth to twins. It was so extraordinary that when I went back to my hotel afterwards, I had this terrific urge to smoke. I've never smoked… And I realised then that it was because I just couldn't bear to be that close to what I'd seen. I needed to put something between me and it, or to damp down the emotions that were provoked in me, and smoking was the strange thing that came to mind, to put up a shield.

This need to put distance between herself and the experience about which she writes continues to be fraught terrain for

Garner. She is not very good at it. She feels for people, deeply and viscerally. She throws herself into traumatic stories with an instinctual, full-blown and personally destructive openness.

In *True Stories* Garner asserts her credentials as an accomplished and longstanding writer of nonfiction. Significantly, a number of her essays are suffused with references to, and discussion of, fiction and poetry. Garner introduces and concludes three pieces by quoting the poetry of Thomas Tranströmer, Thích Nhất Hạnh and Theodore Roethke. In a similar imaginative vein, I am reminded by her final stories of Francis Webb's 'Nessun Dorma'. Webb's narrator wanders in darkness past a maternity home on a night that is 'an abyss and depth of light between/Two shorelines in labour: birth and death'. Written in memory of Jussi Bjorling, 'Nessun Dorma' is a poem of mourning for the great musician and a poem of joy for the birth of infants 'quaking towards light':

> O broad light and tender, lucent aria,
> Lacerate my paling cheeklines with the steep
> Bequest of light and tears, flood me until
> The man is the dawning child; be anathema
> To man-made darkness. No one, no one shall sleep
> Till the cry of the infant emergent, lost and lame,
> Is the cry of a death gone towering towards the Flame.

The American edition of *The First Stone* was released in April 1997, with Garner's Sydney Institute address added as an afterword. It was reviewed by Janet Malcolm in the

7 July issue of the *New Yorker*. She judged the afterword to be unnecessary; no defence was needed against the criticisms of Australian feminists. Malcolm took issue with some aspects of the book. She drew attention to the inappropriate initial letter of sympathy to Gregory. She dismissed Garner's fantasy of a less destructive response—'This time I'm prepared to let it pass'—as inadequate, something akin to 'closing ranks with the abuser'. But Malcolm also classified sexual harassment as being 'on the border between a crime and a mistake'; she thought Garner's depiction of herself as an 'unbalanced person' trying to write a calm and balanced book made *The First Stone* 'an extraordinary book, a book unlike any other study of sexual harassment'; she pointed out that 'Garner's oscillating identifications with harasser and harassed, her lurchings between generations and genders, her alternating states of delusion and perception invite comparison with the coded messages of patients in psychotherapy'; and concluded that the book 'no more needs defending than our dreams do, with which there is no arguing, and which are always true'.

When the October 1997 publication of *bodyjamming* fuelled the simmering debates and repercussions anew, Garner sank into depression. She returned to psychotherapy, this time with a female Jewish therapist in Sydney's east. In the early months she attended once a week, then three times a week. She continued with analysis for two and half years.

Psychotherapy gave Garner access to profound aspects of herself she says she had not previously been brave enough to recognise. As she explained to Susan Wyndham:

> Therapy was extremely useful and very, very tough. Your nose is rubbed again and again in the parts of yourself you would prefer to pretend didn't exist and you are no longer permitted to hide behind the carefully constructed self that you use as your excuse for your own appalling behaviour.

She told me: 'This therapist took it right up to me. She wouldn't let me get away with anything. "So, you were sulking," she would say, or "So, you were feeling sorry for yourself."'

It was the first time Garner had been in analysis where she broke eye contact with the therapist by lying on a couch. Initially she approached each session nervously preparing a list of things to talk about, but she came to appreciate that this anxiety was driven by her continuing need to entertain, to keep someone's attention. Of the many valuable lessons she learned, Garner identifies two of particular significance. That she had sabotaged herself in her approach to Gregory and the Ormond College story. And that she needed to learn to be still, to take her time, and to be silent for as long as was necessary to allow something to surface.

She was inspired by how her therapist would draw connections between whatever came up and what she had previously said. Garner felt liberated to write using a similar method. She no longer had to be in complete control of what she was doing; rather, she could let the narrative flow onto the page and discover later where it might be taking her. This strategy would prove invaluable when the time came for writing *Joe Cinque's Consolation*.

*

In January 1998 Garner discovered that Murray Bail was having an affair. She was devastated. Less than two weeks later she set sail for Antarctica, fulfilling a journalistic commitment made months before. While in Buenos Aires, she chanced to find in a bookshop Françoise Gilot's memoir, *Life with Picasso*. Garner wrote to a friend that 'after she left him, she spent the rest of her life working as an artist herself; and that when he begged her to go back to him she thought, "No, I mustn't give in, because if I do it will be *the same regime all over again*."'

Garner had an exhilarating time in Antarctica. At the voyage's conclusion she spent a day in bliss 'scrambling up a mountain behind Ushuaia on hands & knees'. She determined that on her return she would separate from Bail, get her life together and start 'having FUN'. When Garner landed back at Sydney airport, Bail was waiting to meet her. He told her the affair had finished and that he did not want them to part.

For seven months they struggled to maintain their relationship, but in September 1998 Garner moved out of their Roslyn Gardens flat to a high, sunny apartment nearby in Sydney's Bellevue Hill. She set about composing a long narrative poem, in rhyming couplets, recounting recent events. 'The Hat in the Flat', at twelve pages long, was savagely comic. Garner would later laugh about her obsessive construction of this poem, realising that because she wrote it in strict tetrameters it had a tramping, heavy feel. Only when she re-read Alexander Pope's poetry did she appreciate that she should have used the more fluid iambic pentameter. Garner never published the poem.

With the collapse of her third marriage, Garner was convinced that she lacked the talent to sustain intimacy. She had been distracted and ambitious in her second marriage with Jean-Jacques Portail. She had hoped that in her marriage to Bail she'd have the chance to do things properly. In their eleven years together, Garner often adapted her behaviour to what she thought was expected of her. She became accommodated to the quiet lifestyle of thinking and reading, but she missed the dancing.

When I asked Garner why she married three times, she replied that her father was more comfortable with husbands than boyfriends or partners, and also that as a married woman she felt protected against his power. Years earlier, when Sara Dowse asked about her reasons for marrying, she said that she liked the idea of being married to Bill Garner, that Portail needed Australian residency, and that she could not remember why she married Bail but that she seemed to recall it was her idea. The ritual of a public declaration of commitment appealed to her; it enacted a form of resolution. She spoke about the distracting, almost unbearable intensity of being in love and suggested that, for her, making a public statement through marriage relieved that high level of anxiety and tension and allowed her to get on with life. But 'marriage', she added, 'activates certain archetypes in each of you. Your parents' marriage comes into play.'

Throughout her writing, Garner portrays her parents' marriage as a mismatch of power and influence. No outsider can understand a couple's marriage, but Garner has made clear in her writing and interviews that her self-confidence, both as a woman and a writer, was diminished during her third marriage. In 2009 she read an *ABR* review by Vivien Gaston of two books by artists' wives, Irena Sibley and Judith Pugh. In her journal she wrote: 'A slightly sickened sense of recognition slithers through me: the serving, the self-abasement or at least—abnegation, the attempts to rationalise the man's egotistical demands & serene sense of entitlement & <u>the wife's subservience to these</u>: & suddenly a light-bulb clicks on.'

Bruce Ford had commented at Garner and Bail's wedding that no good would come of two writers living together. In fact, much good did come from their relationship, but its breakdown wreaked havoc. Garner's confidence in her writing was shattered. And she faced something of an existential crisis about the purpose of writing itself.

In 1998 Penguin published *My Hard Heart: Selected Fiction*, which brought 'My Hard Heart', 'The Psychological Effect of Wearing Stripes' and 'What We Say' together with *Honour, Other People's Children* and *Postcards from Surfers*. It was a fortuitous marketing venture because Garner was in no state to be writing new work.

In March 1999 the veteran journalist Tim Bowden telephoned Garner with a story about two female law students on trial in Canberra for killing one of their boyfriends by injecting him with heroin. It was a weird tale of educated young people who were apparently unfazed about attending a dinner party organised to mark a murder and suicide. This story had received considerable press and Bowden believed it should be told properly rather than left to tabloid journalism. Garner was not particularly interested. Through preliminary research she discovered that in October 1997 Anu Singh, a troubled, clever and beautiful woman, had drugged her twenty-six-year-old boyfriend, Joe Cinque, with Rohypnol and over the course of a weekend injected him with lethal doses of heroin. Singh was assisted by her friend Madhavi Rao. The first jury trial of the two girls had run for four weeks before being aborted due to the discovery of new evidence, which the court ruled was properly admissible against Singh but not against Rao. Separate trials were established, and Singh and Rao each chose to be tried by a judge alone. That judge was Ken Crispin. At the time Bowden contacted Garner, Singh's trial was already underway.

Out of politeness Garner agreed to meet Bowden's informant, an impressive young woman tangentially related to the events. While Garner was appalled by what she heard about the drug culture in Canberra, she was not persuaded to change her mind about becoming involved. Then she read the transcript of Singh's emergency call. She was hooked.

So began eight months of commuting to and from Canberra. The salve of work began a process of personal healing. In her journal she recorded:

> I am anxious about the moral indefensibility of this kind
> of work but I am also roused from my personal grief
> and loneliness by the bracing awareness of the reality of
> other people. The relief this brings. Doors and windows
> fully open on every side, even if the view out there is
> one of suffering, madness, destruction and endless loss.

184

Throughout 1999 Garner sat through trials, pored over court transcripts, interviewed as many key players as possible and watched home videos of Joe. She regained something of a sense of independence and strength. She grew happier, and was able to concentrate again. Intellectually and emotionally she was engaged. She cared deeply about Joe Cinque and the people involved in the tragedy of his death. Yet she could not write about it. She could not find a way into the story. And she was moving back to Melbourne. She put her work on the 'Joe Cinque book' to one side.

In 2001 Garner published *The Feel of Steel*, a meticulously structured collection of short essays and pieces of journalism. Its narrative trajectory charts Garner's journey from humiliation and sadness through to a growing sense of strength, purpose and hope. *The Feel of Steel* opens in the final years of Garner's marriage to Bail, tracks through the aftermath of its collapse and emerges out the other side of depression and personal despair. In the course of the book, Garner relocates from Sydney to Melbourne and is returned to family life. She bears witness to her mother's crippling dementia and experiences the joy of becoming a grandmother.

The title of the opening story, 'Writing Home', brings us back to a powerful theme: what might constitute home? For Garner, at this juncture, home is neither Sydney nor Melbourne. She identifies the house in which she was born as 'really home', but that space is ungraspable. In the second story there is an undercurrent of fearful anxiety about dislocation, but that dislocation is less to do with geography than with the fracturing of trust.

Perhaps there is no more radical site of physical and psychological dislocation than Antarctica. By the time Garner sets sail for this frozen, white landscape, the ground has shifted dramatically beneath her. 'Regions of Thick-Ribbed Ice' opens with the suggestion that 'tourist ships to Antarctica, even more than ordinary human conveyances, are loaded down with aching hearts'. 'Deceived wives', 'widowers' and a raft of lonely, sad and sometimes ill characters are said to travel to Antarctica in search of 'solace'. 'And then there are married couples,' writes Garner, setting them apart from this motley wounded group, only to wonder at such a relationship: 'but isn't a couple the greatest mystery of all?'

Garner sails on the *Professor Molchanov*, a Russian ship that comes from a place where 'scores of ships lie at anchor, unused, unwanted, rusting—the detritus of empire'. Within an hour of embarkation her fingers 'have shrunk so thin that [her] wedding ring keeps slipping off'. She is 'too sad to be sociable with strangers'. On shore, her fellow travellers set off in pairs or groups to explore and photograph the surrounds. She trudges, stumps, slogs and stabs her way across the ice, alone. Even an unwelcome penguin, which provides 'companionship of sorts', abandons her.

Garner is in search of blankness on which to project her moods and emotions. She wants to gaze at ice. When the first iceberg rears majestically beside the ship, she admits to being irritated by her 'urge to compare it with something'. The other passengers, free of her self-censorship, launch into comparisons. Similes abound. Garner is furious. She wants desperately to see the iceberg 'only in abstract terms', but she too is driven to simile and metaphor. Language is not up to the task. Nor can it capture her place or feelings in this landscape. She wishes she did not have to write about what she is experiencing, yet she must, not only because she is on an assignment, but also because writing may help her understand what she feels.

Back on land Garner feels cast adrift: 'What if somebody's heart has been broken one time too many? What if this person has become stupid with sadness?…If the part of her mind that used to grasp structure and form has suddenly lost its grip?' She cannot process, let alone remember, what she has read. Garner now hates writing: 'Writing is a sickness, a neurosis, a mania.' She questions the worth of the diaries she has filled. Words come between the self and lived experience. Words make it impossible to appreciate truly the beauty of nature and art. And yet, through words, she is slowly rebuilding her sense of self and her place in the world.

'Tower Diary', crafted from the diary Garner kept in the Bellevue Hill flat, charts her fragility and depression. She is razor thin. She is attuned to strangers' conversations, the pores of their skin, the weeping in the night from warring lovers. She wonders why she is no longer writing fiction and decides she is paralysed by fear and self-consciousness. Yet she is reading Ibsen, Thackeray, Pope. She is keeping a journal. Again, Tennyson's 'The Lady of Shalott' informs her thinking.

She becomes a version of his 'Lady', alone in her tower, weaving her impressions of the outside world. She too must renegotiate the space in which she can create. But unlike Tennyson's 'Lady', she will find her way back into the world and regain her life through writing.

In the years following *The First Stone* Garner took solace from being a member of the congregation at St John's Anglican Church in Darlinghurst, Sydney. Bill Lawton was the minister, a warm and brilliant man. When Garner was at her lowest point in 1997, Lawton read *bodyjamming* and other published pieces critical of her and her work. At the end of 1998 he was forced into early retirement. In her tribute to him when he was leaving the parish, Garner noted: 'the backing he discreetly gave me was informed not token. Once, at early morning service, he spoke up for me: he asked God to help me <u>keep my dignity</u>. What this meant to me, when I was on the ropes, I will never forget.'

In May 1999, at a time when the St John's community was trying to come to terms with having lost their cherished vicar, a visiting archdeacon delivered a sermon about not over-estimating one's worth. Parishioners were furious and upset. Garner wrote to the archdeacon pointing out that she found it disturbing to be preached to 'as if doubt and trouble were not fruitful human states but merely problems to be dealt with by the brisk application of a couple of texts from Romans'. She noted that while she was not one of the more involved members of the congregation, she went to church:

> because life is tough and painful, and because I need to pray and to be cared for and challenged and forgiven and fed and blessed—so it means a great deal to me that the person who preaches should have a grasp of—or at least a respect for—the difficulties that I, and other people like me, have with the whole matter of faith.

Garner has long been drawn to the formal rituals of worship. She takes comfort in the cyclical nature of the church year. In 'Sighs too Deep for Words', she describes how she enjoys the structure of the service and a minister's intelligent explication of the readings. In her self-deprecating manner, she insists that she is inadequate to the task of reading the Bible well. Yet she provides a vibrant analysis of the ways in which the stories' language and structure move, shock, startle and hurt her.

Garner likes the story of the woman at the well. She is a sinner, married many times and currently living with a man not her husband, yet Jesus chooses her to draw water for him and then offers her the water of eternal life. Garner seeks something similar. She wants to be washed clean, blessed, given a fresh start:

> ...there are days, as I go about my business along certain streets, when my past cruelties, my foolishnesses, my harsh egotisms hang around me like a fog—or, rather, when they haunt me like a pack of cards which offer themselves to my consciousness one by one and with clever appropriateness, as if a tormentor's mind were actively choosing and shuffling them, so that their

juxtapositions are forever fresh, always bright and with
a honed, unbearable edge. Because of this I understand
and treasure the Bible's repeated imagery of water, of
washing; and of the laying down or the handing over
of burdens.

She writes that her sister has 'a passionate hatred' for the
parable of the prodigal son and segues into a story in the Book
of Tobit, from the Apocrypha, where the father bestows a
blessing on his daughter:

'Go in peace, my daughter. I hope to hear nothing but
good of you, as long as I live.' That's the blessing I've
been longing for all my life, the one I have given up hope
of getting from my own father and mother. I need it. I
have to have it.

Garner does not receive that exact blessing from her parents,
but in the time she spends with her mother and extended family,
and in the realignment of her relationship with her father, there
is a sense of homecoming and of peace. It is possible to read *The
Feel of Steel* as a parable of the prodigal daughter, sister, aunt.

On her return to Melbourne in 2000, Garner agreed to
do a weekly column for the *Age*. She realised that she needed
to write and publish if she was to feel whole again. She wrote
about her new granddaughter, her nephew, the death of Tess
the blue heeler, gold sandals, a bar mitzvah: 'the smaller the
thing I was going to write about the more fun it was'. A number
of these columns make up the remainder of *The Feel of Steel*.
She concludes 'Tess Bows Out' with the comment: 'Everything
around me is seething with meaning if I can only work out

what it is.' She makes meaning out of being seduced into buying coloured glasses, out of despoiling her beautiful clothes with wine, out of an abortive shopping trip to Freedom Furniture with her father. The stories shine with grace and redemption. The 'I' of these pieces becomes calmer. She begins to laugh more at herself.

In her journals, letters and interviews, Garner asserts that her daughter was the best thing that ever happened to her. With the birth of her granddaughter, she discovers a whole new dimension of passionate feeling: 'At the sight of her I was pole-axed by an emotion unlike any I have ever felt before. The word *love* hardly touches the sides.' She writes about her veneration of this child, about being driven to be with her constantly, about her terror that some ill could befall her. When these pieces appeared in the *Age*, strangers approached Garner in the street, thanking her for sharing her joy. In 'The Nanna-Mobile', Garner is less worried that her books may be forgotten than she would once have been. She has a vision of her daughter and granddaughter walking along a dirt road in conversation: 'They were my future.' She describes the image to her psychoanalyst friend, who interprets her response as a 'collapse of ambition'. Garner begs to differ: 'Collapse? It felt more like a flourishing, an opening out. Ambition may have collapsed, but not me. Not this nanna. She's only just taking off.' It is a remarkable transformation from the broken narrator of the earlier stories.

In the late 1990s Garner's mother had succumbed to the ravages of Alzheimer's. By the time Garner returned to Melbourne, Gwen Ford was in a nursing home. Garner writes about the final months of her mother's life in two related stories in *The Feel of Steel*, and after her death, in 'Dreams of Her Real Self'. To this day Garner feels guilt for being too hard on her mother, for denying her eye contact, for not asking her more questions about her life. For a long time, Garner was angry with her. She felt that her younger siblings were preferred and she was jealous. She could not allow her mother into her life too deeply. They could not talk to each other. 'She didn't know how to be useful to me,' Garner says, 'or maybe I wouldn't let her.' She believes her mother was afraid of her, and she is probably right. As she told Phillip Adams, it is painful to be more educated than one's parents.

Bruce Ford was a graceful dancer, a good storyteller and a strong man. Gwen was not confident. She could not hold a story. Garner now looks back and sees a kind woman overrun by a domineering man. Psychoanalysis helped her understand her self-destructive behaviour in relation to men and her inability to sustain intimate long-term relationships. It took a long time to realise that while she was trying to deal with her father and her lovers, her mother was in the shadows of her psyche and she had never dealt with her. Garner was moved greatly by Colm Tóibín's novel *The Blackwater Lightship*, published in 1999, in which the daughter, called Helen, armours herself against her mother. When Tóibín's Helen is eleven, her father dies and her mother is unable to respond to her needs. Helen copes by shutting her mother out of her adult life. Deep down she resents her mother for not fighting harder for their relationship. Her mother refuses to show her pain.

Garner has felt the longing for a mother figure in her life. In her early adulthood the author and folk singer Glen Tomasetti operated as a maternal figure. She took Helen in, educated her about politics, took her to demonstrations and discussed literature and music. Later Garner became close to McPhee and Gribble. It took her years to realise that she had transferred a maternal role, in an editorial capacity, onto McPhee, and often abused that relationship. Garner's need is not related to age; it is about identifying a senior person who stands behind her, who is protective and steady, who will love her no matter what. For a time, she thought of Amy Witting as her literary mother, later Elizabeth Jolley. Both were older writers who pointed the way for her own work.

In 'Our Mother's Flood 1', Garner writes with tenderness about holding her ailing mother's hand, stroking her hair, looking her in the eye and telling her she was loved. As her mother becomes increasing labile and paranoid, Garner longs to build a phantom house around her, to offer her safe harbour within familiar rooms surrounded by loving family. Always the realist, however, she also names the frustrations and resentments that arise within herself and between family members as they struggle to care for their mother in her declining mental state.

When each of the Ford parents died, their adult children came together to write their eulogies. Over long, rambling conversations, Helen and Catherine took notes and drafted the eulogies for their mother and father respectively. Both Gwen and Bruce had Anglican funerals. Their children stood before the altar together, and each read a paragraph.

The eulogy for Gwen Ford, delivered on 29 August 2001, began with each child mentioning one 'secret intimacy' they'd had with their mother. Helen remembered being taken by herself to the drive-in at Ocean Grove. The other children shared stories that demonstrated Gwen's love, dedication and acceptance of them. They remembered a time when she used to 'play hilariously' with them in the kitchen while their father tried to watch the news in the next room: 'We used to fool around, copying special dance poses we saw in the stage shows she'd take us to. We'd pretend to be Japanese maidens or shaggy-booted peasants...we postured as ferocious hunters on the mighty steppes of Russia. We laughed till we cried, so did Mum.' But Gwen was also timid and her children suggested that perhaps in struggling with that legacy they became a bit 'brutal': 'we've had to toughen ourselves and crash through'. As her Alzheimer's progressed, however, they felt freed from established inhibitions. At last, they said, they could speak to her and each other 'without embarrassment, using endearments...words that, until then, had had no currency in our family'. Bruce visited his wife in the nursing home every day. His sorrow at her death opened a space for new relations to blossom with his children and between his children.

In Melbourne, Garner picked up her ukulele again, rehearsing and making music with her sisters and friend. The essay 'Against Embarrassment' describes how she first discovered the instrument when holidaying in Vanuatu with Jean-Jacques Portail, whom she described as 'a kind but restless man'. She wanted to cradle a ukulele in her arms. Immediately she 'crushed' her longing 'with my usual puritanical savagery', but on her arrival home she bought a ukulele. She hid it away, and took it out whenever she was alone: 'It was so intimate, so un-awe-inspiring.'

A revised version of 'Against Embarrassment' introduces Garner's most recent essay collection, *Everywhere I Look*. Now Garner describes Portail as 'a kind and very musical man', and includes a new paragraph:

> Somewhere in the background of all this, my marriage crashed and my daughter grew up and left home. Next time I looked around I was living in Sydney with a severe modernist to whom the presence of the ukulele in the house would have been an outrage; doormat to the last, I had left it behind in Melbourne.

This later revision reaffirms how much of herself Garner feels she lost in the final years of her marriage to Bail. In returning to Melbourne and taking up her ukelele she reclaims her independent creative spirit. She is home.

Garner took the title for this collection from fencing. After more than forty years she returns to the sport for pleasure, but also as a way of focusing and directing her aggression. Her coach sums up the essential lesson she must learn, as a fencer and as a writer: '"You may be swift," he said sternly…"but you've got to learn to *retreat*."' In training, Garner becomes focused. She grasps, 'for the first time in

[her] life what tactical thinking might be'.

As always, Garner concludes her book with a celebratory gesture towards the future. 'Arrayed for the Bridal' revels in the female emotions and negotiations involved in being appropriately decked out for a white wedding. Garner sits blissfully on the change-room floor, immersed in the personal dramas of brides-to-be, their mothers and attendants. Her dressmaker friend Vanessa provides the ballast in the emotional turmoil and stress surrounding the choice and fit of wedding dresses.

Yet again this lighthearted story is about much more than the actual characters being prepared for their ceremonies. It is also Garner's psychological drama of herself. The things she sees reflected in the shop mirrors map onto her recent psychological states: hysterical anxiety, panicked paralysis, a blinkered view of one's misshapenness, mistakes. Vanessa as psychotherapist, or perhaps as Garner's more mature, more balanced self, is empowered and in control. Garner dedicated *The Feel of Steel* to her psychotherapist, her granddaughter, Olive, and her nephew Karim. Each played a vital part in transforming her life positively in the closing years of the millennium. In a large measure, thanks to them, this book that begins as a work of mourning becomes a work of validation and hope.

In 2015 Genevieve Lacey and James Crabb recorded pieces of music which they hoped would suggest something like a conversation between friends. They matched their disparate musical voices—recorder and classical accordion—with writers they loved to read. Each writer was sent a recording with the request that they 'please write to someone, real or imagined, in response to this piece of music, and the idea "Heard this, and thought of you…".'

Lacey and Crabb sent Garner Bach's Sonata No. 3 in D minor. She wrote to the ship *Professor Molchanov*: 'Four bars in and suddenly it was the summer of 1998 and I was dragging my grubby little broken heart down Las Floridas in Buenos Aires.' She wrote about trudging along the foreign street 'stupified with jetlag and misery'. She recounted seeing the tango dancers, whose feet placement, in their tight choreography, became— like her marriage—'a breathless struggle for ground'. Lacey's recorder and Crabb's accordion took her back to the terrifying storm crossing in the Russian icebreaker. More importantly, they transported her to the 'bright and pure', fiercely clean Antarctic space:

> I understood my chest had been cramped half-shut for all
> my adult life. What you gave me, *Professor Molchanov*,
> was air; and every time I hear Bach played on those
> brilliantly airy instruments, a recorder and an accordion,
> I will think of you.

IO

The Shape of Loss:
Lament and Restitution in
Joe Cinque's Consolation

Remembering is an ethical act, has an ethical value in and of itself.
SUSAN SONTAG, *Regarding the Pain of Others* (2003)

*I had been granted the inestimable privilege of looking into
other people's lives. What I had found there had absorbed my
intellectual and emotional attention for many hours. Unlike the
Cinques, unlike the Singhs, I could walk away.*
HELEN GARNER, *Joe Cinque's Consolation* (2004)

In *Joe Cinque's Consolation* Garner acknowledges, with
the benefit of hindsight, that she went to Canberra because
the breakdown of her marriage had left her 'humiliated and
angry'. She wanted to gaze at women accused of murder and
'find out if anything made them different from me'. Armed
with her journalist's notebook, she envisaged that she would
'slip quietly into court…watch and listen for a while, satisfy
my curiosity, and wander out again at will, unscathed and free
of obligation'.

It was 6 April 1999 when Garner first arrived at the ACT
Supreme Court. Dr Singh was in the middle of giving evidence

at Anu Singh's second trial about his daughter's childhood and subsequent medical and psychiatric history. Garner went in search of a journalist to bring her up to speed on what she had already missed. In recounting these early days her tone is light. She likes journalists because they 'are always good company, full of "facts" and keen to gossip and speculate'. The two female journalists that she encounters fill her in with 'gusto and a fair amount of eye-rolling'. Garner's detachment, however, was short-lived. Exactly one week later she recorded in her journal:

> Seeing Mrs Cinque double over as if stabbed, on hearing her dying son described (in Anu's letter 'seized at remand centre') as 'lying there gasping for breath'—
>
> For the first time I'm <u>hurt</u> by this story—not just incredulous but moved by the horror of it.

In May 1999 she approached the Cinques and Singhs saying that she may want to write about the case. Maria Cinque was positive. She hoped a book would ensure Joe was not forgotten. She wondered if profits from a book might be sufficient to establish a scholarship for disadvantaged children in Joe's name. From his perspective, Dr Singh was keen for people to know the story of how his beautiful, talented daughter was destroyed by mental illness. Indeed, he thought that when the case was over he might himself write a book or make 'a little movie'. Neither knew of Garner's reputation as a writer.

Garner sent them copies of *True Stories* and *The First Stone*. She worried that Maria might be offended by the story of the sex education lesson at Fitzroy High, but the first piece Maria read was 'At the Morgue'. She told Garner the story convinced her that 'we should write a book'. She asked that the first and last chapters be dedicated to her son. For the rest, Garner could tell the 'true story of what happened'. Garner baulked at the 'we', but she packed her tape recorder and headed to the Cinque's house in Newcastle, NSW, for what turned out to be a seven-hour interview followed by dinner. In the book she writes: 'To call the encounter an interview would be to gild the lily. I was too bewildered by their story, and too shaken by their raging anguish and grief, to do much more than listen.' Unknowingly, she had spent the day sitting in the chair reserved for Joe.

When she contacted Dr Singh again, he was more guarded. He agreed to be interviewed and offered that he would help pay for the publication if Garner wanted to write a book about Anu. She demurred. Over afternoon tea in their Sydney home, Dr Singh asked if his family would share in any profits from the book, suggested they write the book together and 'declared roundly, "You must tell the truth! The main character is my daughter!"' Garner recognised the fault lines: 'A book *about her*. A book *about my son*.' In her journal she noted: 'The struggles heading my way are 1) for control of the shape and purpose of the book & 2) ethical.' She would wrestle with precisely these issues for the next five years.

Garner came to build a much stronger rapport with the Cinques than the Singhs. She hoped eventually to be able to call the Cinques friends, but she did not want to push the relationship. She was worried not only about aligning herself too closely with one side, as had happened with *The First Stone*, but also that she would disappoint them. She was also acutely aware that she had the power to cause further pain, on their side, for Anu and the Singhs. On 18 July 1999 she noted:

> Thinking again, over & over, abt the <u>ethics</u> of writing this book: the hurt it might cause to Anu & Madhavi— then every so often comes the thought: BUT THEY MURDERED HIM...Surely, if you murder someone, you forfeit your right to discreet handling? to privacy? The word 'surely' here shows my uncertainty.

In June 1999 Anu Singh was found not guilty of murder but guilty of the manslaughter of Joe Cinque. Due to a finding of diminished responsibility, she was given a sentence of ten years, reduced to a non-parole period of four years, including time already served.

In December 1999, at her second trial, Madhavi Rao was found not guilty of every charge: murder, felonious slaying, attempted murder, and the attempt to administer a stupefying drug. Garner contacted Dr Singh about a follow-up discussion. She was informed that his family did not want to open old wounds. When Rao declined the invitation to speak with her, Garner felt utterly defeated. How could she write another book in which two young women would again be silent? She wrote to the Cinques explaining that without the women's input the book would be too unbalanced. She thanked them politely for their kindness, and for the privilege of having met them and been a witness to their dignity and strength. Maria telephoned. She was bewildered. All she wanted was for Joe to be acknowledged. Anthony, her surviving son, had recently had a breakdown and had attempted suicide. Her life was shattered, her family destroyed and yet she had to remain silent. Why? In the book Garner writes:

> I was dumb with shame. How could I have thought that when I couldn't bend the story to my will I could just lay it down, apologise for inconvenience caused, and walk away? Her son's murder was not an opportunity for me to speculate on images of disharmony or disintegration. It was not a convenient screen on to which I could project sorrows of my own that I was too numb to feel. It was not even a 'story'. It was *real*…Never in my life had I felt so weak, so vain, so stupid.

As Garner has remarked in interviews since, she knew then with 'everything ethical' in her that she had to write this book. She told Maria that she was moving back to Melbourne and promised to think about what she could do. She had to finalise her divorce, find a place to rent, get a paying job and help care for her ailing mother. Despite the demands on her time and energy Joe Cinque was never absent from her thoughts. In her journal she wrote:

> Joe Cinque's murder wasn't a series of facts that I could be professional about, that I could seize and manipulate with my mind. I was helpless in the face of it. It billowed like a dark curtain on every breeze that blew. It seeped into everything I did. It was a stricken land to which my imagination had been exiled. I couldn't find a place to

get back across the border. The only way was to write about it. But I was paralysed.

Every few months Maria would telephone. She enquired about Garner's family, and about progress on the book. Garner dreaded these calls because she could offer no constructive news, yet she commented in her journal that she 'felt enriched' by their conversations and that Maria was always warm, gracious and friendly.

On 2 November 2000 Maria called to say it had now been three years since Joe's death, and that if Garner was not up to writing the book they would have to give the story to someone else. After some discussion, Maria agreed to wait until Easter 2001 before making any decision. A few weeks later Garner came up with what would become her opening sentence, but she could still not find the right voice or shape for the story. By the end of February 2001, as she completed the edits on *The Feel of Steel*, she recorded her conflicting moods about the book, her anxiety about being forced to take a side, and the intense emotional pressure of what she felt was her duty to Maria Cinque. She began to have frightening dreams of betrayal, evidence of her anxiety about exposing the personal lives of living people. She also came to realise that she had to finish the current work in order to strengthen herself for the Cinque book.

Throughout these months she sought counsel from Hilary McPhee about her proposed approach. On 21 March 2001 she wrote:

> I am worried about narcissism, I mean BEING narcissistic
> in the way I want to write this book. What I mean is,

> do you think I can tell it in a really personal way? How I witnessed it and how all the people struck me? This seems my natural way of going about things and the way in which I am drawn to tell the story but I am aware of how it must affect the people I am writing about—you know, feeling that their tragedy has been subsumed in 'MY' story.

McPhee reassured her; it was her great skill to get inside people's heads and operate as a filter for ideas. Garner listened but was not entirely convinced.

A week before the Easter deadline Garner read *Divorce: The Unforgivable Sin?* by Ken Crispin, and was moved by the epigraph from Luke 4:18: 'He hath sent me to heal the broken-hearted.' She wanted to write a book that would enact a form of healing. A few days later she chanced upon Montaigne's 'Of Practice', in which he discusses thinking and writing about oneself. Garner was flooded with relief. She reflected that 'it seemed to go straight to the point of my deepest anxiety about the Joe Cinque book—my urge to write the story from MY point of view, MY sense of it & its meanings'. She copied out the following passage: 'Here you have not my teaching but my study: the lesson is not for others; it is for me. Yet, for all that, you should not be ungrateful to me for publishing it. What helps me can perhaps help somebody else', and followed it with a list of her greatest fears about writing this book, which included: 'being unequal to the task', 'damaging people further', angering the Cinques, intruding on the grief and anxiety of the Singh family, being sued, getting 'lost in the darkness and evil of the story', 'misunderstanding facts' and 'of being & appearing to be officious'.

Garner wrote directly to Anu. She explained that she wanted to discuss 'the intersection of psychiatry and ethics…and how the person in the street is often resistant to psychiatric concepts, preferring to think and speak in unmodulated terms of right and wrong'. Anu's reply in July 2001 said she was familiar with Garner's work and believed her 'to be a responsible and insightful writer'. Anu outlined her own research interests and affirmed that she was interested in meeting with Garner. She hoped to be granted parole in October and preferred to wait until then to meet. Perhaps, thought Garner, there would be a passage into this story after all.

On 23 August 2001 her mother died. Two months later, on 24 October 2001, her beloved friend Axel Clark died. He was fifty-eight.

There was silence from Anu.

Garner's experience in trying unsuccessfully to gain interviews for *The First Stone* precluded her making any more advances. She would have to go ahead, yet again, without any contribution from two young women. About this time, she was musing in 'Woman in a Green Mantle' about the 'dangerous and exciting breakdown of the old boundaries between fiction and nonfiction, and the ethical and technical problems that are exploding out of the resulting gap'. She decided she did not have to be objective. She longed to write a lament for Maria Cinque, and she would. In her journal she noted: 'I don't have to write a book like any other book. I can invent the sort of book that suits the material and my interaction with the material.' She began to type up what she had collected.

In 2002 Garner accepted a teaching position in the creative writing program at the University of Newcastle. It afforded her the opportunity to spend more time with the Cinques and, crucially, to interview Joe's friends. The book was taking shape in her imagination. Yet one critical piece of her enquiry was still missing. In February 2003 she returned to Canberra and interviewed Justice Ken Crispin. Now she was ready to write.

While working on some of the early drafts, she also nursed her sister through the final months of her life. Marie Cole died in June 2003. Garner completed the ninth and final draft of the manuscript on 15 March 2004. It had been a gruelling five years.

Throughout the creative process, Garner toyed with a variety of titles: *Joe Cinque's Apples*, *After Joe Cinque*, *Joe Cinque's Lament* and *Joe Cinque's Consolation*. That final title made her intention plain.

The genre of consolatory writing goes back to Homer. In the twenty-fourth book of the *Iliad*, Achilles consoles Priam on the loss of his son Hector, insisting that 'To mourn avails not: man is born to bear. / Such is, alas! the gods' severe decree.' Classics scholar Elizabeth Gloyn has described the *consolatio* as 'a piece of writing addressed to someone suffering some specific misfortune [and] designed to comfort them with philosophical arguments'. Garner writes her own version of a *consolatio*. She makes no pretence that philosophical argument can assuage the pain of loss; rather she addresses the Cinques' pain through her attempt to provide meaning and understanding.

To make sense of this extraordinary story, Garner turned to the court transcripts—one thousand pages of them. She had sat through most of the proceedings scribbling furiously. Now, at her appointed desk in the office of the Director of Public Prosecutions, she opened the first of four bulging binders. In addition to the transcripts, they contained witness statements, police interviews, psychiatric assessments, crime scene photographs and copies of tendered police evidence.

The transcripts reported the committal hearing, the aborted double trial, Singh's trial and sentencing hearing and Rao's trial. Garner thought they would offer a clear chronology. In fact, she finds, they are 'a mess, full of senseless fast forwards and flashbacks'. It fell to Garner to find coherence. She marked up the transcripts in pink and blue highlighter with comments, underlining and asterisks. Slowly she built a composite picture of the week that ended in Joe's death. She was horrified to realise that there were two dinner parties, not one, that the first attempt on Joe's life was on the Monday evening, and that on the following weekend it took a full thirty-six hours to kill him.

Garner's job was to allow her readers to 'hear' the evidence for themselves, but she selects and arranges excerpts in a way that builds narrative tension. The result is a form of courtroom drama in which Garner discovers the unstable nature of testimony. She doubts there can be a single objective truth. She inserts a vignette of meeting a man from her primary school days in the taxi queue at Canberra airport. Her recollection of seeing him being punished at school for swearing is vivid, yet he denies her version of events. If memory is unreliable, how can anything ever be proved? If memory and testimony are affected by emotion and manipulation, how can a court of law pretend to decide fates using only logic and reason?

When Dr Singh pushed Garner to articulate what she intended to write, she replied that she wanted to 'enlarge my imagination to the point where it can encompass truths as widely separated as your version of events and the Cinques''. If only she could maintain a level of detachment, she could write a balanced story and not have to take sides. But in the face of the Cinques' pain, detachment went out the window. She strives to acknowledge the Singh's suffering: their concern for Anu's mental health, their attempts to help her, their despair at Joe's death. But Joe Cinque and his family's suffering occupy the moral and narrative centre of this book.

Garner's attempts to place herself in the story were fraught. She acknowledged herself to be in a state of rage when she first headed to Canberra. She spoke at length with her psychotherapist about her intense identification with Anu, and she makes that identification clear in the book. When the expert witness, psychologist Dr Kenneth Byrne, categorises Anu as mentally ill due to her mood swings, fragile sense of self, fear of abandonment and impulsivity, Garner and two female journalists laugh and think: '*Call that mental illness? She's exactly like me.*' When Byrne states that she is 'a self-centred, angry girl', who punishes boys and sees them as an 'expendable commodity', Garner reflects: 'Memories from my own selfish and carelessly hurtful youth flashed through my head, scenes I did not care to examine. I shifted in my seat. I had joked with the journalists about it, but this stuff was getting too close for comfort.'

Garner's emotional and instinctual response to Anu is complex. On the one hand, she feels immense hostility towards her. In her journal, however, she records moments of empathy, even tenderness. She is anxious for Anu the night before she is sentenced. She worries about her arriving at Silverwater jail, and weeps for Mrs Singh's agony at knowing her child will be in such a brutal place. When Anu is sentenced and taken down to the cells, Garner begins to shake uncontrollably. She crafts a Dantesque vision of the young woman descending into hell, accompanied by the screams and curses of her victim's mother. When Garner launches an assault on Anu the judgment she is seeking is also on herself:

> Do we identify with a criminal in that we too secretly long to be judged? Popularly, being 'judgemental' is ill thought of and resented. But what if we want our deeds, our natures, our very souls to be summed up and evaluated? A line to be drawn under our acts to date? A punishment declared, amends made, the slate wiped clean?…Anu Singh, with her 'promiscuity', her frantic need to be found attractive by men, her 'using up' of men and 'throwing them away'; her perhaps turbulent relationship with her father; her blaming of a man for everything that was wrong in her life; her crazed desire for revenge on him; her lack of empathy with others, her self-absorption, her narcissism: I was hanging out for judgement to be pronounced on *such a woman*.

Garner has repeatedly confessed to interviewers that she is appalled by the thoughtless cruelty of her behaviour when she was a young woman. She told Susan Wyndham that she did not like to think about 'the narcissism, just crashing from one person to another, wounding people and in fact wounding myself and being numb to it'. Her youthful behaviour was 'quite manic…A very high level of sexual activity without much emotional content'. When she saw Anu's behaviour being pathologised, she was challenged: 'either it's not pathological or my behaviour back then was also pathological.' Near the close of the narrative, Joe's previous girlfriend Rebecca tells her that she 'wanted to save myself for marriage'. A 'thunderstruck' Garner thinks about herself at that age, and 'contemplating the wreckage that was strewn behind me now, the selfish cruelties, the terrible waste, I was flooded with respect for her clarity and her self-command'.

Garner was perplexed by her differing responses to Anu Singh and Madhavi Rao. She admits that without meeting them she 'was like everybody else who had come into contact: one made my hackles go up, while the other aroused a puzzled, muted compassion, a curiously protective urge'. They represented an easily recognisable female doubling: 'One girl wild, seething with hormones and sex, ready to damage herself, needing the ballast of the other who is still a child, prim and cautious.' It was precisely that kind of relationship she had explored in *Two Friends*. But the women also represented, in a Jungian sense, different aspects of herself and, she would argue, of every woman.

Garner wanted to be something more than simply another reporter working on this case. In her journal she wrote about waiting outside the Supreme Court:

> I skulk about, scribbling notes standing up, leaning against a lamp post. Am I <u>one</u> of them, the scavengers, with their cameras and mikes, their stiff coiffures and good teeth—their opinions—their <u>youth</u>? I feel lonely. What am I doing here, at 56, full of curiosity and clashing thoughts, sick with pity for the Cinques, sorrow for the Singhs, curiosity about Anu?

Loneliness and self-doubt fuelled her anxiety. She asked friends and peers for advice. McPhee suggested she build her qualms into the story. Michael McGirr felt that thinking through the process of her doubts would make 'terrific reading in its own right'. Garner mused: 'I would like to write <u>abt the process</u> of slogging thro these questions. Would it hopelessly lack tension/ narrative drive etc? or can I structure it somehow? Or can I hold it together w. my voice?'

The product of these internal musings was a nine-part structure. Garner sets the scene of her initial involvement, then recreates a roughly chronological timeline of events. She charts the passing of time through the changing seasons. She establishes her presence by depicting herself outside the courtroom: trudging through the degraded druggie surrounds of Garema Place, eating in various Canberra restaurants and revelling in the beauty of cloudless skies and morning birdsong. Her voice holds the many narrative strands together, a voice which dances between a troubled, observing first-person self and a more detached, authorial third-person Garner. She becomes what Morag Fraser later aptly termed a 'fallible register of impressions'. She appears to do her thinking through the writing on the page. Of course it is a construct.

As Garner worked her way through the transcripts, the one person she could not find, or feel, was Joe. Inescapably, Anu was everywhere in the documents and got 'bigger, louder, brighter', as Garner read. Garner quotes Malcolm's statement from *The Silent Woman* that the living always side with the dead 'because of our tie to them, our identification with them. Their helplessness, passivity, vulnerability is our own.' She admits that she sided with Joe; she felt protective of him, knowing it was too late. When she returned to the transcripts on her desk in the office of the Director of Public Prosecutions, having been back to Sydney or even just out to lunch, she would stand Joe's photo in front of her and greet him: 'Hello Joe. I'm back. I have not forgotten you.' She longed to steal his photo from these files, to keep him close and safe.

On her third day among the transcripts, she discovered the thirteen crime scene photographs. One juror from the original double trial was excused from duty because he was unable to look at these photographs. The Cinques were advised not to look at them. Garner examines them and invites her readers to bear witness. She follows the police photographer's eye as he traces Joe's trajectory to a corpse on a hard metal gurney. Unlike her, the photographer 'was uninterested in argument and immune to ideas of art', but, like her, he decided what was framed, in focus or relegated to the blurry sidelines. The photographer roams through the couple's Antill Street townhouse with its briefcase of drugs, green apples and eerie detritus of a meal prepared for one, to arrive in the bedroom where Joe's discarded clothes mark a path to his naked body, livid on the floor. The sheets of his bed are 'wrenched askew', 'dragged halfway to the floor' and 'stained'. Beside the bed is a half-drunk coffee in which two cigarette butts float. Garner extends her gaze into the morgue where she describes in loving detail the 'youth and tenderness' of the young man's face, the 'beauty and freshness of his hair' and the 'thin trickle of black muck running from one corner of his gently closed mouth and disappearing under his left earlobe into the dark'. She gazed often at these photos. She found Joe beautiful, tender and almost childlike in death. When she later sent her manuscript to the Cinques, she inserted a warning note before the pages where she had described the photographs.

Around the time Garner discovered these photos, she visited an exhibition of crime scene photographs from the 1940s–60s at the Justice & Police Museum in Sydney. Intrigued, she saw the exhibition a number of times. In her address to the Sydney Writers' Festival in 2015 she spoke about being haunted by one particular photograph of a naked woman whose body was barely discernible in the back of a dark cave. Perhaps this photograph influenced her approach to writing *Joe Cinque's Consolation*. She explained:

> I treasure the memory of this photo because of the
> purity of the recording eye: its unsentimental respect, its

unshowy reverence for the deep calm of a place where a
person has died, or been murdered, or has killed herself;
I would even say the holiness of a place where something
unthinkable and final has happened. Such a place, if
you can bear to stand there, is imbued with a rich and
sacred meaning.

Garner found it challenging to 'stand there' in the Joe Cinque
story; yet she was drawn to the darkness and she knew that
somehow, in the midst of it all, she would find a way to place
Joe. Photography and video recordings were part of her strategy.
It was impossible to resurrect Joe corporeally, but as her opening
sentences signal, she intended to restore him to some form of
visual presence.

> The first time I saw Joe Cinque among his friends and
> family, the first time I ever heard his voice, was in the
> living room of his parents' house in Newcastle, in the
> winter of 1999.
>
> By then, of course, he had already been dead for
> nearly two years.

On the very next page, she reproduces the transcript of Anu's
call to the paramedics as Joe lay dying. It is a gripping and
manipulative narrative strategy. Visually, a vibrant young man
is catapulted from the warm embrace of 'friends and family' to
become an abused and broken body secluded from help. For
Garner the emergency call enacts 'the whole tale in miniature'.
Anu dominates the foreground, but behind her Garner sees Joe:
'the jolting visual flashes of Joe Cinque's death throes—the
close presence, behind the screaming, of a young man's body

in extremis—his limbs, his mouth, his teeth, his heart'.

In *Regarding the Pain of Others*, Susan Sontag argues that some of the most disturbing photographs are those of people who have been condemned to death. The subject appears to be 'forever looking at death, forever about to be murdered'. The viewer is drawn in as a witness and cannot look away. A certain intimacy, perhaps even responsibility, is established between the viewer and the condemned subject. Garner was seeking such an effect. In juxtaposing the opening video with the graphic image of Joe's dying body, she urges us to see and opens up a space of 'if onlys': if only someone had been strong enough to intervene, if only Anu had received effective medical treatment, if only someone had had the moral fortitude to notify authorities, Joe Cinque would not be dead.

For the first two years after Garner returned to Melbourne, she began each day by scouring the newspapers, scissors at the ready. She was drawn to stories about 'murder, trial, punishment', and 'collected horrors, pointlessly, fanatically, in a sort of secret grief'. 'It was,' she writes, 'a long, grinding, obstinately interior process that had nothing to do with intelligence. My files bulged with cuttings that did not enlighten me.' Her files certainly bulged—the sheer volume of material is daunting—but what she read informed her understanding of the psychological, social and ethical forces at play in Joe's killing.

Of primary importance was her need to understand the psychiatric evidence tended. Four expert witnesses were called to give psychiatric assessments of Anu. While all agreed she was in a state of some mental disorder, their diagnoses differed: a major depressive episode; a histrionic personality disorder with delusional and narcissistic features; borderline personality disorder or an eating disorder associated with disturbed body image. Garner was keen to understand more. She interviewed psychiatrists and psychologists, including those who appeared for the Crown. She studied the psychiatric reports and the *Diagnostic and Statistical Manual of Mental Disorders*. She learned about the biochemistry and effects of Rohypnol and heroin. She read about the status of psychiatric evidence. In reading a review of T. M. Luhrmann's *Of Two Minds: The Growing Disorder in American Psychiatry*, she underlined: 'How we conceptualise madness is a moral issue…How we think about culpability for our actions is a moral issue: "Biology is the great moral loophole of our age."'

For much of *Joe Cinque's Consolation*, Garner casts doubt on Singh's defence of diminished responsibility. Ken Crispin's Freudian slip, when he announced in court that he found Singh 'not guilty of murder…but…guilty of murder', played beautifully into the narrative of evidentiary doubt. Garner's discovery of Justice Peter Heerey's paper, 'Expert Evidence', seemed to lend further weight to her scepticism. Heerey pointed out that most judges lack scientific expertise. He discussed the inevitably nuanced nature of scientific truths and noted that on occasions judges may well favour experts because they offer simple explanations, or because their reasoning seems the most logical, or because they are more personable than other experts in court.

At the same time, Garner was also affected by Kay Redfield Jamison's *Night Falls Fast*, a compassionate study of the lives of suicides. Garner credits the book with changing her way of feeling about Anu Singh: 'For the first time, I think, I acknowledged with sorrow and even empathy that she must have been SUFFERING when she did it.'

Garner also read Emmanuel Carrère's *L'Adversaire*, the story of a murder trial in which Carrère aligns himself, through moral and psychological fascination, with the accused, Jean-Claude Romand, a man who had murdered his wife, children and parents. Garner felt that pull. And she was interested in the way Carrère inserted himself into the narrative and examined why he was so fascinated with the story. 'The Adversary,' is one of many names for Satan. Garner wondered if '"Satan", "evil", "the adversary" are just another set of words for the ones psychiatry uses? BPD. Psychosis.' She wondered about the similarities between religious and psychological thinking: 'possession by the devil isn't really that different from BPD, depression, psychotic episode. Janet Malcolm says something similar—those psych terms are just another statement of the "problem of evil".'

The question of evil first arises when Garner picks up, in Crispin's judgment on Singh, the citation of a 1996 decision from the NSW Criminal Court of Appeal dealing with diminished responsibility: 'Whilst the behavior of the accused could legitimately be taken into account in determining whether she had been suffering from an abnormality of mind, abnormal or outrageous acts could be seen as the result of other things such as stupidity or *simple wickedness*.' What is 'simple wickedness'?, Garner asks. 'Was there ever such a thing, or did it die with the arrival of psychiatry?' These questions go to the heart of her enquiry. When she interrogates Crispin he is circumspect: 'I think there are acts which *are* objectively wicked. To some degree the application of psychology doesn't mitigate the wickedness but it *explains* the wickedness.' Garner knows this. She has read Gitta Sereny's books on Mary Bell, in which Sereny demonstrates that, while the act of murdering a child is evil, the perpetrator of the act is not necessarily so.

Having thought about the existence of evil for most of her adult life, Garner is not sure she believes in evil. When she admits that maybe 'in an anxious corner of myself I stubbornly believed' in its existence, she suggests that perhaps 'evil' is a force that inhabits ordinary people when their defences are down. She quotes her Jesuit friend: 'there is a good reason… for the long tradition that speaks of evil in the third person, even gives it a name. It seems to treat the human as a kind of host, like a parasite.'

Part of Garner's difficulty in understanding the Joe Cinque story was the spell-like atmosphere around the events leading up to Joe's death. Nearly every person involved—counsel, judge, witnesses—termed the story 'bizarre'. In interview, Crispin agreed with Garner that Anu Singh seemed able to cast a spell over people. The evidence made clear that her power was tied up with her forceful sexuality. Some critics would later draw parallels with Garner's characterisation of the young women in *The First Stone*. Yet again, they argued, the power she was attributing to a young woman, against a vulnerable man, was 'embodied and highly sexualised'. Others would assert that Garner was evoking the Garden of Eden and casting Anu Singh as Eve, the evil temptress of men. She had even supplied the cue of green apples. Joe Cinque loved apples. On the weekend he lay dying Madhavi Rao, at Anu Singh's request, delivered six green apples to their flat. They remained untouched on the kitchen bench. When Joe's previous girlfriend told Garner that Joe 'really believed that if you ate an apple a day you'd always be healthy', the apples on the bench became, for Garner, symbolic of Joe's innocence in a complex world of dark forces.

Garner thought that perhaps people sometimes clutched at the idea of evil because, if they allowed themselves to understand how something terrible happened, they might have to follow their reasoning all the way to forgiveness. Can one forgive yet punish, she wondered? She filed away cuttings about sentencing: Judges' comments, public outrage at given terms, the influence of psychiatric testimony and the finding of diminished responsibility. She read the *Sentencing Act 1991* (Vic) and later amendments to it (2002), academic legal papers on sentencing and a criminal textbook on the defence of mental abnormalities. She cut out articles that discussed the efficacy of juries and followed high profile jury trials at home and abroad.

When she read Terry Eagleton's response in the *London Review of Books* to Peter Brooks' *Troubling Confessions: Speaking Guilt in Law and Literature*, Garner highlighted: 'The most obvious difference between religious and legal acts of confession is that the former is about forgiveness while the latter is about punishment.' She made a special folder for 'forgiveness' clippings.

In February 2001 the *Herald Sun* reported the death of Barbara Mackay, widow of slain anti-drugs campaigner Donald Mackay, and noted that she had written to the Mafia hitman who murdered her husband, saying she had forgiven him. She was a devout Christian. In her journal Garner wrote: 'What on earth can this sort of "forgiveness" mean?' She was unconvinced about what she saw as the 'falsity of dutiful forgiveness'. In August 2003 South Africa's Truth and Reconciliation Commission delivered their final report. Marina Warner wrote an extended piece on apology and what it means in the modern world for the *Times Literary Supplement*. Garner marked the question: 'Is an apology a plea for forgiveness, which reaches completion only if and when that pardon is granted?'

When Garner first encountered Anu Singh in the courtroom, she was taken aback by the 'ordinariness of her demeanour'. Anu had just 'flashed' the Crown psychiatrist 'a bright smile' and given him 'a little wave'. Garner asks: 'Why wasn't she down on her knees, grovelling for forgiveness? From the Cinques? From the whole human race? Begging for pardon, and with no sense that she was entitled to it, no expectation of ever receiving it?' Later, when she hopes to interview Anu, she wants to ask her about 'her soul'. She also wants to know if Anu considers herself responsible not for 'what happened' but 'for what she had done to Joe Cinque':

> Did words like remorse, repentance, redemption have
> any value for her, or were the categories and processes

of psychiatry sufficient? Did she feel that by spending four years in gaol she had made amends?

And to whom did she believed she owed atonement, if she agreed atonement was due? To the Cinques? To her own parents? Or was it broader, less personal than that—a matter of repairing the rent in the social fabric?

Garner wanted to believe that it might somehow be possible to atone, to heal the 'rent in the social fabric'. She found only one story that 'came anywhere near this longing for the symbolic', and it involved Samoan villagers coming together with the family of a convicted killer to kneel outside the victim's home and 'bear witness to their collective responsibility, to express their grief and shame, and to offer reparation'.

Legally, there are three main reasons for punishment: deterrence, rehabilitation and retribution. Garner felt that punishment had a deeper, more moral purpose to do with restitution for the victim or victim's family. She puzzled over the paradoxical idea that punishment might promote healing for the person convicted. She transcribed into her journal a passage from the postscript to Hannah Arendt's *Eichmann in Jerusalem: A Report on the Banality of Evil*:

> in view of the current confusion in legal circles about the meaning and usefulness of punishment, I was glad that the judgement quoted GROTIUS who, for his part, citing an older author, explained that PUNISHMENT IS NECESSARY TO DEFEND THE HONOUR OR THE AUTHORITY OF HIM WHO WAS HURT BY THE OFFENCE SO THAT THE FAILURE TO PUNISH MAY NOT CAUSE HIS DEGRADATION.

A second passage she took from an essay in *Australian Book Review* by Raimond Gaita: 'how deep is the human need for punishment, not just in the hearts of the victims of crime, but also, sometimes, in the hearts of its perpetrators.' Garner pinned Gaita's comment on the wall above her desk. As she explained in an interview with Susan Wyndham: 'If you acknowledge you've done something bad and wrong but you don't pay for it, you carry it for the rest of your life.' Garner was appalled by such a possibility.

Garner read Primo Levi's memoir *If This is a Man* and was moved by his 'moral dignity' and 'restraint', but she admits she was 'unable to emulate him'. When she left the Cinques' home after that first marathon encounter, she was horrified to discover that, while she said she did not believe in the death penalty, she knew in her heart if anyone harmed her daughter or granddaughter she would want to kill them. She remembered being electrified by the actions of a mother in Germany who smuggled a gun into court and killed the man charged with the rape and murder of her daughter. In her journal she admitted that when she read about that mother her 'heart leapt up in a blaze of exultation':

> I am ashamed of this; and yet I am also ashamed of pretending that I don't feel such bestial things. I am ashamed of myself for lying, and for being too lazy to think it through to the end. Something horrible lies curled up in a secret, violent corner of myself. It is my duty as a decent person, as someone who is mistakenly supposed to know how to think, to examine it, expose it to philosophy and arguments.

In the book she owns her shame and interrogates publicly her unreasoned response:

> Into my thoughts kept seeping fantasies of violent retribution. Of execution. What was happening to me? Like almost everyone I knew, I had always been 'opposed to the death penalty'. I had worn my 'belief' as a badge of decency and reason. But now I saw that I had never thought the matter through. I did not want to have to think it through. I didn't know how to start, and I was too scared of where I might end up.

Garner 'read miserably, wildly, at random'. She 'ploughed through books on depression and mental illness and suicide'. She read memoirs of wounded parents whose children had been murdered, and reams of true crime. For the first time, she read *Crime and Punishment* , and was struck by the way Dostoyevsky investigates questions of atonement and redemption. She read Martin Amis' *Experience*, Conrad's *Lord Jim*, Euripides' *Medea* and Aeschlyus' *The Oresteian Trilogy*.

Again and again, Garner returned to Hannah Arendt's *Eichmann in Jerusalem*. It gave her much pause for thought. Arendt investigates questions of collective guilt, suggesting that those who failed to intervene in the executions may have been more culpable than the perpetrators of the crime because their ability to tell right from wrong remained intact. Of the many passages Garner transcribed, two are particularly relevant. First, was the chief argument against the trial: 'that it was established not in order to satisfy the demands of justice but to still the victims' desire for, and perhaps right to, vengeance'.

Secondly, that a murderer 'is brought to justice because his act has disturbed and gravely endangered the community as a whole, and not because…damage has been done to individuals'. 'In criminal cases,' Arendt suggests, 'it is the body politic itself that stands in need of being "repaired", and it is the general public order that has been thrown out of gear and must be restored…It is, in other words, the law, not the plaintiff, that must prevail.'

In Part Seven of *Joe Cinque's Consolation*, Garner turns to the case against Madhavi Rao. Rao was complicit in Anu's plans to kill Joe. She had been present at both dinner parties, and in the months previous, she had helped Anu research the legal defence of insanity and methods of killing, she provided money for heroin and joined Anu in learning how to inject. On the day before Joe's death, she attempted to placate the anxieties of Bronwyn Cammack—the only person with enough moral courage to attempt to intervene to save Joe's life. On the morning of his death, Rao returned to Antill Street and saw Joe lying unconscious on his bed. He was blue around the lips, but breathing. She did not call an ambulance. She walked away.

Garner felt curiously protective of Rao. She dreaded the possibility that, because Rao was not suffering from a mental illness, she might receive a heavier sentence than Anu. In her journal she noted that she did not want Rao to *be* guilty, but clarified the statement, noting that it was different from not wanting her to be *found* guilty. She wanted to believe in the goodness of this girl.

When the Crown argues that Rao had a duty of care towards Joe, Crispin remarks on the legal complexity of such a duty. Garner switches to her interior voice: '*Difficult?* I thought. Rao should have done something. She did nothing. What's so difficult about that?' She casts herself as an uncomprehending layperson appalled by the spin Rao's barrister Lex Lasry puts on the events of Joe's last days. With deft legal skill, Lasry weaves an argument that Rao had no case to answer. He insists that since Rao had told her friend on the Saturday morning following the dinner party that she was going to cut ties with Anu, she had ended 'the original enterprise'. Joe's murder on the Sunday was 'a whole new enterprise by Anu Singh, and Madhavi Rao had nothing to do with it', he tells the court.

Garner is appalled: 'The hide of this, its cool, hair-splitting audacity, made my head spin. Could anyone really believe in such a mechanistic model of human behaviour?' She reels from his nerve. A shiver passes over her skin. As Lasry constructs Rao as an '*innocent bystander*' who simply went to Antill Street, Garner, along with the public gallery, is swept by a 'wave of incredulity and revulsion':

> With the point of his blade Lasry peeled ethics away from the law. Whatever *moral* duty might have been on a person in her circumstances to act, no *legal* duty was created by those circumstances—unless some responsibility had been *assumed* by Madhavi Rao. Anyway, said Lasry, 'Duty of care and duty to act are not the same thing.'

Garner needed to understand these concepts. She studied cases on negligence and duty of care. She followed up on the various cases cited by counsel, reading judgments from the High Court, the Victorian and New South Wales Courts of Criminal Appeal and from the House of Lords. And she summarised these judgments, transforming reams of typescript into a few sharp sentences:

> A pimp laid a coat over a dying junkie prostitute. A lone burglar, abandoned by his accomplice, dangled on a rope from a hole in a warehouse roof. A man climbed out a window and ran for help from a suicide pact gone wrong. Another stood by while his wife drowned their two children and then killed herself.

Over the course of the book, Garner constructs a seemingly naïve narrative voice. By the time she writes that she had 'never thought of these things before', she has studied dozens of legal textbooks and judgments. She has also read Crispin's 'Ethics and the Adversary System', a research article drawn from his doctoral thesis in which he discusses the gap between morality and justice, and suggests that lawyers operate within a realm of moral ambiguity and 'make no pretence of fighting only for truth and justice'.

She pits her gut reactions against the intellect and reason of the law. A handful of commentators later criticised her for failing to grasp 'the complex issues of law and justice', for resorting to emotional arguments, prejudice and 'unexamined assumptions'. On 17 November 2004 Inga Clendinnen delivered the Lionel Murphy Memorial Lecture. She told a roomful of legal practitioners:

> The Garner narrative is about the failure of law: of justice denied; truth abused; the virtuous injured; another witch on the loose…It exemplifies what you lawyers are up against. It exemplifies the lay person's way of 'doing justice'—through appeals to moral intuitions authenticated by current popular narratives underpinned by folk psychology, with authenticity guaranteed by appeals to public or deep personal experience, and/or mythic archetypes to give temporal depth. Garner's 'heart-felt' narrative is utterly impatient of the slow business of due process and the cautious accretions of the law.

True, Garner appeals to personal experience. She constructs mythic archetypes. She rails against the ragged holes that gape between ethics and the law. She toys with populist ideas about vengeance and justice, only to dismiss them. She is not 'impatient of…due process'.

She is fully aware that emotional and instinctual responses, part of every courtroom drama, must be secondary to the cool reason of legal argument and precedence. That is why she takes her reader so carefully through Lasry's submissions.

Lawyer and literary scholar Penny Pether argued that a 'limitation' of *Joe Cinque's Consolation* lay 'in Garner's stubborn novelist's insistence that the law do more than it can'. Yet Garner writes at the conclusion of her interview with the judge:

> Everything he said was calm and persuasive. It was reason, reason all the way, and I could not see a gap in it…But I was thinking, Where does all the woundedness,

the hatred *go*? What becomes of the desire for vengeance, for a settling of the score?

Do we pretend that this anguish doesn't exist? Is it a load that can only be shouldered by the sufferer? Is this what tragedy means—that you have to carry it inside you, weighing you down, poisoning you, for the rest of your life? I remembered what Maria Cinque had said to the judge: 'How am I supposed, your Honour, to go on?'

She is not asking the law to do more than it can, but she is painfully aware that the rent in the social fabric has not been healed. Garner longs to do something to alleviate the Cinques' torment. 'Was the law,' she asks, 'the wrong place to look for an answer to this question?' The obvious answer is yes, and she knows it. She seeks to enact a different form of justice, the justice of remembrance and of healing.

Garner's methodology resonates with Wai Chee Dimock's argument that literature can deliver a vital form of justice. In *Residues of Justice: Literature, Law, Philosophy* Dimock examines of a diverse group of nineteenth-century American authors on the historical meanings of justice to demonstrate 'its historically problematic relations to the densities and textures of human lives'. She positions literary justice as a 'supplement and a corrective to any legal or philosophical propositions'. She argues that in literature the problem of justice is given a face and a voice and suggests: 'We might think of literature, then, as the textualization of justice, the transposition of its clean abstractions into the messiness of representation.' In *Joe Cinque's Consolation*, Garner appreciates the 'clean abstractions' of the legal process, but she insists that for any true healing to begin there must be an acknowledgment of the 'messiness' of human emotions and motivations and, in this particular instance, a re-presentation of the victim.

After the trial Garner returns to Canberra to interview Ken Crispin. Only then does she report that he was not cold and abstract but warm and personal, that he felt deeply for the Cinques, that he too had lost a child and that he had 'never *seen* a case of diminished responsibility that was as easy to prove as that one'. After a narrative filled with anguished confusion and indignation, Garner acknowledges: 'Sitting there…with this tired, serious, decent man, I felt the self-righteous anger seeping out of me. There was nowhere for me to go with it. All that remained was sorrow and loss.' But there was somewhere for her to go with it. She could transform it into a narrative of mourning, memory and consolation.

Joe Cinque's Consolation gives voice to Maria's lament. The narrative shares a certain resonance with the arias performed in eighteenth-century opera serie. Garner's is the principal voice but her song is accompanied and punctuated by other voices. The moment of narrative crescendo arrives after the sentencing, when Maria Cinque stands in court to curse Anu Singh as she descends through the floor. Garner is 'awe-struck' by Maria's monumental dignity and power:

> Her outburst after the sentence was not a rupture of protocol. On the contrary, we had waited for her to speak, holding open a space for her to utter. It was an honoured and necessary stage of a ritual: a *pietà*. We

listened in respect, almost in gratitude. We needed to
hear the sufferer cry out against her fate, although we
knew that for this pain and loss there could be no remedy.

Garner emailed Kerryn Goldsworthy to ask if there was a
literary equivalent to the *Pietà*, so often depicted in the visual
arts. Goldsworthy thought immediately of Medea and Niobe,
and asked her online reading group for advice. One suggestion
was made many times: Act IV, Scene iv of Shakespeare's *Richard
III*, where Queen Elizabeth, Queen Margaret, and the Duchess
of York mourn for their sons murdered by order of the King.
When the grieving Elizabeth asks the older Margaret to teach
her how to curse her enemies, Margaret responds:

> Forbear to sleep the night, and fast the day;
> Compare dead happiness with living woe;
> Think that thy babes were fairer than they were,
> And he that slew them fouler than he is:
> Bettering thy loss, makes the bad causer worse:
> Revolving this, will teach thee how to curse.

Two questions informed Garner's approach to writing *Joe
Cinque's Consolation*: 'What's the use of one more victim story?'
and 'What fresh understanding can it bring?'. Terry O'Connell,
a former police officer who was by then the director for Real
Justice Australia, told her that a book about the Cinques' story
would be 'of no use to them unless it leaves them in a different
place from where they were before it'. When Maria's Victim
Impact Statement was tendered to the court, Crispin read it in
silence then admitted it as evidence, thus preventing journalists
from being able to quote from it. 'Oh, if only Maria Cinque

could read out the statement in her beautiful accent, to show her strength of character, to give voice to the family's sorrow and rage in a public forum,' Garner writes.

In her journal she wrote of this moment: 'MAYBE I CAN DO THAT FOR HER. THIS WAS THE FIRST MOMENT THE IDEA OCCURRED TO ME.'

Garner sent the manuscript to the Cinques for their approval and blessing. She had no intention of publishing it if it would cause them more pain. They approved—'Helen, it's good'—and *Joe Cinque's Consolation* was published to acclaim. Reviewers wrote of the 'compelling' nature of the book, that it was 'moving, enraging, poignant; always honest, always insightful'. Susan Lever suggested that Garner had written 'a tragic drama of classical proportions' that offered readers 'a deeply moving insight into the shortcomings of our society's humanity and justice'. Some academics were more critical, particularly of the way in which Garner used fairytale and myth to portray archetypal figures. Maryanne Dever, noting that her colleagues refused to read Garner again after *The First Stone*, argued that in exploring an 'exceptional case of a woman who commits an act of fatal violence', Garner was writing about a 'statistical aberration'.

As was the case with *The First Stone*, readers' letters came flooding in. A number of them were from legal practitioners grateful that Garner had made them question their beliefs and their perspectives. Psychiatrists weighed in with personal assessments and suggested diagnoses. Scores of wounded, grieving people wrote to tell the circumstances of their loss. Many requested that Garner write about their experiences.

One man assured her that her story 'wasn't just one more', and went on to relate how the world seemed to close around his brother's death ten years earlier: 'There was something deeply comforting about your book…You wrote about Joe Cinque, but I felt comforted over my own brother. Somehow your compassion struck the universal note, even though it was drawn from the specific.' He commended her decision to place herself in the story:

> Your presence, as both character and narrator, and particularly one striving to make sense of the senseless, all this somehow enclosed the human ugliness within a protective shell, which allowed me, the reader, to be more moved in the end than horrified, more in tune with the world than alienated from it…It wouldn't have been half the book it is if it wasn't for all those little confessions in relation to your own history, your instinctive responses and your own prejudices.

A father who had lost his young son told her: 'I found the subject matter and…the Cinque family's despair so deep that it gave me a strange sort of comfort that someone else could face their terrible trauma as I have endeavoured to do.' An adult son coming to terms with the death of his father wrote: 'Memory, mourning, telling the story of a person, once living, now dead—these are sacraments that the secular can practice. I feel very deeply their value and their necessity. You have done this for Joe Cinque.'

Then there were letters from Joe Cinque's colleagues and friends who were grateful that Garner had helped them understand what had happened. They told her further stories about him. One young man who had worked closely with Joe for some time filled in all sorts of details that confirmed Garner's approach. He thanked her, and worried that she may be 'unjustly criticised for her subjectivity', before signing off with 'you have my deepest respect'. Letters from readers who knew Anu, Joe and Madhavi affirmed that she got them 'exactly right'. A law lecturer from ANU who taught Anu, Madhavi and a number of the students involved, wrote: 'your account is fair and perceptive' and 'your exploration of the ramifications of the tragedy is of great value'.

Perhaps the most gratifying correspondence of all was from readers who sent letters, notes or wishes to be passed on to the Cinques.

In the midst of her creative paralysis, Garner herself had written a heartfelt letter. Back in January 2001, Nicholas Shakespeare had told her he had been discussing *The First Stone* with Gitta Sereny. Garner had sent Sereny a copy of the book with the accompanying letter:

> I would like, if I may, to ask you a question.
> When *The First Stone* appeared, it hit a nerve here…
> I was ferociously criticised by certain sorts of feminists,
> for obvious reasons, but also by historians, and others,
> who thought that the damage done to living people by
> writing about them was so great that it outweighed the

benefits of the open discussion of urgent human problems that such writing can make possible.

I know you have had to endure much worse attacks than these, and that your work has plumbed depths that I can only dream of. For this reason I need to ask you whether you have found a track through this ethical minefield. Is there a track? Or do non-fiction writers have to wake up in a cold sweat for the rest of their lives?

...

What am I asking you? Perhaps just whether you believe, looking back, that it's been worth it.

Sereny never replied. But the Cinques' response and the feedback Garner received, along with the rich and affectionate relationship she went on to develop with the Cinques, were surely answer enough.

At the time Garner was getting to know Maria Cinque, her mother was dementing and dying. Though Garner was several years older than Maria, she felt powerfully drawn to her as an archetypal mother figure. Maria was so much that her mother was not: dominant, fearless, a powerful woman of commanding presence. She had a deep effect on Garner. Garner was drawn to the formality and grace of the Cinque family and their Italian friends. For a second time she felt like the ranging cello in the Schubert sonata she described in 'Recording Angel'. Here she was again, wanting to be drawn into the warm bosom of a family's life. And she was. Her abiding memories are of laughter shared around the Cinque's kitchen table.

Garner's relationship with her father improved after her mother's death. Bruce Ford was still living in his seventh-floor apartment in Melbourne's CBD. He was eighty-nine and his children were worried about him being so isolated. Fortuitously, Garner's next-door neighbour was about to sell her house. Garner's father bought the house and moved in. So began two companionable years for father and daughter.

Bruce Ford died on 30 December 2004. Garner chanced to be the one who was alone with him. Poignantly, for a daughter who had longed for her father's blessing, she writes, in 'Dreams of Her Real Self': 'I blessed him. I sat with him quietly for ten minutes, on a chair by the window.' On the day he died, Alice Garner phoned her mother to tell her that the house next door to her was for sale and that she should buy it. She did.

Garner was exhausted after finishing *Joe Cinque's Consolation*. The years of work and the deaths of Axel, Marie and her parents had taken their toll. She published nothing in the second half of 2004, but early in new year she began writing journalism again.

She began with 'In the Wings', a joyous essay in which she captures the physical, emotional and psychological challenges ballet dancers confront. Twenty years earlier, in 'Recording Angel', Patrick dismisses the lines written on a card pinned to the narrator's window as shallow pop psychology. In fact, those lines—'*What are you waiting for? What are you saving for? Now is all there is*'—were Balanchine's dare to his dancers. As Garner sits through rehearsals and moves behind the scenes, she reads these dancers' bodies and personalities, enthralled by the way in which ballet, as a form, can express either ecstatic heights or unbearable pain and loss with power and grace.

In the second half of 2005 Garner published nine pieces, including six incisive and often humorous film reviews, in the newly established magazine the *Monthly*. In September, in the process of packing up her old house she uncovers photographs from the 1980s and destroys them all; a curious thing to do for someone so intent on cataloguing her life through daily journal entries. In 'Moving Experience' she admits to a proclivity for moving house similar to her father's. In total, she has moved more than twenty-six times. Was she eternally restless? In this essay we find Garner looking outwards towards new perspectives, new horizons:

> those wonderful Jungian dreams that everyone has, of finding in the house another room that you didn't know was there, high up under the roof, a whole extra storey, unused or neglected, but with more windows, sunshine pouring in, a glorious view, and more space than you've ever had before or imagined you deserved. You can't wait to sweep it out and furnish it and begin to inhabit it—to expand into it.

The very next month her old friend Jenya Osborne arrived for a three-week stay. Jenya was in the advanced stages of cancer and came to Melbourne to undergo questionable alternative therapy. In March 2006, she died. Jenya and her visit inform *The Spare Room*. Garner would write the novel in six months, remarking that it seemed to 'burst out' of her.

11

Telling It Like It Is:
Love and Tyranny in *The Spare Room*

*To have a friend…is to know in a more intense way…that one of the
two of you will inevitably see the other die.*

JACQUES DERRIDA, 'THE TASTE OF TEARS' (2001)

*Death will not be denied. To try is grandiose. It drives madness
into the soul. It leaches out virtue. It injects poison into friendship
and makes a mockery of love.*

HELEN GARNER, *The Spare Room* (2008)

In *The Spare Room* the protagonist, called Helen, lives next
door to her daughter, son-in-law and grandchildren. Five-and-
a-half-year old Bessie is a constant presence in Helen's life as
she moves easily between the houses. When Helen's friend
Nicola arrives, the household dynamics are thrown into
disarray. Nicola is extremely ill. Surgery, chemotherapy and
radiation have failed to halt the spread of bowel cancer to her
liver and bones. She comes to Melbourne to undergo three
weeks of treatment at the Theodore Institute.

The novel opens with Helen preparing for Nicola's arrival.
She goes to great lengths to make her spare room as welcoming

237

as possible. Bed linen, floor covering, a mirror, are all carefully chosen. Helen arranges the bedside table and plants geraniums in the window box. She is going to be an exemplary carer. When the newly hung mirror falls and shatters, the portent is less to do with superstition than with facing facts; no illusions will remain in place by the end of this visit. The masks erected by each woman will be brutally shattered.

With Bessie in tow, Helen heads to the airport to collect her glamorous friend but the 'tall, striding' Nicola has been reduced to a 'staggering…old crone'. She needs a wheelchair and Bessie, terrified of being left alone with her, is commanded to go and ask for one. The tussle between friend and grand-daughter—which becomes a tussle between death and life—is established: 'I pushed [Bessie] away from me.' On their arrival home, Nicola's presence displaces Bessie entirely. 'Go home, sweetheart…Go home,' says Helen.

Nicola's treatment includes massive doses of infused vitamin C, which cause her to shudder incessantly. She fronts up to the Theodore Institute for more of it every second day, and her physical reactions become even more extreme. On the less traumatic days, she submits to ozone saunas and peroxide drips. Over the three weeks she imbibes essence of cabbage juice and crushed apricot kernels and struggles to self-administer coffee enemas. Like Nicola, Helen was part of the counterculture movements of the sixties and seventies and therefore accepts, to an extent, her friend's need to believe in the efficacy of alternative therapies. But Helen suspects that Nicola is being cruelly exploited. Her medico friend Leo agrees. When Nicola says that she needs

Helen to believe in the treatment, the tension mounts.

Garner's prose is stripped bare. As Robert Dessaix points out in his *Monthly* review of the novel, Helen's speech is 'almost all subject-verb-predicate—"I put it down...I grabbed her hands...I said...She tried".' Helen strips, bundles and breaks out new linen. She kicks sheets to the laundry and stuffs them in the machine. She tears open the newspaper. She trudges. She speeds on her bike for lemonade which she pulls out of the fridge. She grabs chocolate bullets and shovels them into her mouth. The reader is privy to Helen's barely repressed rage and Nicola's complete unawareness of it.

The way in which Garner marks time, tracing Nicola's symptoms through passages beginning with 'On Tuesday', 'That night', 'On Friday', 'that afternoon', intensifies the claustrophobia of the friends' increasingly volatile relationship, while also emphasising the unrelenting assault the treatment is having on both Nicola's body and Helen's psyche. There are moments of wondrous respite between infusions when the women go to the movies, a magic show, the nursery or on a picnic. They are always followed by the smiling, suffering Nicola taking to her bed.

The spare room is now a place of sickness. The new sheets become one set among many that need continuous washing. The blind is closed to the geraniums. The rug has a strange smell and needs to be removed. Perhaps Helen should adopt a role beyond carer. Both Leo and Helen's sister Lucy suggest that maybe Nicola has come to Melbourne so Helen can tell her she is going to die. But Helen does not want to be the person to dash Nicola's last hope. 'Who was I to tell her she had to drop all weapons and face death?' Eventually, Helen raises the idea of palliative care. Nicola baulks and Helen, aware that she has 'dragged' her friend to face the spectre of death, forces Nicola to explain her reticence. Helen is chastened yet defiant: 'I looked at her there…fighting to hide her terror, and my heart contracted into a knot of pity, love and rage.' The arrangement of those emotions to privilege rage is significant.

Helen is perplexed by her own anger. She knows she is being unkind, but she refuses to back down from her position. After yet another appalling night, Nicola agrees to call the palliative team. Only then does Bessie make a tentative appearance at the back door. Ostensibly, she has been banished because she has a cold. But she has been exiled by death. 'Death was in my house,' Helen muses. 'Its rules pushed new life away with terrible force. I longed for the children next door, their small, determined bodies through which vitality surged.'

Sixteen years earlier, in *Cosmo Cosmolino*, Garner wanted to test the possibility that three different forms of spirituality might be able to coexist and form something whole within a household. In *The Spare Room*, her first work of fiction since *Cosmo*, she returns to investigate how divergent belief systems might interact. Helen has no idea how she can remain detached from her anger in order to 'serve' Nicola. Tactfully, the palliative-care nurse legitimises Nicola's denial of her situation: '"I've learnt that there are people who never, ever face the fact that death's coming to them. They go on fighting to their last breath." She paused. "And it is one way of doing it."' She wonders if Helen is able to accept that Nicola might be such a person.

Earlier in the narrative, Helen's repeated sequences of 'maybes' signal her attempts to be more open-minded:

> What did I know about cancer? Maybe there was something in these cockamamie theories? Maybe they were the future. Maybe Leo was wrong when he said that vitamin C did not shrink tumours. Maybe it *was* unfair that these pioneers had fallen foul of the authorities.

The truth is, she wants Nicola to stop attending the clinic and accept her imminent death in the way Helen's sister Madeleine accepted hers: 'She laid down her gun. She let us cherish her.'

Bessie's first conversation with Helen includes some philosophising about Saddam Hussein and tyranny. Tyranny threads through this narrative. Physically, we witness the tyrannical cancerous destruction of Nicola's body matched only by the tyrannical regimen of treatments to which she willingly submits. Psychologically, there is also something of a tyrannical power play operating between the friends. Nicola's permanently fixed smile, her refusal of proper pain relief and her resistance to palliative care are manipulative and harsh on Helen. Helen's need to wipe the smile off Nicola's face and compel her to get ready to die is forcefully cruel. Their friendship is real and deep, but the laughter and intellectual camaraderie that has bound them together for fifteen years has given way to a sickening falsity. Together they are trapped in their seemingly isolated world of pain, grief, love and fury. Garner takes us into that world; she exposes the harsh realities of caring for a loved one who is dying.

Nicola's body resembles the butternut pumpkin Helen finds sitting on the shed's windowsill: 'The flesh was pale and fibrous, hardly more substantial than dust.' Like the pumpkin, Nicola feels she has fallen between the cracks. She explains to Helen that she cannot face death because, having chosen a life of freedom and independence, she has no legacy. No amount of reassurance can convince her otherwise. Nicola is a bohemian and part of the bohemian ethos back in the *Monkey Grip* days involved forming new configurations of family among friends and lovers. Helen's care for Nicola affirms the legitimacy of those youthful aspirations. But only to a point. When Nicola decides to stay on in Melbourne for spinal surgery, assuming blithely that Helen will continue to care for her, a panicked Helen calls a halt. Three weeks was her limit. Her hospitality is at an end.

On their final day in the house together, Bessie comes knocking when Helen is out. Nicola pretends there is nobody home. Death has fully colonised the once-welcoming heart of Helen's house. Sure enough, when Nicola goes out, Bessie makes her entrance through the front door. She bounces onto the bed and talks to her nanna about death and souls. She takes hold of Helen's wrist and plays with her old, loose skin.

Garner decided to compress the action of the novel into three weeks, culminating in Nicola's death. How to accommodate these requirements when the story was based on real events? She began to write about Nicola's surgery and post-operative care in the same time frame as the rest of the novel. It didn't work. She overcame the technical problem by casting much of the conclusion in the simple past tense that looked into the conditional future: 'I didn't know then, as Bessie and I lay on my bed and reasoned about fate and the universe, that Nicola's mad dream of flying her carers down to Melbourne and putting them up at the Windsor would come true.' In a few short pages Garner traverses the final months of Nicola's life. She writes of the things Helen had not foreseen: coming to love the intimacy of caring again for Nicola in Sydney; of bearing witness to the 'thrilling alto drone' of the Buddhist women who chanted her spirit away and of accounting for herself and her relationship at Nicola's memorial service. Helen discovers Nicola's letter, which validates some of the tortuous emotions the friends experienced over their weeks together:

> I had no idea that before she left my house, Nicola would write me a valedictory letter of such self-reproach, such tenderness and quiet gratitude, that when I came across it, months later, in its clever hiding-place, I was racked with weeping, with harsh sobs that tore their way out of my body, as she had fancied her toxins would rush from hers.

But the narrative swerves back to that afternoon with Bessie and confirms the one thing that Helen was certain of at the time: 'If I did not get Nicola out of my house tomorrow I would slide into a lime-pit of rage that would scorch the flesh off me, leaving nothing but a strew of pale bones on a landscape of sand.' In place of tears there is relief, an acknowledgment of guilt and an honest feeling of failure.

Garner knew she had to kill Nicola in the pages of her text. She told the critic Shannon Burns:

...when she was dead I lay on the floor and I wept and howled and sobbed for half an hour. The book demanded that she should die. But I didn't want to make her die. I'd had to force myself to do it. The reason it was unbearable to me was that while forcing myself to write her death I had to acknowledge the fact that I also have to die. In fact, while it's only mentioned in one tiny moment in the book, a lot of the book's rage was actually the rage at knowing that I also have to die.

The Spare Room was translated into eleven languages. Reviewers everywhere were glowing in their praise. They wrote of the 'elegance and taut style of the narrative voice'; that it was an 'extraordinary, exhilarating novel'; that it fulfilled the brief of 'great fiction' by 'demand[ing] us to reset our moral compass and look at our value coordinates all over again'; and that 'it's a fiction about truth; about witnessing to truth...A hymn to friendship tested to its limits'. James Wood listed it in his *New Yorker* column for the Books of 2009, commenting: '*The Spare Room* is a far more powerful re-writing of Tolstoy's *The Death of Ivan Ilyich* than Philip Roth's much more self-pitying *Everyman*.' In Australia Robert Dessaix praised *The Spare Room* for being 'a quietly devastating book, written with superbly refined ordinariness, on ageing, women's friendship and how to look death in the eye', but insisted that, like *Monkey Grip*, *The Children's Bach* and *Cosmo Cosmolino*, it could not be classified as a novel. As Garner explained to Burns:

It is morally a novel even though it's very closely based on my real experience of those three terrible weeks in my life. By calling it a novel I'm saying: this is not a memoir, this is not non-fiction, this is a novel and there will be things in here that are invented, that didn't really happen, and I'm going to take...every sort of liberty I need to take in order to turn it into the sort I book I want it to be.

Garner had thought she would be a tender and patient carer for Jenya, and was dismayed yet fascinated by her anger. She wrote about that anger in order to understand it further and she wrote the novel as a way of containing, or giving shape to, her intense sorrow. Initially, she named the protagonist Carol, but she wanted to investigate *her* response and she felt compelled to own her anger, hence, the switch to Helen. She knew some readers would find the anger distressing and offensive, but she was convinced that she could not be the only person who had experienced such feelings in this situation. Surely some readers would benefit from her honesty. She was prepared to chance it.

Following publication Garner was invited to talk to audiences of a kind she had not before encountered. She recounts addressing the annual conference for Carers Australia—a support and funding group for people involved in long-term care for family members who are ill or children with disabilities:

> When I started to talk about anger I could see that there wasn't a single person in that room who was offended or surprised. ...At the end a woman in her seventies came up to me and said, 'Helen, we all feel that anger. You must never feel guilty or ashamed about it.' That was a huge relief to me—because there is something shameful about anger, especially if you're a woman.

In September 2011 Garner took part in the Narrative and Healing Symposium I convened at the University of Sydney with Dr Frank Brennan, a palliative care physician, and Ms Joan Ryan, a palliative-care clinical nurse consultant. The day was designed to bring writers, clinicians and counsellors together with members of the public. Garner did not speak much about *The Spare Room*. She noted that, having never had cancer or lost a child or grandchild, she would consider it an impertinence to speak of consolation or healing. Rather, she spoke about the ethical obligations that informed her nonfiction. She spoke about bearing witness to the suffering of others, and the shame and guilt attached to her powerful curiosity about people's suffering. She admitted to being worried that she had given the impression of feasting 'bright-eyed on people's pain'. She described being on Darwin radio following the publication of *The Spare Room* and being taken aback by a comment from a reader that yet again she was forcing her way into the centre of somebody else's pain. On reflection, she said she wished she had responded in the following way:

> I hope what I'm doing in writing is taking someone else's trauma into the centre of <u>me</u> where I can contemplate it and brood over it in some kind of thoughtful and intimate way, and then try and shape it into a piece of writing that will respect its complexity and maybe even relieve some of the pain that the existence of the trauma causes to everyone who is aware of it, not just the person to whom the pain has happened.

12

The Darkness Within: Bearing Witness in *This House of Grief*

Sorrow is the real cause
Of deaths and disasters and families destroyed.
EURIPIDES, *Medea* (431 BCE)

Oh, these matters we worry in our work.
JANET MALCOLM, EMAIL TO GARNER (APRIL 2013)

In September 2005, a year after the release of *Joe Cinque's Consolation*, an item on the evening news caught Garner's attention. A car was being winched out of a dam. Robert Farquharson had been returning his three sons home to their mother, Cindy Gambino, after a Father's Day visit. His battered Commodore left an unremarkable stretch of road and plunged into a deep dam. Farquharson opened his door and swam to safety. Jai, aged ten, Tyler, seven and Bailey, two, drowned. Garner described the scene in the opening pages of *This House of Grief*, published nine years later: 'Night. Low foliage. Water, misty and black. Blurred lights, a chopper. Men in hi-vis and helmets. Something very bad here. Something frightful.' 'Oh Lord', she thought, 'let this be an accident'.

Farquharson claimed that he blacked out due to an episode of cough syncope and regained consciousness only as his car was sinking. He staggered to the road, flagged down a passing car, driven by two young men and gabbled that 'he had done a wheel bearing, or had a coughing fit', insisting they drive him to Cindy's house in Winchelsea. He had to tell her he'd killed the kids.

Two months later Farquharson was charged with three counts of murder. The police relied on forensic evidence and a statement from his longtime friend Greg King that Farquharson had intimated some months previously that he would kill his children in order to punish his wife for ending their marriage. When his committal hearing opened in Geelong on 14 August 2006, Garner was there. Her early plan was to turn this story, set largely within the landscape of her childhood and adolescence, into an essay for the *Monthly*. As it would turn out, that week in the Geelong Magistrate's Court was only the first of many, many weeks she would spend in courts following this case. It proceeded through the committal to two full criminal trials and three appeals over seven years.

There were several irresistible hooks for Garner in this story: an interweaving of betrayal, divorce, depression, evangelical religion, small town loyalties, decent country folk and vulnerable, almost inarticulate young men. Added to these was the curiosity she had developed about detectives and lawyers. Garner's friends and peers questioned her interest. Why would she want to immerse herself in such darkness? Was there some masochistic or self-destructive strain in her personality? She replied that she wanted to find out why men kill their children. She was driven to understand the forces required for seemingly ordinary people to surrender to their darker selves. Robert Farquharson, she insisted, was not a psychopath or a monster. Neither was he evil. He was an unimaginative, boring, ordinary bloke.

The Farquharson case provided Garner with a justification to immerse herself again in a criminal trial, to witness complex and painful intimate stories played out within the highly ritualised structures of the law. When the first trial opened in the Victorian Supreme Court in August 2007, Garner took her place, accompanied by Louise, the brilliant sixteen-year-old daughter of an old friend. She was among familiar faces. The first trial judge was 'Fabulous Phil' Cummins who had presided over the Daniel Valerio murder trials. Farquharson's defence counsel was the son of Jim Morrissey QC, who had successfully prosecuted Paul Aiton, Daniel's killer. The second trial judge was Lex Lasry, previously defence counsel for Madhavi Rao. Garner was drawn into the camaraderie among the court journalists.

Garner knew from the outset that she could do something substantial with this material. She was alert to the 'moral mess' she might find herself in and wondered if she could find a way through it so as not to produce 'a third maimed book'. She was on dangerous territory personally. Within days of the committal opening in August 2006 she told her sister, 'I feel like I'll never get over this.' That same month she published her review of Paul Greengrass's movie *United 93*: 'I'm left with…the same old haunting question: why do stories matter so terribly to us, that we will offer ourselves up to, and later be grateful for, an experience that we know is going to fill us with grief and despair?'

Garner wondered about the wisdom of investing in Farquharson's story at this creative period of her life. She was not to know that she would be required to live with it for seven years. Many times during those years she regretted having become involved. Periodically she would record in her journal the Beckettian mantra: 'I can't go on. I'll go on.' Yet, as before, once she was in this story she was incapable of walking away.

Every day she sat in court. Just before Farquharson's first appeal, she sent a request for an interview, accompanied by a copy of *Joe Cinque's Consolation*, to Cindy Gambino's parents Bev and Bob, and to Farquharson's sisters Carmen and Kerri. All politely declined. Her less direct overtures to Cindy came to nothing. Eventually Cindy signed a media package that precluded her speaking to Garner about the case. After some momentary disappointment, Garner was relieved. She was free to write the story as she saw fit.

This House of Grief is subtitled 'the story of a murder trial'. It analyses Farquharson's first trial and appeal before offering a compressed account of the subsequent second trial, second appeal and High Court application for Special Leave. But it also pays homage to the best of the Australian criminal justice system; it's an absorbing study of human motivations, and a plea for understanding of the devastation men may feel when they lose daily contact with their children.

Garner writes from the centre of the courtroom drama, revelling in its arrogant bluster, friendly concern, passion and pathos. She sketches the leading legal characters. Defence counsel Peter Morrissey—who took silk during the years of proceedings—is a big, somewhat-dishevelled Irishman. He strides into court, high-fives his client, and whistles provocatively the Collingwood club song. He believes in his client's innocence and exudes optimism. Acting Chief Crown Prosecutor Jeremy Rapke QC, is 'a lean, contained-looking man, with a clipped grey beard' and a 'severe', slanted mouth. He is piercingly brilliant, 'formidable in trials' and 'enthralling to watch'. Justice Philip Cummins, a 'silver-haired man in his sixties with an open, good-humoured face', sports a tiny diamond stud in his left ear and bestows on proceedings an air of calm reassurance.

Garner, the fiercely observant writer of the sensual world, deciphers the atmosphere of the courtroom. She describes the 'Homeric' clashes and 'gargantuan' struggles Morrissey undertakes in advancing Farquharson's innocence. She reads counsel's body language and interrogates their strategic manoeuvres. Morrissey fights valiantly for his client, but his 'energy-thieving' cross-examination, mired in intractable technical specifications, is 'catastrophically lacking in narrative'. He loses his audience and seems unaware of the fact. As the hours and days grind on, the air in the court becomes 'a jelly of confusion and boredom'.

Then Rapke gets to his feet, the air clears, focus is restored. When he 'surged into the final curve of his argument…the jury sat engrossed'.

Garner also charts the atmospherics of grief. The courtroom is awash with emotion. Farquharson sits in the dock, 'scared, and small, and terribly lonely', hanging on every word spoken and gesture made by his former wife. When Cindy gives evidence for the first time she speaks 'in a series of soft, gasping cries'. Farquharson leans forward. 'People in the court had their hands over their mouths. The air was filled with a faint rustling.' When Cindy recounts the horror of the night her sons drowned, Farquharson weeps 'soundlessly, without shame, his mouth gaping, his eyes locked on hers':

> A great knotted current of agony surged back and forth between the dock and the witness stand: a flood of terrible compassion. Something was happening to Gambino's voice. It dissolved, it thickened, it throbbed and took on colour; it rose and fell in octaves, like a chant.

Again and again Garner maps 'the day's wild carnage'. In the second trial, having listened to the recording of her emergency call, Cindy staggers 'along, bowed over, clutching herself with both arms like someone who had been shot in the belly'. Court rises.

Jai, Tyler and Bailey drowned when their father's car plunged into a dam, having crossed over the central line of the road, avoided oncoming traffic, charted a course across open ground that involved three distinct steering inputs and narrowly missed the solitary tree at the dam's edge. Garner wants her reader to appreciate the full extent of a murder trial; not only the drama of grief, anger and intrigue, but also the interminable tedium generated by examination and cross-examination about technical evidence. Weeks are spent discussing road cambers, wheel alignment, steering inputs, velocity and the accuracy or otherwise of yellow paint markings, made on the night of the drownings, that supposedly demonstrated the angle of the Commodore's tyres as the car left the road.

How does Garner keep the reader's interest? First, she distills reams of transcript into a few pithy sentences: 'Figures were scattered about like confetti: angles, arcs, radii. The word *infinity* was mentioned.' Next, she injects wry humour. When the inflexible and somewhat unpleasant traffic analyst David Axup mentions the yellow marks she almost squeals:

> *Marks*. The light went out of the juror's faces. A reporter scrawled on my pad, 'Yellow paint mark syncope! Instant and total blackout.' We snorted behind our hands, but soon, while Axup confidently set sail on a sea of *steering ration, friction value, critical radius, cord, middle ordinate*...a familiar stupor enfeebled me.

Garner feels caged by her inability to escape the endless detail. Her heightened, poetic prose liberates the reader: 'They were tackled on road cambers, on steering-wheel turns, on terrain, on tussocks. And always, always, Morrissey dragged their attention back to the burden of his song: the mistakenly angled yellow paint.' Her rhythm and imagery arrest attention:

> By now…the very words 'yellow paint marks' provoked
> a Pavlovian response. The jurors glazed over and turned
> sullen. They rested their chins on their fists. Their eyelids
> drooped. Their necks grew loose with boredom, they
> were limp with it, barely able to hold themselves erect.
> Once I glanced over and saw four of them in a row, their
> heads dropped on the same protesting angle towards
> their left shoulders, like tulips dying in a vase.

Through free indirect speech and quotation she maintains momentum and allows access to unfiltered witness responses. Repeatedly, she uses the present tense to convey immediacy. She paraphrases the hours of police interrogation using short, punchy sentences. She describes much of the courtroom drama in colloquial language. Rapke takes on the look of 'someone who spent his days listening to bullshit'. Morrissey gets a witness 'in a full nelson'. In evidence we hear that 'every man and his dog were out on the street', that Farquharson and his sons 'did rock through the Mount Moraic house' just hours before the fateful events.

When Louise's friends ask her 'if he did it', she thinks it is 'the least interesting question anyone could possibly ask'. Louise's reaction harks back to Garner's response in *The First Stone*, where she wrote that 'the innocence or guilt of [the Master] was to me the least interesting aspect of the story'. While that sentiment may be true in the context of *The First Stone*, it does not fully capture the present situation. Farquharson's culpability may not be so relevant for the grieving families lost in 'an abyss of suffering where guilt or innocence have no purchase', but it is of central legal relevance. His guilt or innocence drives the courtroom contest. Psychologically, it is central for Garner herself. Some part of her wants him to be found innocent of the charges, not because she believes him to be so, but because she cannot bear to countenance the idea that a father would wilfully kill his children.

Alan Gregory, Anu Singh and Madhavi Rao were all accorded judge-only trials. Those verdicts were, in different ways, more open to debate than the verdicts delivered by the juries in Farquharson's cases. Twice he was found guilty on three charges of murder. Having listened to twenty-seven witnesses, seen his police interview and heard the forensic evidence submitted at his committal, Garner felt from early on that Farquharson might well be guilty. But even as the evidence seemed increasingly incontrovertible, she fluctuated. And she was unsettled by her uncertainty.

After the secretly recorded conversations between King and Farquharson were played in court, she could not meet Louise's eye: 'To have my residual fantasies of his innocence dismantled, blow by blow, and out of his own mouth filled me with an emotion I had no name for, though it felt weirdly like shame.' Even so, she insists that she wants 'to think like a juror, to wait for all the evidence, to hold myself in a state where I could still be persuaded by argument.' This time around, she would not rush to judgment.

In the first trial Cindy asserts Farquharson is innocent. Garner surmises that Cindy could not admit to herself that he had killed the boys to punish her because she could not survive the cataract of guilt that would follow. For much of the narrative, Garner tries to take a similar approach. Her original prayer morphs into a kind of magical thinking:

> if only Farquharson could be found not guilty, then the boys would not be dead. Cindy would drive home from court and find them playing kick-to-kick in the yard, or sprawled in their socks on the couch, absorbed in the cartoon channel. Bailey would run to her with his arms out. They would call for something to eat…I could not wait to get home, to haul my grandsons away from their Lego and their light sabres, to squeeze them in my arms until they squirmed. Young boys! How can this hilarious sweetness be snuffed out forever?

Garner mused about Cindy's belief in Farquharson's innocence, and asked herself: 'Who am I to take that away?' She knew she would have to make her narrative 'dance on the head of a pin'. She needed to accommodate as much ambiguity as possible, for as long as possible. The structure of a criminal trial assisted greatly. Garner presents excerpts of the prosecution's case followed by the defence. Just when we might begin to form an opinion, she outlines the prosecution's closing arguments, and then those of the defence. Indeed, her reporting of the entire proceedings from inside the courtroom enables us to learn more about the psychological and psychiatric evidence tendered than did the jurors who were, on occasion, sent outside. Evidence excluded from the trial for legal reasons fleshes out the story.

*

James Ley commented of *This House of Grief*: 'There are no bombs of fury and disgust, no violent fits of nausea.' He is right that there is an apparent restraint in this text absent from Garner's earlier work. In part, Garner's measured tone was inspired by the professionalism of Senior Constable Rebecca Caskey of the Search and Rescue Squad, and that of the detectives and members of the Major Collision Investigation Unit, whom she came to know and admire deeply. Garner wanted to emulate what she felt was 'calm and shrewd and decent' in the police. Her respect is evident in her description of Caskey's dive to locate the sunken Commodore:

> Again, eyes shut and palms exposed, she mimed her fumbling search.
>
> 'And then', she said, 'I felt, slightly protruding from the car, a small person's head.'
>
> On the witness stand she cupped both hands before her face, and delicately moved an imaginary object sideways.
>
> 'I pushed it back in. And I shut the door.'

The tension generated by Garner's simple sentences gives way to a quiet, sacred moment. Cold and wet, Caskey waits at the scene until the car is fully recovered. She looks inside. On the front seat lies the body of the child 'whose head she had touched, and, for a moment, held in her hands'.

Garner finds Caskey's 'tender reverse-midwifery' extremely moving. She slides into another of her magical fantasies imagining the boys as 'water creatures': 'three silvery, naked little sprites, muscular as fish, who slithered through a crack in the car's rear window and, with a flip of their sinuous feet, sped away together in their new element'.

Dominick LaCapra, writing in the context of Holocaust Studies, has championed the concept of 'empathic unsettlement'. He urges historians to get close enough to their subjects to experience a certain level of trauma, and to allow that trauma to direct their work. Empathy does not equate to identification. To prevent over-identification with either subject or trauma, he proposes a 'middle voice' that articulates 'modulations of proximity and distance, empathy and irony'. Garner crafts just such a voice.

LaCapra's approach may help us understand a disturbing interlude in the book. Garner relates an outburst, where in the space of two hours she shifts from a cuddling, doting grandmother to a woman blinded by rage ready to 'land a blow' on her grandson. The incident happened in January 2009, on the third day of a Melbourne heat wave where temperatures hit the mid-40s. Garner was helping her son-in-law mind the two small boys. It was too hot for them to play outside and she had no air conditioning. Tempers frayed. She was shocked by her exploding rage. The next morning, as Melbourne continued to swelter, separated father Arthur Freeman threw his four-year-old daughter Darcey off the Westgate bridge. For the briefest moment when she heard the news, Garner understood that Freeman had snapped and felt 'the line between him & me is wafer thin'.

She included this personal anecdote primarily to debunk the 'sentimental fantasy of love as a condition of simple benevolence, a tranquil, sunlit region in which we are safe from our own destructive urges'. The repeated assertions that Farquharson loved his children and could not, therefore, be capable of harming them rang false. 'Surely,' she writes, 'Freud was closer to the mark when he said, "We are never so defence-less against suffering as when we love".' Her outburst, and her inclusion of it in the book, also gives an inkling of how tense and psychologically fragile she was at the time.

Garner was haunted by a piece of evidence in a witness statement that was never admitted in court. On the day Cindy asked him to move out, Farquharson requested that his GP refer him for a vasectomy. Had Farquharson, all those months earlier, wanted 'to amputate his fatherhood, to annihilate everything that he and Gambino as a couple had brought into being'? Had Farquharson killed his children as payback for Cindy's humiliating rejection of him? Early on Garner writes of visiting the dam and the children's graves with her friend: 'We were women in our sixties. Each of us had found it in herself to endure—but also to inflict—the pain and humiliation of divorce.' Garner knew all too well that humiliations were 'the hardest things to forget', and that the pain of humiliation could lead to a desire for retaliation and destruction. Now, writing at a time when she was no longer fighting a husband or her father, she felt a deep empathy for men who had also been humiliated. She recognised 'their fragility, their sorrows and struggles, their smashed hopes, their stoicism'. Some critics have suggested that Garner excuses Farquharson's actions. She never does. But she tries to find an explanation for them, precisely because he is such an ordinary bloke.

Garner was shocked by the pity she felt for Farquharson. Within the first year of his trials, he had transformed from an awkward, shy man who smiled and held the door for her, to someone who could manage 'only a teeth-baring grimace that did not reach his eyes'. As he shuffles into court she thinks, in an echo of her language from *The First Stone*: '*You poor bastard.*' Although he is known in Winchelsea as 'little Robbie Farquharson', his family call him Rob. Throughout her journals Garner refers to him always as 'Robbie'. She wonders if he inspires the maternal instincts in women. The senior journalist in court repeatedly castigates Garner for her tears and pity for him. Garner knows she will attract the ire of others for her sympathy, but she owns it unashamedly.

Originally she chose four epigraphs. The fourth, deleted in the later drafts, was from Montaigne: 'Every man bears the whole form of the human condition.' Garner's appreciation of Farquharson's full humanity reflected the kind of ethical imagination advocated by her friend Raimond Gaita, whose work she read while writing each of *Joe Cinque's Consolation* and *This House of Grief*.

In July 2014, when launching *A Sense for Humanity: The Ethical Thought of Raimond Gaita*, Garner noted that it was a relief to be among philosophers who did not think she was deluded in feeling pity for Farquharson:

> In these essays, and in work of Rai's that I now remem-
> bered, I found myself in the company of thinkers who
> did not find it bizarre or psychologically weird to pity a

murderer, or to be interested in the processes by which he had arrived at the moment where his foot went through the floor. Instead of railing self-righteously, these philosophers proceeded on the daring principle that 'all human beings, even the foulest criminals, are owed unconditional respect'.

I am all too painfully aware of how far I still am from being able to live out such a towering moral precept. But to see this enormous, astonishing, terrifying challenge expressed once more has quietly removed ten tons of concrete from my shoulders.

At the heart of Garner's sympathy for Farquharson lay the broader question she asks in each of her three major nonfiction works: Who are the victims? As always, the answer is: almost everyone involved.

There are deeper psychological forces at play in Garner. She is moved by the unwavering support and 'relentless loyalty' that the Farquharson sisters offer their younger brother. She mentions her own brother, one among five sisters, a 'treasured boy'. Garner identifies strongly with both of Farquharson's sisters. Throughout her journals she praises them; they are 'terrific', 'honourable', 'reliable'. She draws attention to Kerri's 'big sister' grip on Farquharson's arm as they are photographed leaving court. It is an arresting grip, but more revealing is the interest Garner took in it. Kerri's grip supports the idea that Farquharson was infantile, and that, as the sisters later affirmed to John van Tiggelen, he was dominated by them. Garner invests it with something more.

In June 2008, following an afternoon with Bob and Bev

at their Birregurra home, Garner drove back to Melbourne, acutely aware of her surroundings:

> In the dimming winter light the landscape I cross is very beautiful: long sweeps of blond grassland, cut by windbreaks of cypress…A gentle, & tender light…The sun is going down behind me, the road leads up & down a series of long, smooth, gradual hills. Out the driving window, a moon just before full—round & pale & small in the pure sky…Eventually the sun is almost down, leaving behind it a huge comma of flushed cloud.

She stopped and took a photo which she later pasted on the cover of her fourth journal. She wrote to McPhee about the visit, describing the deep hold that the melancholy Geelong landscape had on her psyche. Garner used to go for Sunday drives through this country with her parents and siblings. Way back in 1963, on the train from Melbourne to Geelong, she had similarly described to Axel how the 'daylight dry desolate ugly country' was 'transformed by bright moonlight into something quite beautiful':

> The moon shone on the crops and turned them silver, and clumps of trees stood up very black and solid on the flat ground. The You Yangs looked almost magic—there was a silvery mist round them and underneath it they were a dim blue. It looked very beautiful—but closer to Geelong even moonlight can't make the country anything less than hideous.

One wonders if some of Garner's sorrow during these years of the Farquharson trials was due to an unrecognised resurfacing of old wounds; an eldest sister separated against her will from younger siblings? Perhaps, even some deep stirring of a memory of returning to Geelong, so many years ago, after she too had lost a child?

For her own self-preservation as well as for aesthetic reasons, Garner knew that she must stand back from the immediate drama. Her narrative control and measured tone are all the more remarkable given how heavily invested she was in the trials. Repeatedly she records feeling '100% alert' and 'razor sharp' in court only to emerge into the outside world and stagger home in a 'stupor of horror'. Over the weeks, and then months and years, she became exhausted and ill, partly due to the demands of straining to hear every word in court, but also because of disturbed sleep. She experienced unsettling dreams of the trial and would wake tired, anxious and confused. She was perplexed by the intensity of her 'persistent, aching, leaking sadness'. At one point she felt that she had become 'porous', absorbing Farquharson's 'states'—'the endless dullness, the stunned plodding'—and the torrent of emotions thrown up by the trial. She described herself as being 'in a sort of hell-paradise'.

Farquharson was found guilty on three counts of murder on 5 October 2007. He was sentenced to three life sentences without parole. The courtroom erupted. Gambino wailed. Her mother collapsed and was carried from court. Morrissey 'stood like a beaten warrior...his face was chalk'. Garner was shocked. She had convinced herself that there was enough reasonable doubt not to convict. At home, she took up the green scarf she had been knitting and marked the verdict with a red stitch. Farquharson's lawyers appealed the decision on numerous grounds. The appeal began on 1 June 2009.

In those intervening years, stories of fathers, and occasionally mothers, killing their children appeared from everywhere; Garner amassed clippings from Canada, Denmark, Germany, France and North America. She read Carolyn Harris Johnson's *Come with Daddy*. She spoke with Johnson and read her as-yet-unpublished research papers. Johnson's work provided her with labels for Farquharson's crime—retaliatory familicide, separation-instigated violence—but he did not fit the aggressive, violent stereotype so often associated with domestic violence of this kind. Garner searched for something more. Justice Cummins said in sentencing that Farquharson had 'formed a dark contemplation'. But how did Farquharson come up with the idea to drive into the dam? One week after the verdict, an electrician told Garner about a Transport Accident Commission television advertisement that had aired in 1996. As a warning against driver fatigue, it showed a man at the wheel of a car that plunged from the road into a dam. His family did not survive, but he did. Had that advertisement lodged somewhere in Farquharson's mind? Even so, Garner reasoned, a thought or image was not an action: how could he go through with the act of drowning his kids?

She interrogated her network of psychiatrist, psychologist and psychoanalyst friends. Why do men kill their children after marriage break-ups? She read up on similar cases. She attended the 2012 Freud Conference in Melbourne, hoping to gain insight from discussions about the psychoanalytic understanding of killing. But she was no closer to comprehending such dark human motivation.

Garner turned to literature. In Alice Munro's story 'Dimension', she discovered a more violent version of the Farquharson story. Munro's Lloyd slays his three children. His young wife persists in making the trek to visit him in prison only to be turned away. In E. L. Doctorow's story 'Edgemont Drive', a man instructs his wife that 'to know a man's car is to know him. It is not useless knowledge.' Javier Marias' story 'While the Women Are Sleeping' offers a more than plausible scenario to explain why Greg King might not have told his wife about Farquharson's threat to kill his children for revenge. Garner realised that Colm Tóibín's *The South* 'is the same story'. Meanwhile, Veronica Hegarty, the protagonist of Ann Enright's *The Gathering*, gives a convincing explanation as to how the seeds of self-destruction may be sown in the mind of a depressed man. From James Joyce's story 'Counterparts' Garner transcribed: 'All the indignities of his life enraged him… The barometer of his emotional nature was set for a spell of riot.' And, even more poignantly, from 'A Painful Case': 'No one wanted him: he was outcast from life's feast.' The Azaria Chamberlain case and Lindy's seemingly unnatural behaviour after her daughter's disappearance also hung over this trial. Garner re-read *Evil Angels*.

But the great work that shadowed this story was Euripides' *Medea*. When John Leonard, reviewing Anne Carson's new translation of Euripides' four plays, argued that Euripides 'invented Medea's appalling infanticide as an understandable, if not excusable consequence of her profound suffering', Garner wondered:

> How can it be that for centuries we have contemplated Medea's 'blazing fury' and her dreadful crime as 'understandable, if not excusable', while to mention a contemporary wretch like Robert Farquharson in the same breath as an expression like 'profound suffering' would strike us as outrageous, even ludicrous? His wife cut him loose, he limped off to his father's, and the GP put him on Zoloft. Where's the grandeur in that?

Garner was determined that she would not suffer the same kind of paralysis she experienced while trying to write *Joe Cinque's Consolation*. But the many years spent in trials and appeals meant that public reporting of the case was sub judice. She had to be patient. In May 2008 Lindy Cameron and Fin J. Ross's *Australian True Crime: Killer in the Family*, which included a chapter on the Farquharson case and sported a photo of him on the cover, was pulled from the shelves. In October 2008 John van Tiggelen contacted Garner saying he was sorry to be 'butting in' but he had been looking at the transcripts from the trial and was planning on doing a story about the Farquharson family's 'inability to come to terms with something this dark within'. He also told her 'another book' was being written. A proprietorial Garner was unsettled by the news, but there was nothing she could do. In the coming months, while she waited for the first appeal to start, she recognised that the hiatus was a gift. It allowed her to spend more time with her small grandsons and prepared her for writing the book by driving home 'the reality of the drowned children, [and] the unbearable reality of the Farquharson and Gambino families' loss'. She felt 'tied to the leg-rope of non-fiction', however, and wondered how she could break free. She consoled herself that it would probably only be one more year.

In early 2009 Garner sent Justice Ken Crispin—the judge from Anu Singh's trial—a copy of Theo Hobson's *Times Literary Supplement* review of James Q. Whitman's *The Origins of Reasonable Doubt: Theological Roots of the Criminal Trial*. At this critical juncture, Crispin sent her a copy of his new book, *The Quest for Justice*, saying that he had been re-reading *Joe Cinque's Consolation* and 'pondering again some of the questions you asked; questions to which I still do not have wholly adequate answers'. It was the fillip she needed. If she could not fully understand Farquharson's actions or motivations, then at least she could frame the questions.

Following the June 2009 appeal, Garner produced a draft manuscript titled 'The Dam'. It was dull. The details of the case overwhelmed her. She could not let enough of them go. McPhee offered her a radical critique. Ashamed, Garner destroyed the version with McPhee's notes. She could not contain the story in any meaningful way. She was fearful of the ethical burden she had taken on. She began a fresh page in her journal, paraphrasing British psychologist Marion Milner: 'I have nothing. I am nothing.'

Milner's *An Experiment in Leisure*, first published in 1937, is a seminal text for Garner. Milner writes about her search for meaning, creativity and self-acceptance in the face of radical uncertainty and insecurity:

> Whenever I felt the clutch of anxiety, particularly in relation to my work, whenever I felt a flood of inferiority lest I should never be able to reach the good I was aiming at, I tried a ritual sacrifice of all my plans and strivings. Instead of straining harder, as I always felt an impulse to do when things were getting difficult, I said: 'I am nothing, I know nothing, I want nothing,' and with a momentary gesture wiped away all sense of my own existence. The result surprised me...not only would all my anxiety fall away, leaving me serene and happy, but also, within a short period...my mind would begin... throwing up useful ideas on the very problem which I had been struggling with.

This paragraph is one of three from Milner that Garner typed out and stuck to the wall above her desk. The other two speak similarly of letting go, of accepting the futility of feeling unequal to the task of writing, of sitting still and waiting for the 'crystallisation' of ideas that will come 'after the corruption, blackness and despair'.

By 3 September 2009 Garner had produced a revised 30,000 words. She later likened the process to 'dragging great shaggy ropes of seaweed out of my guts'. There was little to be salvaged from that draft either. On 17 December 2009 the Victorian Court of Appeal delivered its judgment and ordered a retrial. Farquharson was to be released on bail.

*

The second trial began on 20 April 2010. It turned out to be profoundly different from the first. Most significantly, Cindy Gambino had reversed her position. She now believed Farquharson to be guilty and she was, as Garner wrote, 'mad with rage'. The emotional tone and social dynamics of the courtroom radically changed. Cindy's shift of allegiance caused a rupture in the previous seating arrangements.

Garner found a seat on her own, but the Farquharson camp believed she was on the Gambino side, and radiated a quiet hostility towards her. So too did the defence legal team. In the breaks she took refuge in the Supreme Court library.

Without Louise, and with none of the former camaraderie among the journalists, she was lonely. Van Tiggelen sat with the Farquharson family. Garner recognised the relationship. He was 'like me with the Cinques'; he was 'their writer'.

This time around Farquharson took the stand. It was excruciating to witness. He admitted only to being 'annoyed' or 'upset' by the marriage break-up, yet, falling for the prosecution's tactics, rose up in anger to contest the right of Cindy's new partner to drive the better car. As one commentator noted, it was 'like watching some poor animal dying'.

Garner redeems the moment by shifting her focus to the love and support offered to Farquharson by a Christian 'motherly woman' with tangential connections to his family. It is her lead-in to another fantasy of healing.

June 2010. Garner heads to a Fitzroy pub to hear her sister sing in the Melbourne Mass Gospel Choir. The first song is 'about the water of salvation…rising up the body':

> By the time the sixty-strong choir burst into 'Jesus
> Dropped the Charges', I had air-lifted the whole mighty
> throng of them plus the band and the audience and the
> entire dramatis personae of the court out through the
> roof…to the banks of the nameless dam, where we threw
> down our swords and sang and shouted and testified
> together, while the three children in pure white robes
> were raised gasping and dripping from the depths and
> restored all perfect to their mother's arms.

Next morning, when she returns to 'Court Eleven, where the Old Testament spirit of retributions still reigned', she resists her urge to shout Amen in response to the day's ceremonial opening. In *Joe Cinque's Consolation*, Garner longed to ask Ken Crispin about his thoughts on atonement, forgiveness and healing, but she knew her line of questioning would be inappropriate: 'But we weren't in a church. We were in the Supreme Court, the temple of reason. So I said nothing.' In *This House of Grief*, she cannot maintain that distinction.

Garner seeks sanctuary in the courtroom partly because, like a church, it operates through established formal ceremony. But she discovers that being open and vulnerable in church is different from being open and vulnerable in a court of law. She needed the court to be upstanding. She felt 'patriotic' when, for example, Justice Lasry 'bent over backwards and tied himself in knots to make [the retrial] fair'. In the opening pages, Garner admits to approaching the Supreme Court each time with a 'surge of adrenalin and a secret feeling of awe'. By the time she was awaiting judgment in Farquharson's second trial she had extended her respect for the institution to the building itself. She was ashamed of the shabbiness of certain fittings and fixtures. On 21 July 2010 she unclogged the bubbler in the courtyard and scrubbed it clean with toilet paper and soap from the bathrooms. She knew she was 'in a state'. The next afternoon Farquharson was again found guilty of three counts of murder and sentenced to thirty-three years in prison.

It was at this time that Garner chanced to hear on the radio Jimmy Webb's *Wichita Lineman*, a song of isolation, loneliness and being battered by love. She emailed Imre Saluzinsky: 'I'm thinking *Wichita Lineman* expresses the tragedy of that poor bastard Robbie Farquharson. Wish I could tell the story as a country & western song.'

The verdicts in Farquharson's trials set off a media feeding frenzy. Cindy appeared on *60 Minutes* and, over the coming years, gave five interviews to *Woman's Day* and *New Idea*. When it came time to write, Garner wanted to smash through the sentimental, sensational tone of the magazine and tabloid articles. She realised that sentimentality was 'a kind of numbness' or 'frozenness':

> What Kafka meant when he said, 'A book must be an axe for the frozen sea within us'. Sentimentality as ICE. It protects us from the pain of real feeling. We have to use the 'grieving, bloodstained language of art'. A language violent in its simplicity and directness.

She wanted to 'drag' this story 'up out of trash territory & into Greek myth where it belongs.' And the years of patiently waiting for the court proceedings to end would ultimately give Garner the necessary space and perspective to write this story in such a way.

Crucially, by that time Garner had access to Cindy's voice through her media appearances and through Megan Norris' *On Father's Day: Cindy Gambino's Shattering Account of Her Children's Revenge Murders*. She also became friendly with Bob and Bev Gambino and spoke with them over the years. She had interviewed some of the expert witnesses, including a number of people not mentioned in the book. On 28 March 2011 the ABC's *Australian Story* aired the episode 'Across the Night Sky', which included interviews with Farquharson's sisters and close friend. At the time it appeared certain that Farquharson's lawyers would appeal the second conviction, van Tiggelen resigned from his position at *Good Weekend* and gave Garner the transcript of his interview with Kerri and Carmen. It was, he said, the least he could do for them.

On 4 October 2011 Garner's beloved friend and former publisher Diana Gribble died. Garner delivered one of four short eulogies at her funeral, paying tribute to her 'aura' and acknowledging how much she 'loved and valued her realistic assessments'. Garner began the third draft of the Farquharson story. From Michael Greenberg's *Hurry Down Sunshine* she transcribed: 'Idiot compassion—you destroy yourself by entering the suffering of others, while doing nothing for them.' At the very least, her book might be able to 'shine a light on the need to improve the possibility of men being able to articulate their feelings'.

On 17 November 2011 Farquharson's lawyers lodged the papers for a second appeal. The next month Garner's sister admitted being too bored to finish reading Garner's third draft of the manuscript. She did not want to know more about this man who had been found guilty twice, and could not understand why Garner persisted. Garner once again contemplated dropping the whole project, but she could not break free. Then, in February 2012, she received a letter from a police officer's wife. In part it read:

> The issue of why men kill their children is enormously important…Your book will also be read by people like my husband, the police detective, who may gain an insight that will help him deal with the issue on a professional level. Or at least gain a sense that his own bewilderment is shared.

The poet and editor Felicity Plunkett has called *This House of Grief* a 'brilliant, poetic work of jurisprudence'. In the strictest legal sense, it may not qualify as a work of jurisprudence, yet Garner is charting her own brand of legal philosophy. Throughout the book, she uses an unnamed, retired criminal barrister as a touchstone for advice. His voice is engaging, informative and, at times, critical. Garner was worried about the concept of reasonable doubt and no amount of research could quell her anxiety.

When the barrister asks her opinion as to Farquharson's guilt or innocence, she fudges and, in a familiar move, casts herself as a guileless layperson. She raises the question that informed so much of her response in *Joe Cinque's Consolation*:

> I wanted to ask him about gut feeling. I knew he would say it had no place in court. But what *was* it? Wasn't it really a kind of semi-conscious reasoning, shaped by the many weeks of evidence? A lightning-fast, instinctual matching up of the phenomenon in question against every similar one you had ever come across, in all your life's dealings with other people?

Garner is not as naïve as she makes out. As James Ley observes in his review: 'Garner's wider interests demand that a certain lack of understanding be preserved in order to create her books' characteristic open-ended contemplative space.' She calls this crucial open-endedness the 'cloud of unknowing'. Milner is again instructive:

> one day I read 'the opposite of thinking clearly is being muddled. To be conscious of being muddled is a horrible experience. To avoid it we may even be tempted to shut our minds and swallow a belief, ready-made, from some expert authority.' This made me wonder, if it were true that false thinking comes even partly from the horrible experience of being muddled, then would not one way out be to learn how to accept the experience of being muddled? I knew only too well how strong was the impulse to be certain, to lay down the law, to have things in black and white. But my mind had now driven me on to become aware of this other mood, the acceptance of emptiness, and to discover that whenever one achieved

this there was then no need to force one's thinking into
a misleading clarity.

Garner was convinced that, if she could keep her book
'hovering lightly within that cloud', it might 'enlighten' rather
than increase suffering. She took heart from an opinion piece
by psychoanalyst Peter Ellingsen, in which he wrote about
crafting a coherent article as a witness to the Tiananmen Square
massacre. Garner underlined the following:

> Staying with the anxiety would have brought me closer
> to the gaping hole—the subjective crisis—that such an
> event evokes…I knew I was not as sure as the sentences I
> wrote, that my nouns and verbs cracked under the weight
> of what I saw. But I did not know that it is through
> these cracks—the gap which arises—that the light gets
> in…We distance ourselves to get perspective …But this
> distancing—searching for sense and plausibility misses
> something.

Ellingsen's paragraph sums up much of Garner's method in
writing nonfiction.

In Garner's criminal 'jurisprudence', the law proceeds by
means of logic, reason, precedent and authority, but she insists
that it is open to the subjectivity of jurors, the accused, witnesses,
practitioners and judges. She respects the traditional attire of
wigs and gowns, and understands that they signify how counsel
and the judiciary operate as officers of the court, but she also
sketches a richer story. She offers a glimpse of the barristers'
private lives. Jeremy Rapke is absent from court on significant
Jewish days of worship and celebration. One morning, Peter

Morrissey acknowledges his wife watching from the gallery. Garner signposts the physical toll of the first trial by describing Morrissey's persistent, barking cough and Rapke's exhaustion. She draws attention to the emotional and psychological demands made upon the advocates. Deftly, she presents them as variously triumphant, effective, flustered and beaten.

Throughout the years Garner spent researching and writing *This House of Grief*, she continued participating in annual workshops run by the Judicial College of Victoria. Every August she worked with judges and magistrates on legal writing and reasoning. In 'Looking for the Story', her opening address to participants in 2013, she said that the difficulty she experienced when reading some legal judgments was less to do with her ignorance than it was to do with the way the judgments were written. She insisted that the judges and magistrates were 'the custodians of the richest, the most dramatic and poignant of human stories'.

Garner loves talking at the barristers' breakfasts organised by Clerk Michael Green and held at Melbourne's Owen Dixon Chambers. In May 2016, during her fourth Green's List appearance, she articulated a version of her jurisprudence developed over the past decade spent observing trials and working with the judiciary. She 'thought of the law as a vast poem about the terribleness and the beauty of life, like religion or philosophy'.

Was it a murder–suicide? Did Farquharson hit the water and suddenly want to live? Was it planned revenge by an unimaginative man who had not thought about anything beyond the 'fantasy of one clean stroke that would put an end to humiliation and pain?' Garner asks, yet cannot answer, these questions. She accepts the verdicts: '*Dura lex sed lex. The law is hard, but it is the law.*' She is not angry as she was after the trials of Singh and Rao, but still she is 'horrified, sad and frustrated'.

Garner agrees with Inga Clendinnen's argument in *Reading the Holocaust* that we must always keep trying to think the unthinkable because otherwise the terrible things people do will simply be labelled as 'evil' and considered beyond understanding. In the course of her research Garner discovered that 325 children had been killed by a parent in Australia over a thirteen-year period from July 1989 to June 2002. In May 2011, as she struggled with her drafts, Ramazan Acar stabbed his daughter while texting the toddler's mother and posting her murder on Facebook. The unthinkable had reached new heights. The many individual cases Garner researched stand behind her closing sentences: 'The children's fate is our legitimate concern. They are ours to mourn. They belong to all of us now.'

Garner never knew Jai, Tyler and Bailey. As a grandmother, she was drawn especially to Bev Gambino. While the jury was out in the second trial the two women accidentally met up in the street. It would have been Tyler's twelfth birthday. 'What sort of boy was he, Bev?', asks Garner, and in that moment ensures Tyler and his brothers remain at the centre of this story. Their innocence is reinforced by Garner's allusion to the jugs of water in the courtroom and W. H. Chong's cover image of three half-filled glasses of water, seen from below, as if from a child's perspective.

On 16 August 2013 the High Court dismissed the case Farquharson's lawyers had brought for Special Leave to appeal the second guilty verdict. The trials had finally come to an end. Garner was free to write. By the early months of 2014 the manuscript was complete, and *This House of Grief* was published on 20 August 2014. Garner hand-delivered a signed copy to the office of the Major Collision Investigation Unit.

The reviews were glowing. The book described as 'magnificent', 'compelling', '[t]ender and electrifying'. Having commented on Garner's 'exceptional lyricism', Felicity Plunkett stated: 'Garner's spare, clean style flowers into magnificent poetry.' James Ley wrote of Garner's 'mastery'. He judged *This House of Grief* to be the best of Garner's three nonfiction books, observing that she 'has perfected a kind of negative capability in which she acts as a focal point for the book's themes, which are channelled through her reactions but resonate far beyond them'.

The first of the congratulatory letters to arrive came from the Victorian Chief Justice, The Hon. Marilyn Warren AC, who found the book 'utterly rivetting'. As a judge she praised the way in which *This House of Grief* sought to educate, rather than merely entertain, the general public about the 'demands of the criminal justice system'. Praise followed from a raft of lawyers, including the three silks involved in the trials. Farquharson's support person wrote a note of thanks saying that while the book was 'not my miracle', she was comforted that it was more 'open ended' than it might have been. Justice Lex Lasry told

Garner that his wife loved the book but that he could not read it. The submergence videos, he said, were the worst part for him. He never wanted to revisit them.

Lasry's aversion was mirrored, to an extent, in the general readership. Stephen Romei captured that response when he wrote about being at the Kibble Awards where extracts from the shortlisted books are read aloud by high school students: 'It's a moment to relax, sip some wine, whisper a comment to your neighbour about this book or that. And so it was—until we came to Helen Garner's *This House of Grief.*' The crowd fell silent as the student read the passage about Rebecca Caskey's dive into the dark water of the dam. 'The room was still and tense. We were waiting, quietly, politely, for something deeply unpleasant to be over.' Despite being assured the book was a masterpiece that deserved serious attention, Romei admits he resisted reading it. When he did, he likened it to Dostoyevsky's *Crime and Punishment.*

As Garner set about publicising the book, the physical and psychological toll of the seven years became startlingly obvious. In October 2014, while speaking to journalism students at La Trobe University, she suffered an attack of transient global amnesia. She was forced to cancel all public appearances and rest for some months. When she fronted the sell-out Sydney Writers' Festival crowd in May 2015, she began a little tentatively. Her talk—'On Darkness'—traversed the territory of trauma she had navigated in writing both *Joe Cinque's Consolation* and *This House of Grief.* The address danced lightly between pain and gentle humour. About ten minutes in, something shifted.

Garner began to relax and enjoy herself, to perform. I could not help but think that the battle-scarred, self-flagellating Garner who had spent so many years writing about and living with pain, rage and humiliation, had all the while been serving a necessary apprenticeship. Early on in her journal she had written: 'I was BORN to do this kind of work.' It turns out, she was right. A few days prior to her address she received an email that delivered unexpected affirmation:

> Dear Helen, On Thursday I will attend your session on writing about darkness with ten dedicated colleagues who make up the child death and child protection review team for the NSW Department of Family and Community Services. This team write review reports on as many as 80 deaths of children every year. They write about hard subjects and distressing stories, nearly all of which are set against a back drop of poverty and disadvantage. Your writing has inspired the work of this team and I wanted you to know just how important it has been for them to have a mentor who writes with such honesty and clarity. The team is so looking forward to this presentation to keep them strong in the important work they do.

But the trauma had not worked its way through her body yet. A few weeks later Garner was struck down with pneumonia.

13

Versions of Herself:
Everywhere I Look

A biography is considered complete if it merely accounts for six or seven selves, whereas a person may well have as many as a thousand.

VIRGINIA WOOLF, *Orlando* (1928)

In the cover image of *Everywhere I Look* Garner stands centred. She looks directly into the camera lens. Once the full cover is opened, however, she shifts to one side of a group of people. Suburban life appears to go on around her. In the essays and diary extracts that make up this collection, Garner is a shifting presence, observing from both the centre of the action and from a distance. In most entries, she stands behind the lens recording herself recording.

In his 2016 Sydney Writers' Festival address, Julian Barnes touched on the relationship between photography, representation and biography. Admitting to his suspicion of biography, Barnes asked his prospective biographers to include the caveat: 'This is not how I was. This is how I looked when I was being biographised.' The biographer—or literary portraitist—interprets a life through her own imaginative, cultural and political filters. In crafting a coherent narrative, she chooses what to include, omit or emphasise. There are always alternative biographies of the same subject that might be written.

Everywhere I Look can be read as one possible biography of the writing persona that is Helen Garner. As always, Garner has carefully selected and arranged her pieces. Their publication dates, with one exception, span the sixteen years since she returned to Melbourne in 2000, but their content looks back to her childhood and through to the present day. Garner marks out her journey from a lonely, somewhat dislocated individual to a grounded, more confident woman surrounded by friends and family. Along the way she lets go a little of her 'puritanical savagery' and 'defensive primness'. Throughout the entries she is gently chastised by friends and loved ones. More forcefully she castigates herself, but there is also a sense of deepening self-acceptance, even a cautious equilibrium.

Her publisher Michael Heyward proposed putting this collection together as a means of restoring Garner to balance after the battering she had taken writing *This House of Grief*. He was surprised by the speed with which she assembled the work. Perhaps the timing was perfect for this particular project. Garner and I had been discussing her life and work quite intensely over the previous year. In *Everywhere I Look*, Garner seizes control of her own representation. She sketches a series of self-portraits.

We see a woman revelling in sharing the lives of her treasured grandchildren. She enters into their games, dinks them home from the crèche, makes up stories and takes them seriously. We see a woman who dances alone in her kitchen. A 'sopha'-leaping, vodka-slugging Austen fan. From a different angle, we meet a woman who befriends a lonely traveller, ladies on a suburban train and a hospital volunteer. We witness how acutely Garner observes and records her world, a world where Shostakovich and Dürer sit comfortably alongside Felix the Cat, *Mad Men* and Gary Cooper, and where children, movies, music, literature and politics are all woven together.

Garner offers two explicit images of herself. The first is as a sturdy, battle-scarred kitchen table. To a trained eye its damage is glaring; it is held together by 'crudely jammed' pieces of 'raw', splintered wood. In the right circumstances, however, the table radiates a 'warm, dark glow'. And its cobbled construction lends it a certain strength. In her second portrait she is both the obstreperous, destructive brat and the obedient older sister from *Supernanny*: 'aspects of myself…in their eternal struggle for dominance or recognition'.

In *Everywhere I Look* Garner offers three large excerpts from her diaries, the third previously unpublished. Polished, moving, witty and revealing, these snippets offer insights into her life, imagination and writing practice. Garner says that she does not regret burning her diaries for the years prior to 1980. The diaries she has kept since then are legendary, not least because no one has seen them. The New York-based literary anthology *Freeman's* published 'This Old Self', another set of extracts, in August 2016. These spare, poetic diary fragments signal Garner's command of yet another distinctive literary form.

The more humorous, outward-looking perspective that informs much of this collection stands in sharp contrast with the dark tone of *This House of Grief*. To date, reviewers have been rapturous in their response, commenting on the perfection and economy of Garner's prose, the beauty, depth and honesty of her observations, the uniqueness of her voice and the sense of joy that infuse so many pieces. Anna Goldsworthy, in her review for the *Monthly*, concludes that Garner's writing in *Everywhere I Look* 'expresses a hard-won grace'. 'It brings you closer to the world, and shows you how to love it.' Felicity Plunkett writes warmly about the 'tender, witty and whimsical' nature of the work, while also acknowledging the 'unsettling savagery' of Garner's moments of wrath. She identifies how 'shame and admirable honesty [are] balanced against defiance' in these moments. Shame, honesty and defiance structure this entire collection. As Garner grapples with each of them, she also articulates her sense of gratitude, need for atonement and increasing self-acceptance.

We meet again the terrifying Mrs Dunkley. Now a wiser, gentler Garner acknowledges more fully the debt she owes and the truth of Mrs Dunkley's existence: 'I saw you at last, my teacher: an intense, damaged, dreadfully unhappy woman, only just holding on, fronting up to the school each morning, buttoned into your black clothes, savagely impatient, craving, suffering: a lost soul.' 'Dear Mrs Dunkley' was first published in 2011. So too were Garner's tribute to Jacob Rosenberg, two diary extracts and 'Suburbia'. At that time, she was mired in the darkness of the Farquharson trials. These pieces reflect her search for, and celebration of, moments of gratitude and grace. They form part of her larger declaration of thanks for the blessings of friendship and family.

In 'Suburbia' Garner re-examines her 'bohemian contempt' for her parents' social world of the 1950s. Having discovered the benefits and satisfactions of suburban existence, she feels compelled 'to speak up, now that it's too late, for my parents, and my parents' friends—those shy, modest, public-spirited people'. Age has afforded her a broader, more mellow perspective on her parents' lives. In 'Dreams of her Real Self', Garner confesses to the barriers she erected between herself and her mother, and lacerates herself for them. She articulates how much she misses her mother and longs to atone for the cruelty she dealt her. Garner concludes 'Dreams of her Real Self' with the story of a photograph from 1943. She is six months old, 'still an only child', being nursed by her 'strong', capable mother, a woman not yet stricken with grief by the loss of her beloved brother to war: 'She is my mother, and I am content to rest my head upon her breast.' Back in 1992 Garner made a copy of this photo into a postcard and sent it to Peter Craven, thanking him for his review of *Cosmo Cosmolino*.

In the essay Garner also writes about her father's difficult personality traits and mentions again that his mother died when he was only two. Some years earlier, she realised how profoundly that loss may have shaped him. When he showed her the 1915 *Hopetoun Courier* notice of his mother's death,

Garner spied a small article at the bottom of the page about 'little Bruce Ford' being taken to hospital with severe convulsions. He was treated with strychnine injections. The toddler had been literally convulsed with grief. In their eulogy for him, Bruce Ford's children suggested that he may well have held on to that 'deep and inconsolable sorrow' for his whole life. They acknowledged: 'He left us floundering, in frequent fits of shabby sibling rivalry and jealousy, in his long, cold lapses of attention and love.' But they also celebrated his strength and their shared bond in loving him and each other.

Garner writes most of this collection from within her new configuration of family; she is the Nanna embraced by and embracing her daughter's family next door. In 'Before Whatever Else Happens', however, she tempers the narrative of joy surrounding her grandchildren with a reflection on her early mothering years. Garner admits that she was competent and had a sense of humour but that she was not sufficiently adult. There is quiet regret, a coded apology. And heartfelt admiration: 'But there she goes across the yard, my daughter. With her light firm step.'

Janet Malcolm, in her essay on her abandoned autobiography, writes: 'Autobiography is an exercise in self-forgiveness… The older narrator looks back at his younger self with tenderness and pity, empathizing with its sorrows and allowing for its sins.' In these self-portraits Garner neither forgives, nor justifies, the actions of her younger self but she does appear to ease up a little on her self-contempt. The 'I' of these pieces becomes increasingly assured and playful. The 'white calico and paint', once sufficient to project an acceptable veneer, has given way to a deeper confidence.

In March 2016 Garner told Phillip Adams that being older allowed her to 'see all sides of a question', and be less quick to judge. With experience, she said, 'everything becomes richer and more interesting'. Garner revels in the liberation that age has brought her. She also admits to making 'a pest of myself to some extent'. In 'The Insults of Age', Garner exchanges her 'convalescent sofa' for a night out. In Swanston Street she observes a 'lanky white' schoolgirl mocking and frightening women of Asian appearance. Garner is livid: 'In two strides I was behind the schoolgirl. I reached up, seized her ponytail at the roots and gave it a sharp downward yank. Her head snapped back. In a voice I didn't recognise I snarled, "Give it a rest darling".' The startled girl runs off. Garner falls back in step with her companion. This essay stirred a familiar controversy. Some online posts applauded Garner's takedown of a bully. Others decried her inappropriate use of violence to express her rage. Anecdotally, there was mention in some academic circles that Garner was once again too ready to attack young women.

Garner laughed out loud while writing the essay. It was, she said, the best fun she'd had in years. She wasn't backing away from her actions one little bit. At the same time, she knew she had crossed a dubious line:

> Everyone to whom I described the incident became convulsed with laughter, even lawyers, once they'd pointed out that technically I had assaulted the girl. Only my fourteen-year-old granddaughter was disapproving.

'Don't you think you should have spoken to her? Explained why what she was doing was wrong?'

Shortly after its publication Garner sent me a postcard depicting an irate Madame Hare confronting a cheeky young rabbit: 'Did you pull my tail?' On the back she had written: 'So my attack had a literary precedent!'

In delivering the 2006 Judith Wright Memorial Lecture, the poet Fay Zwicky noted that the 'personality of many writers has a built-in ambivalence, awkward for the writer to live with and equally difficult for the reader to understand'. She spoke of the struggle, begun early in a writer's life, between 'the need for privacy and the need for recognition'. She also suggested that for some writers the 'desire to please the world fights the impulse to tell the world what's wrong with it'. In conversation with Jennifer Byrne, Garner admitted that for a long time she, like Simone de Beauvoir before her, wrote 'in order to be loved'. Experience has taught her to surrender some of that need. Hence there is a heightened sense of mischief—even delight—when she provocatively owns her opinions and examines her less appealing character traits in these essays.

The central ambivalence in Garner's personality is the way that her powerful self-belief is married to a fragility fed by self-doubt. I interviewed many people in the course of assembling this literary portrait who spoke of Garner's honesty and brutal self-examination. Her longtime friend and colleague Michael Gawenda identified a key, seemingly contradictory, aspect of Garner's writerly persona:

Helen has the ability to be an intense observer of people including strangers even when she seems to be relaxed, even when she seems to be shy and reluctant to ask difficult and prying questions. She can seem, uncertain, tentative, but really, she knows exactly what she is doing. Helen has this capacity to make herself invisible, make people forget that she is examining them, listening to them, watching the way they look and sound. She is a ruthless and fearless writer.

Epilogue:
No Sense of an Ending…

*You never have the sense of an ending when you are
writing about a living subject.*

DEIRDRE BAIR, 'IN SEARCH OF THE REAL SIMONE DE BEAUVOIR' (1992)

*Why do books of letters move us as biographies do not?
When we are reading a book of letters, we understand…the rapture
of firsthand encounters with another's lived experience.*

JANET MALCOLM, 'A HOUSE OF ONE'S OWN' (1995)

Garner is famous for her letters, postcards and, more recently, emails and texts. Her richly varied forms of communication populate the archives of writers across the country and the world. As a twenty-year-old, Helen joked to Axel Clark: 'One day these letters will be famous—"The Life, Loves and Letters of Helen Ford".' She envisaged neither her fame nor that Axel would keep and later archive her early correspondence. Despite giving me permission, Garner was troubled to think that I had read her early private epistles, because she continues to feel guilt for her youthful narcissism and personal failures. For my part, I was struck by the consistency of her voice and imaginative drive over five decades. The letters confirm that from her undergraduate days Helen sought to understand herself and her relationships primarily through reading and writing. Her lived and imaginative worlds were inextricably intertwined from the start.

Garner has had a handful of letters to editors published. In 1994 she wrote to *Quadrant*, defending Manning Clark's kindness and generosity. She suggested that Peter Ryan—who had written an angry essay about Clark's histories—should moderate his tone in order to engage in reasoned debate. In September 1995 she sent a brief response to the reports about Jenna Mead's Sydney Institute address to the *Age*, the *Australian* and the *Sydney Morning Herald*. Then in February 2002, she signed a joint letter to the *Age*, along with Peter Carey, David Malouf, Tim Winton, David Williamson, Tom Keneally and Richard Flanagan, protesting mandatory detention for refugees. The writers pleaded for 'more compassionate practices', asserting that the 'the issue of this policy—hatred, scapegoating and denial of human rights—threatens to corrode the soul of our nation'.

In 2010 Garner was one of five women invited as part of a Women of Letters event to 'pen a letter to the night they'd rather forget', and to perform that letter at Melbourne's Trades Hall. She did not follow the brief. Instead, she wrote a series of fragmentary notes to people, living and dead, hoping they would 'add up to one big letter': 'The Letter I Wish I'd Written'. Garner wrote to her grandfather, to some old family friends and to her science teacher. She addressed a lonely old woman with whom she briefly shared a bench in the Carlton Gardens in 1969, her grandmother who gave her a typewriter when she was fourteen but from whom she was later estranged, a classmate from her daughter's primary school and the manager of the Fitzroy Baths. In the final pieces, she wrote to the now accomplished Muslim doctor who kissed her on a summer evening in 1957 at Ocean Grove and concluded with 'a thankyou letter' to her husbands.

Garner thanks her first husband for giving her 'a new name, a daughter, and grandchildren'; her second for teaching her to 'speak a language I had only ever known in books'. To Murray Bail she states: 'you scared the shit out of me with a painful but somehow awesome demonstration of what an artist will do to clear the decks for work'. She admits that in the marriages there was 'a lot of misery', but she is grateful that each husband gave her 'a completely fresh gift of laughter'. She seeks mutual forgiveness before bestowing a blessing on her husbands and offering that there is no longer anything to forgive.

In 'The Letter I Wish I'd Written', Garner acknowledges the sometimes painful truth about her quick-tempered spontaneity and regrets that her thoughtlessness and self-absorption precluded moments of kind companionship. The letter affirms her desire to make amends. Yet she also writes that she will never forgive herself for not having been attuned sufficiently to the suffering or loneliness of others. I asked two people who have known Garner for over forty years about her shame for past actions or omissions. Raimond Gaita judged Garner's self-interrogation to be 'absolutely proper'. The way in which she continues to say 'this is what I did', and to feel remorse for it, he explained, is evidence of her deeply ethical nature. David Malouf, approaching the question from a literary rather than philosophic viewpoint, speculated that perhaps Garner regretted not being sufficiently self-reflexive in her youth.

In 2005 Sara Dowse asked Garner how she would like to be remembered. Knowing that it might sound 'trivial', she replied: 'I would like people to remember me as someone who was fun to be with…I'd like people to miss me when I'm gone and think, God we used to laugh, we used to dance.' She said that she would love to know that something she wrote made her reader laugh. Laughter, she explained, 'is some kind of deep erotic connection you can make with people'.

Garner's friends and family attest that while she can be self-absorbed, impatient and 'a real pain in the arse', she is also open, playful and funny. Helen Elliott identifies 'a fundamental lightness and loveliness in her…A sort of tenderness towards the world similar to that shown by George Herbert, with whom she identifies.' Catherine Ford captures a sense of shared sisterly humour when she writes of Garner's importance in her life: 'Beloved sister, mentor, texting buddy, fellow member of an important club dedicated to raising awareness about the totally suss and utterly overblown national appreciation of Nicole Kidman's acting chops.' James Button delights in how Garner's correspondence abounds with 'jokes, shouts of excitement or fury, snatches of writing she has loved and expressions of fellow feeling'.

The ways in which Garner will be remembered by readers are still unfolding. She should be remembered as a brilliant stylist.

As a writer who has taught us how to see and feel the texture of the everyday, natural world. As a champion of interior lives and the domestic sphere. As a writer prepared to journey into the heart of trauma, absorb the darkness she finds and transform it, often at great personal cost, for the reader. As a writer who dissects gender relations and the complexity of human emotions and motivations, as a boundary-crosser who has redefined and shaped literary genres to accommodate her material.

In the mid-1990s the controversy surrounding *The First Stone* was one of a number of political and cultural events that sparked much discussion about the role of public intellectuals in Australian life. In 1997 Robert Dessaix conducted a series of interviews with noted commentators for Radio National, later publishing an edited collection, *Speaking their Minds: Intellectuals and The Public Culture in Australia*. Garner featured on radio and in print. Dessaix modified Stanley Fish's basic definition of a public intellectual for Australian conditions. Garner fitted the bill:

> an independent thinker and performer who, working from some core area of expertise, takes as his or her subject issues related to the public good…and, by the grace of the media and an outstanding ability to communicate with many publics…has the attention of a considerable segment of educated Australia. And denies it.

Garner absolutely denies the title. Yet in March 2005 the *Sydney Morning Herald* ranked her eighth in its list of the top 100 Australian living public intellectuals. She was one of three women included in the top ten, along with Germaine Greer and Inga Clendinnen.

Garner has never made any secret of the disappointment she experiences when her books miss out on literary prizes. She says that she has grown a thicker skin since publishing *The First Stone*, but she continues to be sensitive to negative criticism or to any impression that her work, particularly her nonfiction, may be overlooked. In 2016 she was awarded the prestigious Donald Windham–Sandy M. Campbell Literature Prize for the body of her nonfiction work. She felt tremendous validation knowing that her 'three big tormentuous non-fiction works' had been recognised as literature. Back in 2004, however, she was 'stung' when *Joe Cinque's Consolation*, which she cared about deeply and had worked so hard to write, did not seem to 'meet with literary favour'. When some critics insisted, four years later, that *The Spare Room* was not a novel, Garner withdrew for a time from the literary world. 'I stopped going to festivals and launching other people's books and writing cover endorsements.' She built for herself 'a weird lonely but *free* space' outside of Australia's writing culture and she felt that in order to keep functioning she had to stay out there. Nam Le, discussing Garner's 'straight-on grace and crazy generosity', captures this sense of Garner as a lonely observer:

> It's hard to overstate how much she's helped other writers, by action as well as example, and yet, in the best way, she's not really 'part' of the writing community—she's in it but not of it. I think of Helen somewhat as a totem pole on our local landscape: silent, upright, observant,

> acceptant of every manner of meaning, drawing weather
> and copping shit but still there, outlasting it all, just there.

In his preface to *The Portrait of a Lady*, Henry James employs the metaphor of the house of fiction, with its many and varied shaped windows and balconies, to describe how the artist, at some remove, perceives 'his' world and shapes that unique perception into a particular literary form. Garner, notebook and pen always at the ready, has lived her adult life as James' watcher. The image of her cycling through Fitzroy and Carlton, sitting in court or conversing around her kitchen table may seem far removed from James' disembodied 'pair of eyes' watching the world through 'a field-glass'. One would not readily think to paint a portrait of Garner 'perched aloft', peering through an aperture in a 'dead wall', and yet she has been offering just such an image of herself. Remember what she has told us about her sense of detachment, her constant struggle to find the appropriate form for her material, her dismissal of the artificial boundaries of genre? The rooms in Garner's house of writing are far more carefully crafted and connected than they may appear.

When we read Garner's work together as an organic whole, we can appreciate more fully *how* Garner writes about her experiences, which, as Philip Roth argues, takes us a long way to understanding *why* she writes about them.

There can be no sense of an ending to a study of a writer still in full creative flight. I now find it impossible to answer Heyward's question about what I consider to be the most significant book in Garner's oeuvre. The ways in which Garner's writing and life interweave, shape each other and send out rhizomic connections to other writing, writers and readers, suggest to me that her life and work whisper, worry, laugh and sing to each other. Garner's work is not 'one book' of what she makes of her world and her life as she has lived it; rather her work and her life are perhaps best thought of as a complex, sometimes discordant, always modulating musical score.

Indeed, in the course of my final edits to this manuscript I was surprised to learn of a new interest Garner was pursuing. Hilary McPhee suggested I ask Garner about their small reading group. I assumed this was the group, now in its fifth year, that had tackled the great works of Western literature. I emailed Garner: 'Do you have another tale to tell me?' She replied:

> The new group: It happened like this: one day Hil was sad because she wasn't in a reading group. I said, How about we start one? She goes, OK, what'll we read? HG: How about poetry? How about the Sonnets? HMcP: Ooh yes, but wait – how about the psalms? HG Fabulous – who'll we invite to join? Hilary suggested Peter and Colin. HG: OK you invite them, let's meet on Monday at yr place. I'll bring my King James bible.

> She emails: the blokes are keen and would love to do the psalms.

> A week later at 7 pm we rock up to her place with a ragtag bunch of bibles—three old King James, the Book of Common Prayer, and my Jerusalem Bible which I thought might be useful because of the footnotes. Hil has a fire going in the living room and a tray of cheese & biscuits and two bottles of wine one white one red.

I refrain from laying down the no-drinking rule that we have in the Milton/Homer/Virgil/now Shakespeare group I also belong to. Someone says, 'We've never been in a reading group—how do you do it?' HG: 'Well, one person starts reading and goes for a while and then the next one takes over, and so on round the ring.' I forget who started, anyway away we go, ripped into Psalm one changing every few verses. Then we read a whole psalm each. After half an hour Hilary says, 'we're going too fast, I can't absorb it, could we read each one twice?' great idea. We do this, with profit. An hour later we spontaneously look up and start talking about what we're reading. Peter knows a lot about different translations and the history of how and when they happened…At the next meeting, a fortnight later, I bring the Revised Standard Version and someone comes up with the brilliant idea: to read each psalm in four different translations: Peter the KJV, Hil the Book of Common Prayer, me the Jerusalem, and Colin the Revised Standard. This works so well we're completely bowled over. And fascinated by the different takes on the same text—the feel of the translators' struggles.

What I notice is how our immersion in a (mighty) text brings everyone to his (or her) best self. Everyone becomes serious. We read as well as we can, slowly and carefully until we get the hang of it, stopping and going back a verse when we haven't quite grasped it.

Is that a story?

Helen

Notes

Introduction: Sketching an Outline

This chapter draws on interviews with James Button and Jenny Sages.

p1: 'For me, particularly…' 'Helen Garner in Conversation with Jennifer Byrne Part 1', youtube.com/watch?v=DREsUqM-INg, published 2 May 2013.

p1: 'because we experience…' David Shields, NonfictioNow Melbourne 2012: 'Nonfiction: The Art of Truth—Writerly Perspectives', 23 November 2012, youtube.com/watch?v=8rfsXsBg3IU, published 28 January 2013.

p2: 'Thank you for telling me…' Garner, 'Death in Brunswick', *Monthly*, November 2012, themonthly.com.au/issue/2012/november/1351733118/helen-garner/death-brunswick.

p3: 'almost pure invention' Janet Malcolm, *The Journalist and the Murderer*. New York: Knopf, 1990, 159.

p3: 'is the worst…' Garner, 'Why writers hate being asked if their work is autobiographical,' *Australian Women's Weekly*, 1985, 291.

p4: 'the intriguing biographical…' Philip Roth, interview with Hermione Lee, 'The Art of Fiction', *Paris Review* no. 84, theparisreview.org/interviews/2957/the-art-of-fiction-no-84-philip-roth.

p5: 'It was a wonderful encounter…' Simon Elliot, 'True Stories: The Story Behind the Creation of the Portrait of Helen Garner by Jenny Sages', *Portrait Magazine*, 1 June 2005. portrait.gov.au/magazines/16/true-stories.

p6: 'Writing is how…' James Button, interview with author, 13 June 2016.

p7: 'close and immediate engagement…' Kerryn Goldsworthy, *Helen Garner*. Melbourne: Oxford University Press, 1996, 10.

PART 1: Letters to Axel

p9: 'I think it's…' Garner, interview with Leigh Sales, *7.30*, 28 March 2016.

1: Writing Home

This chapter draws on interviews with Sally Ford and Judith Whitworth, the unpublished eulogy for Bruce Ford (January 2005) and Garner's personal diary from 2003. Additional information came from the Papers of Axel Clark in the NLA, and two recorded interviews with Garner, conducted by Hazel de Berg (October 1982) and Sara Dowse (March 2005), from the NLA Oral History Collection.

p11: 'There are no beloved...' Garner, 'A Scrapbook, An Album', *True Stories*, Text: Melbourne, 1996, 60.

p11: 'beautiful', 'foreign', Garner, 'Writing Home', *The Feel of Steel*, Picador: Sydney, 2001, 4.

p11–12: 'yanked', 'sneak up', 'stab' ibid., Garner, 6; 'We are women...' ibid., 77.

p12: 'a vivid, obstreperous character', 'never read a book' Garner, 'Dreams of Her Real Self', *Everywhere I Look*, Text: Melbourne, 2016, 93.

p12: 'impatient, rivalrous, scornful', 'unpredictable possessiveness...' Garner, Eulogy for Bruce Ford.

p13: 'If I poked...' Garner, 'Sad Grove by the Ocean', *True Stories*, 44; 'Why would I go in...' ibid., 46.

p13: 'get away from bookshop drudgery...', Garner to Clark, 29 January 1965.

p15: 'Gosh I'm sick...', 'in close touch...', 'There is such a tremendous gap...' Garner to Clark, 14 January 1965.

p16: 'tremendously impressed' Garner to Clark, 3 January 1963.

p16: 'no, I'm not like Sue Bridehead...' Garner to Clark, 2 January 1965.

p16–17: 'tight-strained nerves', 'everything she did...', 'I cannot humiliate...' Thomas Hardy, *Jude the Obscure*. London: Macmillan and Co., 1951, 122 &133.

p18: 'I got a beaut comment...' Garner to Clark, 6 August 1963.

p18: 'My memories of university...' Garner email to author, 19 December 2014.

p18: 'I am suddenly remembering...' Garner email to author, 19 December 2014.

p19: 'unpredictable possessiveness...' Garner, Eulogy for Bruce Ford.

p19: 'I think he is going to forbid...' Garner to Clark, 17 June 1966.

p20: 'is our first universe,', 'nooks and corridors', 'all our lives...', 'localization of our memories', 'Topoanalysis...would be...' Gaston Bachelard.

The Poetics of Space. trans. Maria Jolas. Boston: Beacon Press, 1992 (1958), 8.

p20: 'can't understand why…', 'have a hard shell…' Garner, 'Sad Grove by the Ocean', 42.

p20: 'hopeless at history, the past is a kind of blank…' 'Helen Garner on her Influences and Inspirations'. Sydney Writers' Festival 2008, youtube.com/watch?v=SKcfvPbF4gQ, published 2 May 2013.

p21: 'Yes, but in that house' Garner, 'A Scrapbook, An Album', 72.

p21: 'image, symbol, site and space' Kerryn Goldsworthy, *Helen Garner*, 28.

p21: 'I think I had better…' Garner, interview with author, 11 August 2015.

p22: 'threads between things' David Malouf, *12 Edmondstone Street*. St Lucia: University of Queensland Press, 1985, 52.

p22: 'Wilde and Swift and Berkeley had trodden' Garner to Clark, 5 July 1967.

p24: 'I was rather keen…', 'I feel that Ford…' Charlotte Wood, 'Do you take this man's name?', *Sydney Morning Herald*, 27 July 2002, smh.com.au/articles/2002/07/26/1027497411079.html.

p24: 'I was one of the La Mama widows…', 'left out and lonely…' Liz Jones, Betty Burstal and Helen Garner, *La Mama: The Story of a Theatre*, Fitzroy, Vic: McPhee Gribble/Penguin Books, 1988, 12.

p25: 'pretty angry', 'bourgeois individualism' Garner, Anna Greive and James Manche (dirs.) The Pram Factory, Lindfield, NSW: Film Australia, 1994.

p25: 'wrestling with our feelings…', 'mould them into…', 'facile and self-indulgent' Garner, 'betty can jump', *dissent: a radical quarterly* 28, Winter 1972, 47–50.

p26: 'buzz' Christos Tsiolkas. 'Helen Garner's *Monkey Grip*,' ABC TV, 30 September 2014.

p27: 'for a single beat…' Garner, 'Why Does the Women Get All the Pain?', *True Stories*, 36.

p27: 'own uncertain experience…', 'emotionally ecstatic…' Garner, *Digger* 8, December 2–16, 1972, 1.

p28: 'ga-ga with love', 'but then we…' Garner, 'Bisexuality: Joining the Middle', ibid., 9.

p28: 'popular four-letter words', 'the male and female…' Garner, 'Beware the wrath of caretakers', *Digger* 10, 13–27 January 1973, 6.

p28: 'debauch and corrupt…' Richard Neville 'Richard Neville in his own words', Radio National, abc.net.au/news/2016-09-05/richard-neville-founder-of-oz-magazine-in-his-own-words/7814136, accessed 27 January 2017.

p29: 'Shit, fuck, bum, cunt' Meg Clancy, 'The Pram Factory: Personal Memoirs', pramfactory.com/memoirsfolder/Clancy-Meg.html, accessed 27 January 2017.

p29: 'a bottler' Garner to Clark, 23 December 1972.

p30: 'Things I wrote…' Garner, 'The Art of the Dumb Question', *True Stories*, 3; 'howled', 'hinted that one…' Garner, ibid.

p31: '<u>most peculiar</u> attitude…', 'tiptoed…', 'I am quite sure…' Garner to Clark, 17 April 1975.

p31: 'all events described…' Garner to Clark, 17 April 1975.

2: 'The blind, needing self': *Monkey Grip*

This chapter draws on interviews with Jane Clifton and Sally Ford and material from the McPhee Gribble archive in the Baillieu Library, University of Melbourne.

p33: 'In the journal…' Susan Sontag, 'On Keeping a Journal', 31 December 1957, David Rieff (ed.), Susan Sontag, *Reborn: Journals and Notebooks 1947–1963*, New York: Picador, 2009, 166.

p33: 'I have started…' Garner to Clark, 4 December 1975.

p34: 'uncontaminated by trends…' Kate Jennings, *Mother I'm Rooted: An Anthology of Australian Women Poets*, Kate Jennings (ed.), Fitzroy, Victoria: Outback Press, 1975.

p34: 'to tell us rather diffidently…' Hilary McPhee, *Other People's Words*. Sydney: Picador, 2001, 142.

p35: 'a bit bumpy…', 'it was as if…' ibid., 143.

p35: 'tremendous', 'truthful', Barbara Giles, 'Reviews,' *Luna* 1978, 42.

p35: 'a good old-fashioned love story', R. F. Brissenden in Katherine Brisbane, R. F. Brissenden and David Malouf, *New Currents in Australian Writing*, Sydney: Angus & Robertson, 1978, 26.

p35: 'Immoral and sordid', *Australian*, cited by McPhee, *Other People's Words*, 143.

p35: 'careless and unstructured', 'perverse', 'repetitious', Irina Dunn, 'The Fringe and the Core', *Nation Review*, 3 November 1977, 17.

p35: 'not a book for the prudish', Veronica Schwartz, 'Multiplying and Dividing,' *Australian Book Review*, June 1978, 64.

p35–36: 'Head prefect', 'at the centre…', 'Mr and Mrs Average…' Jan

McGuinness, 'Helen the Stirrer', *Melbourne Herald*, 27 December 1977, 21, 32.

p35: 'the scatological verb' Peter Pierce, 'Conventions of Presence', *Meanjin* 40.1 (1981), 113.

p36: 'wrong kind of publicity' John Larkin, 'Different Style of Living and Surviving,' *Age*, 22 October 1977, 24.

p36: 'audacious', 'Helen Garner has published…' Peter Corris, 'Misfits and Depressives in the Raw,' *Weekend Australian*, 5–6 November 1977, 12.

p36: 'half of Carlton…' Mark Rubbo, *Australian Book Review*, October 1984, 2.

p37: 'I write entirely…' Joan Didion, 'Why I Write,' *New York Times Book Review*, 5 December 1976, montgomeryschoolsmd.org/uploadedFiles/schools/whitmanhs/academics/english/Why%20I%20Write%20Didion.pdf, accessed 27 January 2017.

p37: 'Why the sneer…' Garner, 'I', *Meanjin* 61.1, 2002, 40.

p37: 'in the Diary…' Anaïs Nin, *On Writing*. Gremor Press, 1947, quotes reproduced at brainpickings.org/2013/09/20/anais-nin-on-writing-1947, accessed 27 January 2017.

p39: 'impolite, brashly explorative…' Suzanne Edgar, 'A Feminism That's Almost Priggish,' *Canberra Times*, 4 March 1978, 12.

p39: 'a coldness', 'nervous' Garner to Clark, 7 February 1979.

p40: 'Garner's women characters…' Susan Lever, *Real Relations: The Feminist Politics of Form in Australian Fiction*, Sydney: Halstead Press with the Association for the Study of Australian Literature, 2000, 108.

p40: 'a fast faker' Garner, *Monkey Grip*, 8.

p41: 'Stupidly for something…' ibid., 47.

p41: 'This honest book…' Sean O'Beirne, 'What I Loved', *Readings Monthly*, September 2014.

p41: 'where the sign read…', 'only testing the water…' Garner, *Monkey Grip*, 2; 'what it means…' ibid., 147–148.

p41: '*Monkey Grip*'s particular …' Lever, *Real Relations*, 110.

p42: 'wished that women…' Hélène Cixous, 'The Laugh of the Medusa', Translated by Keith Cohen and Paula Cohen. *Signs* 1:4, Summer 1976, Chicago: The University of Chicago Press, 1975, 876.

p42: 'romantic, exclusive' Garner, *Monkey Grip*, 156.

p42: 'like a very complicated…' ibid., 192.

p42: 'getting a Carlton letter' Jane Clifton, *The Address Book*, Camberwell, Victoria: Viking, 2011, 304.

p43: 'I did despicable things…' Ponch Hawkes, 'The Pram Factory: Personal Memoirs', pramfactory.com/memoirsfolder/Hawkes-Ponch.html, accessed 27 January 2017.

p43: 'more story', 'passion on the page' Colin Talbot, email to author, 23 January 2017.

p44: 'such unstructured fiction…rejecting, illuminating' Tegan Bennett Daylight, 'A phone call to Helen Garner.' *Australian*, 3 November 2012, theaustralian.com.au/arts/review/a-phone-call-to-helen-garner/story-fn9n8gph-1226508428981.

p44: 'artless…naïve and appallingly revealing', Garner 'Helen Garner's *Monkey Grip*', documentary, ABC TV 30 September 2014.

p44: 'Ms Garner is…' Corris, 'Misfits and Depressives', 12.

p45: 'The kids begin…' Garner, *Monkey Grip*, 9–10.

p45: 'attenuated weeping' ibid., 66.

p46: 'the one about…' ibid., 7.

p47: 'sheltered…to see what was…', 'bludger because I…', 'At 35 you'd think…' McGuinness, 'Helen the Stirrer,' 32.

p47: 'McPhee Gribble are about…' *Monkey Grip* launch invitation, [archive], Baillieu Library.

p48: 'easy nor an early…', 'heroin addiction…their full humanity' Joyce Nicholson, Anne Summers and John McLaren. 'National Book Council Annual Awards for Australian Literature: Judges' Report.' *Australian Book Review*, October 1978, 30–31.

3: Ruptures and Dislocations: *Honour & Other People's Children*

This chapter draws on interviews with Jane Clifton and Sally Ford, and material from the McPhee Gribble archive.

p49: 'that mighty institution…' Garner, 'Going the Bloody Hard Way: Notes on Micheline Lee's *The Healing Party*', *Monthly*, 7 June 2016, themonthly.com.au/blog/helen-garner/2016/07/2016/1465264597/going-bloody-hard-way.

p49: 'I finally dragged…' Garner to McPhee and Gribble, 24 May 1977.

p50: 'I wrote this…' Garner to McPhee and Gribble, 13 April 1978; 'people have started…' ibid.

p51: 'through the streets…' Alice Garner, *The Student Chronicles*, Carlton, Victoria: Miengunyah Press, 2006, 86.

p51: 'nervously working on…' Garner to McPhee and Gribble, 6 October 1978.

p52: 'weird sort of politeness…', 'clichéd Carlton type', 'ORDINARY LOOKING', 'current hero' and discussion of *La Femme qui pleure* and casting, Garner to Ken Cameron, 30 January 1979.

p53: 'three main characters…', 'short stabs, very little…' ibid.

p54: 'another layer of the despised…Australian STORY FILM', response to Mad Max, Garner to McPhee and Gribble, 16 May 1979.

p55: 'stern advice' Garner to McPhee and Gribble, 8 June 1979.

p55: 'Helen came to…' McPhee, *Other People's Words*, 157.

p55: 'We've both been …' McPhee to Garner, 31 July 1979.

p55: 'Of course I felt…' Garner to McPhee, 8 August 1979.

p56: '…Things mattered…pain and loss' Chris Wallace-Crabbe, 'Genesis', *The Emotions are Skilled Workers*. Sydney: Angus & Robertson, 1980, 4–6.

p57: 'On summer nights…' Garner, 'Honour', *Honour & Other People's Children*, Melbourne: McPhee Gribble, 1980, 1; 'lack of interest…' ibid., 18; 'himself into a bunch…' ibid., 3.

p58: 'a force-field', 'it was hatred…', 'some half-gagged…' ibid., 26–27; 'smelled coldly of…', 'rattled her fist …' ibid., 6; 'wash-house' ibid., 25; 'the house of…' ibid., 26.

p59: 'She wept bitterly…' ibid., 52.

p59: 'faultless in its structure…' Jefferis, 'Men and women and children,' *Sydney Morning Herald*, December 1981.

p59: 'A work of art' Marion Halligan, 'Excellence in Brevity', *Canberra Times* 2 May 1981.

p59: 'you would never…' Summers, 'View from the ghetto', *National Times*, 23–29 November 1980, 44.

p60: 'What am I…' Garner, *Honour & Other People's Children*, 46'; 'moment of blessing', 'Jenny felt a…' ibid., 23.

p61: 'They hung in…' ibid., 56.

p62: 'harness of gloom' ibid., 85; 'in the tentative…' ibid., 73.

p62: 'self-consciously "a writer"' Garner, 'The Art of the Dumb Question.' *True Stories*, 5; 'I tried to apply…' ibid., 6.

p63: 'the same degree…they strike me' Garner, 'I', *Meanjin*, 42.

p64: 'Powers of observation…' Garner, 'A world apart', *Eureka Street* 5.10, December 1995, 29.

p64: 'You may start…' Garner, 'The Art of the Dumb Question', *True Stories*, 6.

4: A Blessing on this House: *The Children's Bach*

This chapter draws on material from the Scripsi archive in the Baillieu Library, University of Melbourne, the McPhee Gribble archive and the Papers of Axel Clark.

p65: 'a young woman…' Mark McKenna, *An Eye for Eternity*, Melbourne: Miegunyah Press, 2011, 508.

p66: 'terribly impressive' ibid., 508. 'Often after breakfast…', '[i]n Garner…', 'it was a typical…' ibid., 509.

p67: 'conscious compromise', 'inexorably refused', 'she was stone…' Henry James, *Madame de Mauves*, ebook, The University of Adelaide, 17 December 2014.

p68: 'an obsessive memory…' McKenna, *Eye for Eternity*, 48.

p68: 'She must be…' Garner, *The Children's Bach*, Ringwood, Victoria: Penguin, 1996 (1984), 6.

p68: 'after I've been with you…' Garner to Axel and Alison Clark, 17 November 1985.

p68: 'there would be…' Kate Grenville and Sue Woolfe, *Making Stories: How Ten Australian Novels Were Written*. Sydney: Allen & Unwin, 1993, 64.

p69: 'like trying to make…' Garner, *Australian Women's Weekly*, 291.

p70: 'order she would…' Garner, *The Children's Bach*, 22; 'someone saves it…' ibid., 1.

p70: 'The Angel in the House', 'confined to the home…' victorianpoetry-poeticsandcontext.wikispaces.com/The+Angel+in+the+House, accessed 27 January 2017.

p71: 'saint' Garner, *The Children's Bach*, 78; 'perfect' ibid., 38; 'contained, without needs…' ibid., 26; 'tremble with holding…' ibid., 48.

p71: 'probably the greatest…', 'the almost *moral*…', 'to perceive form…' Garner, *Making Stories*, 68.

p71: 'Take out the clichés…' Garner, *The Children's Bach*, 89.

p72: 'Polyphony: which is…' E. Harold Davies (ed.) *The Children's Bach*, Melbourne: Allen, 1933, v.

p72: 'weaves her characters' loves…' Don Anderson, 'A Tale of Modern Love: *The Children's Bach*', *Hot Copy: Reading and Writing Now*, Ringwood, Victoria: Penguin, 1986, 35.

p72: 'It occurred to me…' Anne Olivier Bell, assisted by Andrew McNeillie (eds). *The Diary of Virginia Woolf, Volume Three 1925–1930*, New

York: Harcourt Brace Jovanovich, 1980, 339.

p72: 'what happens in…', 'The War or that kind of thing…' Shelagh Rogers, 'Interview with Helen Garner', *Australian and New Zealand Studies in Canada* 1, 1989, 36.

p72–73: 'men fuck girls…' Garner, *The Children's Bach*, 18; 'rules', 'modern life' ibid., 28.

p73: 'because there is…' Rogers, 'Interview with Helen Garner', 36.

p73: 'I have a young…' Garner to Clark, 31 August 1984.

p74: 'their fingers met…' Garner, *The Children's Bach*, 57; 'Perhaps there was…' ibid., 65; 'that the day…' ibid., 88; '*The Children's Bach*…' Garner, *The Children's Bach*, 29.

p74: 'moral' Ellison, *Rooms of their Own*, 141.

p75: 'tough-talking radical', 'I've always loved children…' Eleanor Wachtel, 'I'm Writing to Save Myself: An Interview with Helen Garner', *Australian and New Zealand Studies in Canada* 10 (1993), 65.

p75: 'dream again…' Garner, *The Children's Bach*, 95.

p76: 'and Athena will…' ibid., 96.

p76: 'One or two people…' McPhee, *Other People's Words*, 245.

p77: 'There are four…' Don Anderson, 'A master is rescued', *National Times*, 20–26 June 1986, 34.

p77: 'Please give my regards…' Raymond Carver to Craven, 26 July 1984.

p77: 'It is so painstakingly…' Garner to Craven, 26 July 1984.

p78: 'this rush of emotion…' 'Helen Garner's Consolation', *Brisbane Times*, 16 June 2008, brisbanetimes.com.au/news/books/helen-garners-consolation/2008/06/15/1213468225536.html.

5: Boundary Riding: *Postcards from Surfers*

This chapter draws on the McPhee Gribble archives in the Baillieu Library, University of Melbourne.

p81: 'an urgent sense…' Garner, 'Tutto Sereno', *The Feel of Steel*, 94.

p81: 'big blunt', 'looked as if…' Garner, 'Postcards from Surfers', *Postcards from Surfers*, Melbourne: McPhee Gribble, 1989 (1985), 9.

p83: 'who's not going…' 'Women like us…', Garner, 'The Life of Art', ibid., 62.

p83: 'I was all over…' Craig McGregor, 'The Gospel According to Garner,' *Good Weekend Magazine*, 29 February 1992, 30.

p84: 'Philip has turned…' Ray Willbanks, *Speaking Volumes: Australian*

Writers and Their Work, Ringwood, Victoria: Penguin, 1992, 95.

p84: 'bend the bars...' Garner, 'Civilisation and its Discontents', *Postcards from Surfers*, 96.

p85: 'I turn forty-one' Garner, 'A Happy Story', ibid., 105; 'I am finally...' ibid., 106.

p85: 'almost dazzlingly confident...' Katherine England, 'Joyful Shocks of Recognition', *Advertiser Magazine*, 8 March 1986, 20.

p85: 'the fine sense of scale', 'intriguing' Nicholas Jose, 'Reviews in Brief', *Age Monthly Review* 5.10 (March 1986), 22.

p86: 'position as one of...' McPhee, *Other People's Words*, 244.

p86: 'idiosyncratic vision...' Kathryn Kramer, 'A Pleasant Discord', *New York Times*, 7 December 1986. nytimes.com/1986/12/07/books/a-pleasant-discord.html.

6: Relinquishing Control: *Two Friends* and *The Last Days of Chez Nous*

This chapter draws on material from the McPhee Gribble and Scripsi archives in the Baillieu Library, and an interview with Peter Craven.

p87: 'My method of work...' Garner, *The Last Days of Chez Nous & Two Friends*, Melbourne: McPhee Gribble, 1992.

p87: 'rough, obsessive, unstoppable' Craven to Catherine Ford, 18 December 1982.

p88: 'seemed exact', 'In Garner small...' Craven, 'The Successful Transition of Helen Garner', *Age*, 14 October 1992, 4.

p89: 'saw a little story...' 'dragged', 'really, in a funny sort...', Garner in Gerry Turcotte (ed.) *Writers in Action: The Writer's Choice Evenings*, Sydney: Currency Press, 1990, 164–165.

p89–90: 'Ah, I LOVE *Two Friends*...', 'I had to learn...' Garner, interview with author, 11 August 2015.

p91: 'to write "a gay comedy...', 'bones of the plot', 'BETH and JP...' Garner, McPhee Gribble archive.

p92: 'dense crazy little...' ibid.

p92: 'Do you think...' Garner, *Last Days of Chez Nous & Two Friends*, 45.

p92–93: 'not a bad performance', 'it's simply a pity...', '[Judy] Davis (or Helen Morse)' Craven, 'The Successful Transition of Helen Garner'.

p93–94: 'it seemed a gift...', 'A spire, no matter...', 'qualities of air...', 'the very image...', Garner, *Last Days of Chez Nous & Two Friends*, xi–xii.

p95: 'Dear Peter, I suppose...' Garner to Craven, 31 October 1992.

7: The House of the Spirit: *Cosmo Cosmolino* and Other Stories

This chapter draws on material from the Papers of Hilary McPhee, NLA, the Scripsi archive, an interview with Ed Campion and the author's correspondence with Tim Winton.

p96: 'I feel as if…' Garner in Turcotte (ed.), *Writers in Action: The Writer's Choice Evenings*, Sydney: Currency Press, 1990, 172.

p97: 'to shift the focus…' Garner 'Germaine Greer and the Menopause', *True Stories*,133; 'essential stage…' ibid., 136.

p97: 'learn the language…' Garner, 'On Turning Fifty', *True Stories*, 141.

p97: 'an obscure longing…' Garner, *Making Stories*, 72.

p97: 'strange, crazy dream-richness' ibid., 70.

p97: 'the doors open…' Drusilla Modjeska, *Second Half First: A Memoir*, North Sydney: Knopf, 2015, 84.

p98: 'This style was…' Garner, 'Dreams, the Bible and *Cosmo Cosmolino*', *True Stories*, 121–122.

p98: 'I was very influenced…' Susan Wyndham, 'Femme Fatale', *Sydney Morning Herald*, 17 July 2004, 25.

p99: 'Nothing can be sole…' Garner, 'What We Say', *My Hard Heart*, Ringwood, Victoria: Penguin, 1998, 19; 'Words which people…' ibid., 18.

p100: 'one of those…' ibid., 17; 'independent breath…', 'I gave him my…', 'You've made a mess…' ibid., 21.

p101: 'the one doing…' Garner, 'The Psychological Effect of Wearing Stripes', *My Hard Heart*, 9.

p101: 'is perhaps closer…', 'no realist framework…', 'a kind of dream…' Goldsworthy, *Helen Garner*, 55.

p102: 'laid out with…' Garner to McPhee, 30 October 1989.

p103: 'Oh yes now…that scared me' Garner, email to author, 13 August 2015.

p103: 'the way the stories…', '<u>waiting</u> (the world's)…' Garner to McPhee, 9 February 1990.

p104: 'They hurt with…' Garner, 'A Visitation', *Cosmo Cosmolino*, Melbourne: McPhee Gribble, 1992.

p106: 'I don't remember…' Garner, 'My First Baby', *Everywhere I Look*, 199.

p106: 'would not be…' Garner, interview with author, 11 August 2015.

p107: 'after I had…' Garner, email to author, 18 August 2015.

p107: 'I feel gloomy…' Garner to McPhee, 27 February 1990.

p107: 'wicked ways' Ramona Koval, 'The Terrible Strength of Angels,' Introduction to *Cosmo Cosmolino*, Melbourne: Text Publishing, 2012, ix.

p107–8: 'to think things...so I do' Garner to Clark, 22 December 1962.

p108: 'cowardice' Garner to Craven, 15 November 1988.

p108: 'mighty force' Tim Winton, correspondence with author, 22 March 2016; 'star-struck...quite worldly' ibid.

p108–9: 'the bodies and...roadtrain of evangelicalism', 'I remember a card...' ibid.

p110: 'soon after the...' Garner, 'Recording Angel', *Cosmo Cosmolino*, 3.

p110–11: '*oldest...most loyal...*' ibid., 7; 'sad girl', problem...' ibid., 17. 'It dropped through...' ibid., 12.

p111: 'Have you ever...', 'like a judge...' ibid., 19.

p112: 'He was a small...' ibid., 22.

p112: 'I was very defensive...' Garner, interview with author, 11 August 2015.

p112–13: 'complicated, angry, frightened...', 'He said he...' Garner, 'A World Apart,' *Eureka Street*, 30.

p113: 'panicky', 'clearly unpublishable', 'I can't quite...' Garner to McPhee, 24 April 1990.

p113: 'I didn't start shaking...' Garner, 'Death', *True Stories*, 229.

p114–15: 'a bird uttered...' Garner, 'A Vigil', *Cosmo Cosmolino*, 38; 'In the passion...' ibid., 44; 'calm stone gaze', 'unbearable diamond... living, living, living' ibid., 47; 'out onto the...', ibid., 47.

p115: 'head girls', Moya Costello, 'Head Girls and Helen Garner's Women', *Imago* 9.3 (Summer 1997), 3–12.

p116: 'bruised', 'heart of the...' 'Cosmo Cosmolino', *Cosmo Cosmolino*, 64; 'a white-washed tomb...', 'nothing but bones' ibid., 66; 'ribcage', ibid., 79; 'Behind her left...' ibid., 88.

p117: 'the pleasure of serving...' 'skull', ibid., 57; ibid., 120.

p117: 'It's quite simple...' Garner, 'Sighs Too Deep for Words', *The Feel of Steel*, 81.

p117: 'of course the failure...', 'when writing this...' Garner to Craven, 1 August 1991.

p118: 'tears of bliss' Garner, 'Cosmo Cosmolino', *Cosmo Cosmolino*, 192.

p118: 'grapplings with spirituality...of meaningless hyperprose' John Nieuwenhuizen, 'Style without grace,' *Australian Book Review*, April 1992, 17.

p118: 'move into religion…', 'insubstantial', 'just the same…', 'soon as writers…' Susan Chenery, 'The Cosmos of Helen Garner.' *Australian Magazine*, 29 February–1 March 1992, 17.

p119: 'a more wondrous', 'write something that…' Garner, 'Dreams, the Bible and *Cosmo Cosmolino*', *True Stories*, 122.

p119: 'purple', Fiona Capp, 'The Ultimate Deadline: Journalism and Fiction', *Australian Book Review*, February–March 1995, 34, and Jenna Mead, 'Politics, Patriarchy and Death', *Island 53* (1992), 67.

p119: 'the framing had…' Garner, 'Cosmo Cosmolino', *Cosmo Cosmolino*, 176.

p119–20: '*The Children's Bach* was…the finest sense' Winton, correspondence with author 22 March 2016.

Part II: Questions of Judgment

p121: 'The characters of nonfiction…' Janet Malcolm, *The Journalist and the Murderer*, New York: Alfred A. Knopf, 1990, 149.

8: *The First Stone: Some Questions About Sex and Power*

This chapter draws on interviews with Ross Gibb, Brian Stonier, Hilary McPhee, David Malouf, Barbara Mobbs and Drusilla Modjeska. Additional material came from the Papers of Helen Garner and the Papers of Hilary McPhee in the NLA.

p123: 'In a work…' Malcolm, *The Silent Woman: Sylvia Plath & Ted Hughes*. New York: Knopf, 1995, 154.

p125: 'good faith', Jenna Mead and Amanda Lohrey, 'Sexual Harassment and Feminism', *RePublica* 2, 1995, 166.

p125: 'totally and emphatically' Garner, *The First Stone*, Picador: Sydney, 1995, 13; 'feminists pushing fifty…at the time?' ibid., 15.

p125: 'heartbreaking…warmest good wishes', Garner to Alan Gregory, 25 August 1992.

p126: 'moment of irrational…' David Malouf, interview with author, 21 March 2016.

p126: 'the thoroughbred…tearing her fetlocks' Barbara Mobbs, interview with author, 30 November 2015.

p126: 'quite dumb…feel myself to be' Garner, 'The Art of the Dumb Question: Forethought and Hindthought about *The First Stone*,' *LiNQ*

24:2 (October 1997), 10–11; 'awareness of that…' ibid., 11.

p127: 'felt the first stab…' Garner, *The First Stone*, 37; 'Helen you have been…' ibid., 70.

p128: 'shot herself…hand too early' Janet Malcolm, 'Women at War: A Case of Sexual Harrassment', *New Yorker*, 7 July 1997, 73.

p129: 'in my psyche…' Garner, 'The Art of the Dumb Question: Forethought and Hindthought about *The First Stone*', 12.

p130: 'haunted'. Garner, *The First Stone*, 39.

p131: 'Helen, this story…' Garner, *The First Stone*, 70.

p132: 'Again and again…on the brakes' ibid., 175.

p132: 'seems to engage…' Shirley Hazzard, Letter to Helen Garner, 30 December 1995.

p132: 'her uneconomical, exhausting…' Garner, *The First Stone*, 142.

p133: 'put the whole thing…' ibid., 71; 'some obscure reason' ibid.; 'finding out things…' ibid., 72.

p133: 'the Ormond drama…' Goldsworthy, *Helen Garner*, 73.

p134: 'tragically bereft', 'a relatively minor…', 'sexual harassment', 'abuse of power' Garner, *The First Stone*, 165–166; 'old fear of…' ibid., 145; 'I functioned from…' ibid., 71–72.

p136: 'hate' ibid., 151; 'retribution', 'out of date…', 'terrifically at a disadvantage' ibid., 97; 'priggish, disingenuous…' ibid., 93; 'constant stress on passivity…' ibid., 99.

p137: 'revenge of the powerless', 'slave' Friedrich Nietzsche, *On the Genealogy of Morals: A Polemic*, trans., Douglas Smith, Oxford: Oxford University Press, 1996 (1887), 20.

p137: 'bruises upon bruises' Garner, 'Killing Daniel', *True Stories*, 164.

p138: 'right from the…propaganda for war' Garner, *The First Stone*, 100; 'pretty', 'conservative' ibid., 58; 'daring beauty…authority and power' ibid., 59.

p138: 'What's wrong with…' Elspeth Probyn, 'Re: Generation. Women's Studies and the Disciplining of *Ressentiment*,' *Australian Feminist Studies* 13:27(1998), 134.

p139: 'I thought…at fifty…' Garner, *The First Stone*, 40; 'pathetic bravado', 'I practically pleaded…' ibid., 106.

p140: 'So this is…' ibid., 97.

p140: 'grim-faced Presbyterians…among their legs' ibid., 35.

p140: 'say more to…' Goldsworthy, *Helen Garner*, 82.

p140: 'putty in the hands…' Garner, *The First Stone*, 202.

p141: 'nervous sweat', Candida Baker, *Yacker: Australian Writers Talk About Their Work*, Sydney: Picador, 153.

p141: 'priggish', 'puritan' 'conflating the genuinely…' Goldsworthy, *Helen Garner*, 79.

p141: 'I dreaded discovering…' Garner, *The First Stone*, 146.

p144: 'the famous novelist', 'talking to your…' Cassandra Pybus, 'Cassandra Pybus reviews Helen Garner's *The First Stone*', *Australian Book Review*, May 1995, 6–8.

p145: 'implacable ambiguities…' Ihab Hassan, 'Australia', *World Literature Today* 69.4 (Autumn 1995), 865.

p145: 'thunderstruck', *'embarrassed'*, 'I behaved like…' Garner, *The First Stone*, 174; 'What *is* this fear…' ibid., 209; 'felt intensely foolish…', 'stupidest of all…' ibid., 208; 'was I, like…' ibid., 209.

p147: 'What is disappearing…' Jane Gallop and Geraldine Doogue, 'Consenting Adults?', ABC Radio *24 Hours*, November 1993, 49.

p147: 'The erotic will…' Garner, *The First Stone*, 161.

p148: 'But feminism too…' ibid., 202.

p149: 'The struggle for…' Zoe Heller, 'Ill-founded outrage', *Times Literary Supplement*, 13 August 1993, 11.

p150: 'craziness' 'Helen Garner in Conversation with Jennifer Byrne Part 1'.

p150: 'rips open what…' Frank Rich, 'Review: Oleanna; Mamet's New Play Detonates the Fury of Sexual Harassment.' *New York Times*, 26 October 1992, nytimes.com/1992/10/26/theater/review-theater-oleanna-mamet-s-new-play-detonates-the-fury-of-sexual-harassment.html.

p151: 'the risk of sanitizing…teachers and students' Margaret Talbot, 'A most dangerous method', *Lingua Franca*, January–February 1994, 40.

p151: 'Packwoods and Woody…or as rapists?' Erica Jong, 'Fear of Flirting: Let Sense Prevail', *Washington Post*, 8 December 1992, 5; 'I am working…' ibid., page.

p152: 'victimhood', 'power feminism' see Naomi Wolf, *Fire with Fire: The New Female Power and How It Will Change the 21st Century*, New York: Vintage, 1993 & Katie Roiphe, *The Morning After: Sex, Fear and Feminism on Campus*, Boston: Little, Brown and Co., 1993.

p153: 'if only the whole…' Garner, *The First Stone*, 222.

p154: 'a less cruel…' ibid., 222.

p154–55: 'the freedom to…' Janet Malcolm, *The Silent Woman*, New York: Alfred A. Knopf, 1995, 41; 'Writing cannot be…' ibid., 176.

p155: 'a man accused…' Garner, *The First Stone*, 15; 'just poor bastards' ibid., 99.

p155: 'sympathetic rendering...' Marilyn Lake, 'Three Perspectives on Helen Garner's *The First Stone*', *Australian Book Review*, September 1995, 26.

p156: 'shifting speculations' Garner, 'The Fate of *The First Stone*', *True Stories*, 170.

p162: 'robust discussion' Ross Gibb, interview and correspondence with author, 19 October 2016.

p164: 'feeding off' Pybus, *ABR* May 1995, 8.

p164: 'envy...hatred...' Jenna Mead, '*The First Stone*: Feminism and Non-fiction', The Sydney Institute, 20 September 1995, *The Sydney Papers* (Spring 1995), 127.

p164: 'charges and counter-charges...' Marilyn Lake, *Australian Book Review*, 27.

p165: 'primal' Garner, 'The Fate of *The First Stone*', *True Stories*, 170; 'these young idealists...' ibid., 175.

p165: 'confusion', 'ignorance' Mead, 'Pity not she who casts the first stone', *Sydney Morning Herald*, 16 August 1995.

p166: 'More perplexing, however...' Virginia Trioli, *Generation F: Sex, Power and the Young Feminist*, Port Melbourne: Minerva, 1996, 21.

p167–68: 'extra efforts...general ignorance' Rosi Braidotti, 'Remembering Fitzroy High', in Jenna Mead (ed.), *bodyjamming*, Milsons Point, NSW: Vintage, 1997, 128.

p169–70: 'persuaded by Garner's...very empowering indeed' Zora Simic, 'Response: On Reading "The First Stone" Ten Years Later,' *Lilith: A Feminist History Journal* vol. 15 (2006), 18–31.

p171: 'a kind of robustness...' Modjeska, email to author, 16 October 2015.

p171: 'The spirit of...' Garner, 'A Scrapbook, An Album', *True Stories*, 69.

p171: 'vanity and pride...' Garner, 'The Art of the Dumb Question: Forethought and Hindsight about *The First Stone*' (1997), 11.

9: Asserting Her Credentials: *True Stories* and *The Feel of Steel*

This chapter draws on Sara Dowse's interview with Garner and unpublished material: the eulogy for Gwen Ford, Garner's tribute to the Reverend Bill Lawton and her correspondence with the archdeacon, from the Helen Garner archive held at Baillieu Library.

p173: 'opposite me sits...' Garner, 'Five Train Trips', *True Stories*, 204.

p174: 'favourite character in…' Garner, 'The Art of the Dumb Question', *True Stories*, 2.

p174: 'capricious, lazy, ill-humoured…', 'a little misfortune' William Makepeace Thackeray, *The Rose and the Ring*, 1854, ebook, University of Adelaide, 17 December 2014, ebooks.adelaide.edu.au/t/thackeray/ william_makepeace/rose, accessed 27 January 2017.

p175: 'bleak story of…' Garner, *True Stories*, 166; 'What happened to…' ibid., 168.

p176: 'sceptical, ironic but…' Garner, 'Marriage', *True Stories*, 217.

p176: 'changed her way…' 'Ramona Koval Talks to Helen Garner About *True Stories*, a Collection of her Non-fiction Work Over Twenty-five Years', Ramona Koval, *Australian Book Review*, May 1996, 24.

p176: 'conviction' Garner, 'Death', *True Stories*, 229.

p176: 'if you watch…' Garner, 'Ramona Koval talks to Helen Garner…', 24.

p177: 'I saw a woman…' ibid.

p178: 'an abyss and depth…', 'O broad light…' Francis Webb, 'Nessun Dorma', in Toby Davidson (ed.), *Collected Poems: Francis Webb*, Crawley, WA: UWA Publishing, 2011, 345.

p179: 'This time I'm…' Malcolm, 'Women at War', 75.

p180: 'Therapy was extremely…' Susan Wyndham, 'Wiping away the tears', *Sydney Morning Herald*, 25–26 August 2001, *Spectrum*, 7.

p185: 'really home' Garner, 'Writing Home', *The Feel of Steel*, 6.

p186: 'tourist ships to…greatest mystery of all?' Garner, 'Regions of Thick-Ribbed Ice,' *The Feel of Steel*, 13; 'scores of ships…', 'have shrunk so…', 'too sad to…' ibid., 14.

p187: 'urge to compare…' ibid., 16; 'only in abstract terms' ibid., 17.

p187: 'What if somebody's…' Garner, 'Woman in a Green Mantle', *The Feel of Steel*, 35; 'Writing is a sickness…' ibid., 37.

p189: 'there are days…' Garner, 'Sighs too Deep for Words', *The Feel of Steel*, 80–81.

p190: 'a passionate hatred', 'Go in peace…' ibid., 84.

p190: 'the smaller the thing…' Wyndham, 'Wiping away the tears', 7.

p190: 'Everything around me…' Garner, 'Tess Bows Out', *The Feel of Steel*, 152.

p191: 'At the sight…' Garner, 'The Nanna-Mobile', *The Feel of Steel*, 188.

p191: 'They were my future', 'collapse of ambition…just taking off.' ibid., 190.

p195: 'a kind but…un-awe-inspiring' Garner, 'Against Embarrassment',

Best Australian Essays 2003, Melbourne: Black Inc., 2003, 212.

p195: 'a kind and...', 'Somewhere in the background...' Garner, 'Whisper and Hum', *Everywhere I Look*, 5.

p195: '"You may be...' Garner, 'The Feel of Steel 2', *The Feel of Steel*, 204.

p197: 'Four bars in...' Garner, 'Dear Professor Molchanov', in Genevieve Lacey and James Crabb (eds.), *Heard This and Thought of You*, ABC Classics, Sydney, 9.

10: The Shape of Loss: Lament and Restitution in *Joe Cinque's Consolation*

This chapter draws on the Papers of Helen Garner and Hilary McPhee in the NLA. Additional material came from Sara Dowse's interview with Garner.

p198: 'Remembering is an...' Susan Sontag, *Regarding the Pain of Others*. New York: Farrar, Straus and Giroux, 2003, 115.

p198: 'I had been...' 'humiliated and angry', 'find out if...', 'slip quietly into...' Garner, *Joe Cinque's Consolation*, Sydney: Picador, 2004, 121.

p199–200: 'are always good...' ibid., 30; 'a little movie' ibid., 76; 'to call the encounter...' ibid., 85; 'declared roundly...' ibid., 188.

p200: 'A book *about her*...' ibid., 80.

p202: 'I was dumb...' ibid., 270.

p202: 'everything ethical' Garner, interview with Sara Dowse, 15–16 March 2005.

p205: 'dangerous and exciting...' Garner, 'Woman in a Green Mantle', *The Feel of Steel*, 42.

p206: 'To mourn avails...' *The Iliad of Homer translated by Alexander Pope*, Volume 4, bartelby.com/203/191.html, accessed 27 January 2017.

p206: 'a piece of writing...' Elizabeth Gloyn, 'Consolatio', lizgloyn. wordpress.com/2011/06/27/consolations-and-grief-in-the-ancient-world, accessed 25 January 2017.

p207: 'a mess, full...' Garner, *Joe Cinque's Consolation*, 141.

p208: 'enlarge my imagination...' ibid., 188; '*Call that mental*...' ibid., 38; 'a self-centred...', 'expendable commodity', 'Memories from my...' ibid., 44.

p209: 'Do we identify...' ibid., 66.

p210: 'the narcissism, just...', 'quite manic...', 'either it's not pathological...' Susan Wyndham, 'Femme fatale', 25.

p210: 'wanted to save…', 'thunderstruck', 'contemplating the wreckage…' Garner, *Joe Cinque's Consolation*, 324; 'was like everybody…', ibid., 231; 'One girl wild…'ibid., 232.

p210: 'a fallible register…' Morag Fraser, '*Joe Cinque's Consolation*', *Age*, August 14 2004, theage.com.au/articles/2004/08/11/1092102517082. html.

p212: 'bigger, louder, brighter', 'because of our…' Garner, *Joe Cinque's Consolation*, 178.

p212: 'was uninterested in…' ibid., 142.

p213: 'wrenched askew', 'dragged halfway…', 'stained' ibid., 143–144; 'youth and tenderness', 'beauty and freshness', 'thin trickle of…' ibid., 144.

p213: 'I treasure the memory…' Garner, 'On Darkness', *Everywhere I Look*, 145.

p214: 'The first time…' Garner, *Joe Cinque's Consolation*, 3; 'friends and family' ibid.; 'the whole tale…' ibid., 178; 'the jolting visual…' ibid., 21.

p215: 'forever looking at…' Sontag, *Regarding the Pain of Others*, 55.

p215: 'murder, trial, punishment', 'collected horrors…', 'it was a long…' Garner, *Joe Cinque's Consolation*, 275.

p216: 'not guilty of…' ibid., 68.

p217: 'Whilst the behaviour…' ibid., 80.

p218: 'Was there ever…' ibid., 80; 'I think there are…' ibid., 314; 'in an anxious…' ibid., 152; 'there is a good…' ibid., 153; 'bizarre' ibid., 75.

p219: 'embodied and highly…' Anthea Taylor, 'Victims and Vixens', *Politics and Culture* 4 (2005), politicsandculture.org/2010/08/17/ victims-and-vixens-2, accessed 25 January 2017.

p219: 'really believed that…' Garner, *Joe Cinque's Consolation*, 325.

p220: 'is an apology…' Marina Warner, 'Who's sorry now?', *Times Literary Supplement*, 1 August 2003, 10.

p220: 'ordinariness of…', 'flashed', 'a bright smile', 'a little wave', 'Why wasn't she…' Garner, *Joe Cinque's Consolation*, 51; 'her soul', ibid., 289; 'what happened' ibid., 115; 'for what she…', 'Did words like…' ibid., 289.

p221: 'rent in the…' ibid., 280; 'came anywhere near…' ibid., 290; 'bear witness to…' ibid.

p221: 'in view of…' Hannah Arendt, *Eichmann in Jerusalem: A Report on the Banality of Evil*, New York: Penguin Books, 1994 (1963), 287.

p222: 'If you acknowledge…' Wyndham, 'Femme Fatale', 25.

p222: 'moral dignity', 'restraint', 'unable to emulate him' Garner, *Joe Cinque's Consolation*, 280.

p223: 'Into my thoughts...' ibid., 87; 'read miserably...', 'ploughed through books...' ibid., 280.

p225: '*Difficult?* I thought...' ibid., 241; 'the original enterprise', 'a whole new enterprise...', ibid., 244; 'The hide of this...' ibid., 242; '*innocent bystander*' ibid., 244; 'wave of incredulity...' ibid., 245; 'With the point...' ibid., 247.

p226: 'A pimp laid...' ibid., 256; 'never thought of...' ibid., 247.

p226: 'the complex issues...', 'unexamined assumptions...' JaneMaree Maher, Jude McCulloch & Sharon Pickering. '"[W]here women face the judgement of their sisters", review of *Joe Cinque's Consolation* by Helen Garner', *Current Issues in Criminal Justice* vol. 16, issue 2 (November 2004), 233.

p227: 'The Garner narrative...' Inga Clendinnen 'Making Stories, Telling Tales: Life, Literature, Law.' 18th Lionel Murphy Memorial Lecture, 17 November 2004. lionelmurphy.anu.edu.au/memorial_lectures.htm, accessed 27 January 2017.

p227: 'limitation', 'in Garner's stubborn...' Penny Pether, 'The Prose and the Passion: Penny Pether Searches for an Australian "Constitutional Epic" in our Recent Literature and Cinema', *Meanjin* 66.3, September 2007, 43.

p227: 'Everything he said was...' Garner, *Joe Cinque's Consolation*, 318–319.

p228: 'Was the law...' ibid., 280.

p228: 'its historically problematic', 'supplement and a...', 'We might think...' Wai Chee Dimock, *Residues of Justice: Literature, Law Philosophy*, Berkeley: University of California Press, 1996, 9–10.

p229: 'never *seen* a case...' Garner, *Joe Cinque's Consolation*, 315; 'Sitting there...' ibid., p317; 'awestruck', 'Her outburst after...' ibid., 131.

p230: 'What's the use...', 'What freshness can...' ibid., 281.

p230: 'Oh, if only...' Garner, *Joe Cinque's Consolation*, 114.

p231: 'Helen it's good' Susan Wyndham, 'Femme Fatale', 25.

p231: 'moving, enraging, poignant...' Kate Grenville, *Australian*, 9 December 2006.

p231: 'a tragic drama...' Susan Lever, 'Truth found under another stone', *Sydney Morning Herald*, 21 August 2004, 9.

p231: 'exceptional case of...' Maryanne Dever, 'Hanging Out for

Judgement?', *Australian Women's Book Review* 16.2 (2004).

p235: 'I blessed him...' Garner, 'Dreams of Her Real Self', *Everywhere I Look*, 92.

p235: '*What are you...*' Garner, 'Recording Angel', *Cosmo Cosmolino*, 7.

p236: 'those wonderful Jungian...' Garner, 'Moving Experience', *Monthly*, September 2005, republished as 'White Paint and Calico' in *Everywhere I Look*, 16.

11: Telling It Like It Is: Love and Tyranny in *The Spare Room*

p237: 'To have a friend...' Jacques Derrida, 'The Taste of Tears', *The Work of Mourning*, Pascale-Anne Brault and Michael Naas (eds.), Chicago: The University of Chicago Press, 2001, 107.

p237: 'Death will not...' Garner, *The Spare Room*, Melbourne: Text Publishing, 2008, 89.

p238: 'tall, striding', 'staggering...' ibid., 1; 'I pushed [Bessie]...', 'Go home, sweetheart...' ibid., 12.

p239: 'almost all subject-verb-predicate...' Robert Dessaix, 'Kitchen-table Candour: Helen Garner's *The Spare Room*,' *Monthly*, April 2008.

p239: 'On Tuesday', ibid., 41, 163, 'That night', ibid., 39, 63 'On Friday', ibid., 118, 'That afternoon' ibid., Garner, *The Spare Room*, 92, 171.

p240: 'Who was I...', 'dragged', 'I looked at...', ibid., 69; 'Death was in... vitality surged', ibid., 80.; '"I've learnt that...' ibid., 94–95.

p241: 'What did I know...' ibid., 37; 'She laid down...' ibid., 35.

p242: 'The flesh was...' ibid., 17.

p243: 'I didn't know...' ibid., 189; 'thrilling alto drone' ibid., 192; 'I had no idea...', 'If I did not...' ibid., 193.

p244: '...when she was dead...' Shannon Burns, 'Shannon Burns Talks with Helen Garner', *Wet Ink* 24 (September 2011), 32.

p244: 'elegance and taut...' Kate Bateman, 'A Taut Telling of a Tough Treatment', review of *The Spare Room*, *Irish Times*, 2 August 2008, irishtimes.com/news/a-taut-telling-of-a-tough-treatment-1.925914.

p244: 'extraordinary, exhilarating novel' Olivia Laing, 'A Passionate End to a Bohemian Rhapsody', *Guardian*, 6 July 2008, theguardian.com/books/2008/jul/06/fiction.reviews.

p244: 'great fiction', 'demand[ing] us to reset...' Mukherjee, Neel, review of *The Spare Room*, *Times*, 28 June 2008, neelmukherjee.com/2008/06/the-spare-room-by-helen-garner, accessed 27 January 2017.

p244: 'it's a fiction...' Davies, Stevie. 'A Literary Revelation from the Final Chapter of a Life,' review of *The Spare Room*, *Independent*, 17 July 2008, independent.co.uk/arts-entertainment/books/reviews/the-spare-room-by-helen-garner-5475274.html.

p244: '*The Spare Room* is a far more...' James Wood, 'James Wood on the books of 2009', *New Yorker*, 9 December 2009, newyorker.com/books/page-turner/james-wood-on-the-books-of-2009.

p244: 'a quietly devastating...' Dessaix, 'Kitchen-table Candour'.

p244: 'It is morally...' Burns, 'Shannon Burns Talks with Helen Garner', 28.

p245: 'When I started...' ibid., 30.

12: The Darkness Within: Bearing Witness in *This House of Grief*

This chapter draws on Garner's research material for This House of Grief, *which has now been deposited in the NLA. It is yet to be catalogued. Additional material came from Garner's unpublished eulogy for Diana Gribble, her unpublished launch speech for* A Sense of Humanity: The Ethical Thought of Raimond Gaita *and her unpublished opening address to participants in the Judicial College of Victoria workshop.*

p247–48: 'Night. Low foliage...', 'Oh Lord...' Garner, *This House of Grief: The Story of a Murder Trial*, Melbourne: Text Publishing, 2014, 2.

p248: 'he had done...' ibid., 10.

p250: 'I'm left with...' Garner, 'The Rules of Engagement', *Everywhere I Look*, 180.

p251: 'a lean, contained...to watch' Garner, *This House of Grief*, 7; 'silver-haired man...' ibid., 8; 'Homeric' ibid., 24; 'gargantuan' ibid., 156, 'energy-thieving' ibid., 136, 'catastrophically lacking...', 'a jelly of...' ibid., 23.

p252: 'surged into the...' ibid., 185; 'scared, and small...' ibid., 7; 'in a series...', 'people in the court...' ibid., 30; 'soundlessly, without...', 'a great knotted...' ibid., 35, 'the day's wild...' ibid., 235, 'along, bowed over...' ibid., 231.

p253: 'Figures were scattered...' ibid., 154, '*Marks*. The light...' ibid., 166, 'They were tackled...' ibid., 22.

p254: 'By now...the very words...' ibid., 73; 'someone who spent...' ibid., 7; 'in a full...' ibid., 242; 'every man and...' ibid., 12; 'did rock through...' ibid., 43; 'if he did it', 'the least interesting...' ibid., 115.

p254: 'the innocence or...' Garner, *The First Stone*, 40.

p254–55: 'an abyss of...' Garner, *This House of Grief*, 37.

p255: 'To have my...', 'to think like...' ibid., 92.

p256: 'if only Farquharson...' ibid., 93.

p257: 'There are no...' James Ley, 'Gut Instinct', *Sydney Review of Books*, 19 December 2014, sydneyreviewofbooks.com/this-house-of-grief-helen-garner.

p257: 'calm and shrewd...' Garner, 'On Darkness', *Everywhere I Look*, 149.

p257: 'Again, eyes shut...in her hands' Garner, *This House of Grief*, 46–47; 'tender reverse-midwifery', 'water creatures', 'three silvery, naked...' ibid., 49.

p258: 'empathetic unsettlement', Dominick LaCapra, *Writing History, Writing Trauma*, Baltimore and London: John Hopkins University Press, 2001, 42; 'middle voice', 'modulations of proximity...', ibid., 26, 30.

p258: 'land a blow...' Garner, *This House of* Grief, 114; 'sentimental fantasy...' ibid., 44.

p259: 'Surely Freud was...' ibid., 45; 'to amputate his...' ibid., 57; 'We were women...' ibid., 2–3.

p260: 'only a teeth-baring...' ibid.,185; '*You poor bastard...*' ibid., 186.

p261: 'relentless loyalty...', 'a treasured boy' ibid., 146; 'big sister' ibid., 19.

p262: 'daylight dry desolate...less than hideous' Garner to Clark, 28 December 1963.

p263: 'stood like a...' Garner, *This House of Grief*, 196.

p264: 'formed a dark...' ibid., 204.

p265: 'to know a man...' E. L. Doctorow, 'Edgemont Drive', *New Yorker*, 26 April 2010, newyorker.com/magazine/2010/04/26/edgemont-drive.

p267: 'pondering again some...' Ken Crispin, email to Garner, 25 March 2009.

p268: 'dragging great shaggy...' Garner, NonfictioNow, 'An Evening with Helen Garner, 22 November 2012, youtube.com/watch?v=8rfsXsBg3IU, published 23 January 2013.

p269: 'annoyed', 'upset' Garner, *This House of Grief*, 272; 'like watching some...', 'motherly woman' ibid., 273; 'about the water...' ibid.

p270: 'By the time...', 'Court Eleven, where...' ibid., 274.

p270: 'But we weren't...' Garner, *Joe Cinque's Consolation*, 319.

p270: 'patriotic', 'bent over backwards' Garner, *This House of Grief*, 251; 'surge of adrenalin...' ibid., 6.

p273: 'brilliant, poetic work...' Felicity Plunkett, 'Helen Garner and Our Terrible Projections: Helen Garner and the Corridors of Empathy,'

Australian Book Review, September 2014, 16.

p274: 'I wanted to…' Garner, *This House of Grief*, 190.

p274: 'Garner's wider interests…' James Ley, 'Gut Instinct,' *Sydney Review of Books*.

p274: 'cloud of unknowing' Garner, *This House of Grief*, 261.

p274: 'one day I…' Joanna Field (Marion Milner), *An Experiment in Leisure*, London: Virago, 1986 (1987), 232.

p275: 'Staying with the…' Peter Ellingsen, 'Haunted by details missing in the struggle for objectivity,' *Age*, 4 June 2009, 19.

p276: 'thought of the law…' Garner, email to author, 22 May 2016.

p276: 'fantasy of one…' Garner, *This House of Grief*, 250.

p277: *Dura lex sed…*' ibid., 197; 'The children's fate…' ibid., 300; 'What sort of…' ibid., 294.

p278: 'magnificent' Peter Craven, 'Robert Farquharson Murder Case Takes Helen Garner Into the Abyss', Review *This House of Grief*, *Weekend Australian*, 23 August 2014, theaustralian.com.au/arts/review/robert-farquharson-murder-case-takes-helen-garner-into-the-abyss/news-story/0e9af664ab31bb6f9efd401b2b5f84d1.

p278: 'compelling' Kate Clanchy, '*This House of Grief* by Helen Garner Review—a Triumph by One of Australia's Greatest Writers', *Guardian*, 8 January 2016, theguardian.com/books/2016/jan/08/this-house-of-grief-helen-garner-review.

p278: '[t]ender and electrifying' Review '*This House of Grief*', *Saturday Paper*, 23 August 2014.

p278: 'Garner's spare, clean…' Plunkett, 'Helen Garner and Our Terrible Projections', 292.

p278: 'mastery', 'has perfected' Ley, 'Gut Instinct', *Sydney Review of Books*.

p278: 'utterly rivetting', 'demands of the…' Marilyn Warren CJ to Garner, 26 July 2014.

p279: 'it's a moment…', 'the room was' Stephen Romei, 'Garner's Farquharson Book *House of Grief* an Uneasy Masterpiece,' *Australian*, 1 August 2015.

13: Versions of Herself: *Everywhere I Look*

This chapter draws on the eulogy for Bruce Ford and an interview with Michael Gawenda.

p281: 'A biography is…' Virginia Woolf, *Orlando: A Biography*, Oxford:

Oxford University Press, 1992 (1928), 295.

p282: 'This is not...' Julian Barnes, 'Some of My Best Friends are Biographers,' Sydney Writers' Festival address, Roslyn Packer Theatre, 19 May 2016. Transcribed by author.

p282: 'puritanical savagery' Garner, 'Whisper and Hum', *Everywhere I Look*, 4.

p282: 'defensive primness' Garner, 'While Not Writing a Book: Diary 1', *Everywhere I Look*, 74.

p283: 'crudely jammed', 'raw', 'warm, dark glow' Garner, 'Some Furniture', *Everywhere I Look*, 8–9.

p283: 'aspects of myself...' Garner, 'White Paint and Calico', *Everywhere I Look*, 11.

p283: Garner does not regret burning her diaries, Gideon Haigh, 'True Voices', *The Weekend Review*, 30–31 March, 1986, 3 and 'Helen Garner in Conversation with Jennifer Byrne Part 1'.

p284: 'expresses a hard-won...', 'It brings you closer' Anna Goldsworthy, 'Felled by Grace', *Monthly*, April 2016, themonthly.com.au/issue/2016/april/1459429200/anna-goldsworthy/felled-grace.

p284: 'tender, witty, whimsical', 'unsettling savagery', 'shame and admirable...' Felicity Plunkett, 'Helen Garner's Tough Gaze and Tender Touch', *Sydney Morning Herald*, 8 April 2016, 26.

p284: 'I saw you...' Garner, 'Dear Mrs Dunkley', *Everywhere I Look*, 31.

p285: 'bohemian contempt', 'to speak up...' Garner, 'Suburbia', ibid., 23.

p285: 'still an only child', 'strong', 'she is my mother...' Garner, 'Dreams of Her Real Self', ibid., 105.

p286: 'deep and inconsolable...', 'He left us...' Garner, eulogy for Bruce Ford.

p286: 'But there she...' Garner, 'Before Whatever Else Happens: Diary 3', *Everywhere I Look*, 110.

p286: 'Autobiography is an...' Janet Malcolm, 'Thoughts on Autobiography from an Abandoned Autobiography,' *Forty-One False Starts*, 298.

p287: 'see all sides...', 'everything becomes richer...', 'a pest of...' Garner with Phillip Adams, *Late Night Live*.

p287: 'convalescent sofa', 'lanky white', 'In two strides...', 'Everyone to whom...' Garner, 'The Insults of Age', *Everywhere I Look*, 213–214.

p288: 'So my attack...' Garner postcard to author, June 2015.

p288: 'personality of many' Fay Zwicky, 'Between Two Worlds', The Judith Wright Memorial Lecture 2006, delivered at Sydney Grammar

School, 10 September, *Five Bells* 13.4 (2006), 15–21.

p288: 'in order to be...' 'Helen Garner in Conversation with Jennifer Byrne Part 1'.

p289: 'Helen has the...' Michael Gawenda, interview with author, 11 June 2016.

Epilogue: No Sense of an Ending...

This chapter draws on interviews with Raimond Gaita, David Malouf, Helen Elliott, Sally Ford, Catherine Ford, James Button and Nam Le.

p290: 'You never have...' Deidre Bair, 'In Search of the Real Simone de Beauvoir', ABC Radio *24 Hours*, April 1991, 34.

p290: 'Why do books...' Janet Malcolm, 'A House of One's Own', *Forty-One False Starts*, 87.

p290: 'One day these...' Garner to Clark, 24 November 1962.

p291: 'more compassionate practices', 'the issue of...' 'Letters to the editor', *Age*, 13 February 2002, 14.

p291: 'pen a letter...', 'add up to one...' Garner, 'The Letter I wish I'd written', *The Lifted Brow* no. 8 (2010), 39–40.

p292: 'absolutely proper' Raimond Gaita, interview with author, 18 March 2016.

p293: 'trivial', 'I would like...', 'is some kind...' Dowse, interview with Garner, 15–16 March 2005.

p293: 'a real pain...' Sally Ford, interview with author, 16 June 2016.

p293: 'a fundamental lightness...' Helen Elliot, interview with author, 9 June 2016.

p293: 'beloved sister, mentor' Catherine Ford, correspondence with author, 25 May 2016.

p293: 'jokes, shouts of...' James Button, interview with author, 13 June 2016.

p294: 'an independent thinker...' Robert Dessaix (ed.), *Speaking their Minds: Intellectuals and Public Culture in Australia*, Sydney: ABC Books, 1998, 29.

p295: 'three big tormentuous...' Garner, email to author, 23 June 2016.

p295: 'stung...I stopped going...', 'a weird lonely...' Garner, email to author, 9 September 2013.

p295: 'straight-on grace...', 'It's hard to...' Nam Le, email to author, 5 July 2016.

p296: 'his', 'pair of eyes', 'a field-glass', 'perched aloft', dead wall' Henry
    James, *The Portrait of a Lady*, Harmondsworth, Middlesex: Penguin,
    1977(1881), ix.
p297: 'the new group…' Garner, email to author, 26 June 2016.

Additional Sources

Introduction: Sketching an Outline

Ellison, Jennifer. *Rooms of their Own*. Ringwood, Victoria: Penguin
　Books, 1986.
Malcolm, Janet. 'Forty-One False Starts'. In *Forty-One False Starts:
　Essays on Artists and Writers*. New York: Farrar, Straus and Giroux,
　2014, 3–38.

Part I: Letters to Axel

1: Writing Home

Deling, Bert (dir.). *Pure Shit*. Apogee Films, 1975.

2: 'The blind, needing self': *Monkey Grip*

Brett, Judy. 'Publishing, Censorship and Writers' Incomes, 1965–1988.' In
　Laurie Hergenhan (ed). *The Penguin New Literary History of Australia*.
　Ringwood, Victoria: Penguin Books, 1988, 455.
Carey, Peter. *The Fat Man in History*. St Lucia: University of Queensland
　Press, 1974.
Goldsworthy, Kerryn. 'Australian Literature 101: Helen Garner: *Monkey
　Grip*.' Wheeler Centre, 26 April 2012. wheelercentre.com/broadcasts/
　australian-literature-101-helen-garner-monkey-grip
Moorhouse, Frank. *The Americans, Baby: A Discontinuous Narrative of
　Stories and Fragments*. Sydney: Angus and Robertson, 1972.
Pierce, Peter. 'Conventions of Presence.' *Meanjin* vol. 40, no. 1, 1981,
　106–113.
Wakoski, Diane. *The Motorcycle Betrayal Poems*. New York: Simon and
　Schuster 1971, 16–18.

3: Ruptures and Dislocations: *Honour & Other People's Children*

Dutton, Geoffrey. 'Author opens a locked-in world'. *Bulletin*, 13 January
　1981, 56.

326

Garner, Helen. 'Eight Scenes from a Friendship'. In *Tim Winton: A Celebration*. Hilary McPhee (ed.), Sydney: Pan Macmillan, 1999, 3–8.

Part II: Questions of Judgment

8: *The First Stone: Some Questions about Sex and Power*

Bail, Kathy (ed). *DIY Feminism*. St Leonards: Allen & Unwin, 1996.

Davis Mark. *Gangland: Cultural Elites and the New Generationalism*. Sydney: Allen & Unwin, 1997.

Else-Mitchell, Rosamund and Naomi Flutter (eds.). *Talking Up: Young Women's Take on Feminism*. Spinifex: North Melbourne, 1998.

Huck, Peter. 'Treachery in Types'. *Australian*, 8 June 1993.

Lumby, Catherine. *Bad Girls: The Media, Sex and Feminism in the 90s*. Sydney: Allen & Unwin, 1997.

Mead, Jenna (ed.). *bodyjamming: Sexual Harassment, Feminism and Public Life*. Sydney: Random House, 1997.

Miller, George (dir.). *Gross Misconduct*. Becker Entertainment Magna Pacific, 29 July 1993.

Summers, Anne. 'Shockwaves at the Revolution'. *Good Weekend Magazine*, 18 March 1995.

9: Asserting Her Credentials: *True Stories* and *The Feel of Steel*

Tóibín, Colm. *The Blackwater Lightship*. Picador: London, 1999.

10: The Shape of Loss: Lament and Restitution in *Joe Cinque's Consolation*

Carrère, Emmanuel. *L'Adversaire*. Paris: POL, 2000.

Crispin, Ken. *Divorce: The Unforgivable Sin?* Sydney: Hodder and Stoughton, 1988.

Crispin, Ken. 'Ethics and the Adversary System'. Canberra 1996.

Heerey, Peter. 'Expert Evidence'. Paper delivered to the World Intellectual Property Organisation Asia–Pacific Regional Colloquium for Judiciary, New Delhi, 6 February 2002.

Jamison, Kay Redfield. *Night Falls Fast: Understanding Suicide*. New York: Knopf, 1999.

Luhrmann, T. M. 'Of Two Minds: The Growing Disorder in American

Psychiatry'. *Times Literary Supplement*, 27 October 2000, 10.
Sereny, Gitta. *The Case of Mary Bell: A Portrait of a Child who Murdered.* Pimlico: Random House, 1995 (1972).

12: The Darkness Within: Bearing Witness in *This House of Grief*

Bryson, John. *Evil Angels*. Ringwood, Victoria: Viking, 1985.
Clendinnen, Inga. *Reading the Holocaust*. Melbourne: Text Publishing, 1998.
Enright, Ann. *The Gathering*. London: Jonathan Cape, 2007.
Harris Johnson, Carolyn. *Come with Daddy: Child Murder–Suicide After Family Breakdown*. Crawley, Perth: University of Western Australia Publishing, 2005.
Hobson, Theo. Review of James Q Whitman's *The Origins of Reasonable Doubt: Theological Roots of the Criminal Trial, Times Literary Supplement*. 6 February, 2009.
Joyce, James. *Dubliners*. London: Jonathan Cape, 1954 (1914).
Marias, Javier. 'While the Women are Sleeping,' *New Yorker*, 2 November 2009. newyorker.com/magazine/2009/11/02/while-the-women-are-sleeping
Munro, Alice. 'Dimension,' *New Yorker*, 5 June 2006. newyorker.com/magazine/2006/06/05/dimension.
Tóibín, Colm. *The South*. London: The Serpent's Tail, 1990.

13: Versions of Herself: *Everywhere I Look*

Garner, Helen. 'This Old Self'. *Freeman's: The Best New Writing on Family*. Melbourne: Text Publishing, 2016, 291–295.

Awards

Awards for Works

2016 Winner Windham–Campbell Prize—Nonfiction.
2006 Inaugural Winner Melbourne Prize for Literature.

***This House of Grief* (2014 nonfiction)**

2016 Winner Western Australian Premier's Book Awards—Nonfiction.
2016 Winner Western Australian Premier's Book Awards—Premier's Prize.
2015 Winner Ned Kelly Awards for Crime Writing—Best True Crime.

***The Spare Room* (2008 novel)**

2009 Winner Barbara Jefferis Award.
2008 Winner Victorian Premier's Literary Awards—The Vance Palmer Prize for Fiction.
2008 Winner Queensland Premier's Literary Awards—Best Fiction Book.

***Joe Cinque's Consolation* (2004 nonfiction)**

2005 Joint Winner Ned Kelly Awards for Crime Writing—Best True Crime.

***True Stories: Selected Non-Fiction* (1996)**

1997 Winner Nita Kibble Literary Award.

***The First Stone: Some Questions about Sex and Power* (1995 nonfiction)**

1995 Winner Eros Foundation Book of the Year Award.
1995 Winner Booksellers Choice Award.

'Did Daniel Have to Die' (*Time Magazine* 1993)

1993 Winner Walkley Award for Best Feature Writing.

Two Friends (1986 telemovie)

1987 Winner New South Wales Premier's Literary Awards—Television Writing.
1987 Winner Australian Film Institute Awards—Best Telefeature.

Postcards from Surfers (1985 short story)

1986 Winner New South Wales Premier's Literary Awards—Fiction.

The Children's Bach (1984 novella)

1986 Winner Festival Awards for Literature (SA)—Award for Fiction.

Monkey Grip (1977 novel)

1978 Winner National Book Council Award for Australian Literature.

Helen Garner's Books

Monkey Grip. Melbourne: McPhee Gribble. 1977.
Honour and Other People's Children. Melbourne: McPhee Gribble. 1980.
The Children's Bach. Melbourne: McPhee Gribble. 1984.
Postcards from Surfers: Stories. Melbourne: McPhee Gribble. 1985.
Last Days of Chez Nous and Two Friends. Melbourne: McPhee Gribble. 1992.
Cosmo Cosmolino. Melbourne: McPhee Gribble. 1992.
The First Stone: Some Questions About Sex and Power. Sydney: Picador. 1995.
True Stories: Selected Non-Fiction. Melbourne: Text Publishing. 1996.
My Hard Heart: Selected Fiction. Melbourne: Viking. 1998.
The Feel of Steel. Sydney: Picador. 2001.
Joe Cinque's Consolation. Sydney: Picador. 2004.
The Spare Room. Melbourne: Text Publishing. 2008.
This House of Grief: The Story of a Murder Trial. Melbourne: Text Publishing. 2014.
Everywhere I Look. Melbourne: Text Publishing. 2016.

Text and Image Permissions

Extracts from *The First Stone* and *Joe Cinque's Consolation* by Helen Garner (Pan Macmillan) are reproduced with kind permission from the author and publisher.

Extracts from *Monkey Grip*, *Honour and Other People's Children*, *The Children's Bach* and *Postcards from Surfers* (Penguin Random House) are reproduced with kind permission from the author and publisher.

An extract from 'Nessun Dorma' by Francis Webb reproduced with kind permission from Therese Nelson and Maria Meere.

Extracts from 'Genesis' by Chris Wallace-Crabbe reproduced with kind permission from the author.

Plate section image credits (in order of appearance):

Photo of Helen with Axel: courtesy Helen Garner.

Letter to Axel (22 March 1966): Papers of Axel Clark, 1926–2001, NLA MS Acc 11.079, Box 18, folder 4.

Letter to Axel and Ali (31 July 1985): Papers of Axel Clark, 1926–2001, NLA MS Acc 11.079, Box 18, folder 4.

Handwritten 'White Eyes' lyrics: Papers of Axel Clark, 1926–2001, NLA MS Acc 11.079, Box 18, folder 4.

Photos of Scotchmer St Mural: Paul Brennan 2017.

'Jack K' transcribed note: NLA MS Acc 16.094 (not yet catalogued). Box description: Farquharson journal 3, 19 November 2007 to 25 February 2008. Reproduced with kind permission from Jack Kirszenblat.

'Did you pull my tail' postcard: courtesy Bernadette Brennan.

'An Open Letter to Helen Garner': Papers of Helen Garner, 1990–2005, NLA MS 9265/6/5, Box 11.

Photos of Helen on the couch alone and with her granddaughter: © Jenny Sages 2002.

Photo of Helen as a baby with Gwen Ford: courtesy Helen Garner.

Photo of Helen with her parents: courtesy Helen Garner.

Photo of Helen with Tim Winton: © Cathryn Tremain/Fairfax Images, first published in the *Age*, 10 May 1986.

Acknowledgments

Thank you to Helen Garner for the trust she placed in me, for her generosity of spirit and for the laughter. Thank you also to Michael Heyward, Elena Gomez and the team at Text Publishing for making this a much shorter and better book that it would otherwise have been.

Some key figures in Helen Garner's life and work chose not to be interviewed for this book. I respect their decision. I would like to thank those people who did share with me their insights about Garner and her work: Hilary McPhee, Peter Craven, Judith Whitworth, Sally Ford, Catherine Ford, David Malouf, Raimond Gaita, Helen Elliott, James Button, Michael Gawenda, Barbara Mobbs, Jenny Sages, Edmund Campion, Tim Winton, Drusilla Modjeska, Jane Clifton, Nam Le, Brian Stonier, Ken Crispin, Colin Talbot and Ross Gibson.

One of the great pleasures in researching this book was meeting Jenny Sages, a brilliant artist and wonderful woman. Thank you Jenny for so generously allowing me to use your beautiful photographs of Helen Garner.

Thanks also to my wonderful brother Paul Brennan for the Scotchmer Street photographs, and to Sally Ford for alerting me to the mural's existence. Thank you to the current owners of the house, Rosalba Fogliani and Andrew Wilkinson, for allowing me to share with readers their unique piece of history.

I would like to extend a heartfelt thanks to the staff in

the pictures and manuscripts branch at the National Library of Australia. Their knowledge, professionalism and diligence was exceptional. They provided me with unstinting, invaluable assistance. My thanks also to the staff in the special collections archives at the Baillieu Library, University of Melbourne, and the staff at the National Archives of Australia.